ZONED OUT

Regulation, Markets, and Choices in Transportation and Metropolitan Land-Use

Jonathan Levine

Resources for the Future
Washington, DC, USA

Printed in the United States of America

An RFF Press book
Published by Resources for the Future
1616 P Street NW
Washington, DC 20036–1400
USA
www.rffpress.org

Library of Congress Cataloging-in-Publication Data

Levine, Jonathan (Jonathan C.)
  Zoned out : regulation, markets, and choices in transportation and metropolitan-land-use /
Jonathan Levine.-- 1st ed.
    p. cm.
  Includes bibliographical references and index.
  ISBN 1-933115-14-9 (hardcover : alk. paper) — ISBN 1-933115-15-7 (pbk. : alk. paper)
  1. Zoning—United States. 2. Land use—United States. 3. Real estate development—United
States—Planning. 4. Transportation—United States—Planning. 5. Cities and towns—United
States—Growth. I. Title.
  HT169.7.L48 2005
  333.73'17'0973—dc22   2005018353

The paper in this book meets the guidelines for permanence and durability of the Committee on Production Guidelines for Book Longevity of the Council on Library Resources. This book was typeset by Peter Lindeman. It was copyedited by Sally Atwater. The cover was designed by Rosenbohm Graphic Design. Calthorpe Associates of Berkeley, California, generously provided the cover art, © Calthorpe Associates, 1995.

ISBN 1-933115-14-9 (cloth)   ISBN 1-933115-15-7 (paper)

About Resources for the Future *and* RFF Press

Resources for the Future (RFF) improves environmental and natural resource policymaking worldwide through independent social science research of the highest caliber. Founded in 1952, RFF pioneered the application of economics as a tool for developing more effective policy about the use and conservation of natural resources. Its scholars continue to employ social science methods to analyze critical issues concerning pollution control, energy policy, land and water use, hazardous waste, climate change, biodiversity, and the environmental challenges of developing countries.

RFF Press supports the mission of RFF by publishing book-length works that present a broad range of approaches to the study of natural resources and the environment. Its authors and editors include RFF staff, researchers from the larger academic and policy communities, and journalists. Audiences for publications by RFF Press include all of the participants in the policymaking process—scholars, the media, advocacy groups, NGOs, professionals in business and government, and the public.

CONTENTS

Acknowledgments   vii

1   Market Failures and Planning Failures   1

2   Travel Behavior Research and the "Market"   21

3   Marketlike Interpretations of Land-Use Controls   50

4   The Harms of Regulatory Exclusion   67

5   Is Zoning State Regulation or a Local Property Right?   86

6   The Limited Power of Smart-Growth Regulation   109

7   Developers, Planners, and Neighborhood Supply   123

8   The Demand for Transportation and Land-Use Innovation   149

9   A New Foundation for Policy Reform   171

Notes   203
References   207
Index   219

To Noga

ACKNOWLEDGMENTS

I am grateful for the help I had from friends, colleagues, students, family, and supportive institutions in creating *Zoned Out*. The Taubman College of Architecture and Urban Planning at the University of Michigan supported the sabbatical that enabled me to write the book. Princeton's Woodrow Wilson School of Public and International Affairs provided an environment that was both stimulating and highly conducive to research; thanks especially to Julian Wolpert, Chris Eisgruber, Kathy Applegate, and Cindy Schoeneck for making me feel welcome during my stay there. The Mineta Transportation Institute in San Jose, California, supported much of the empirical research presented in the later chapters. The Urban Land Institute in Washington, D.C. provided access to its data for a nationwide survey of developers. *Transportation* and the *Journal of Planning Education and Research* graciously allowed the reprinting of material that was included in journal articles.

William Fischel and Eytan Sheshinski offered critical economics insights in early conversations about the ideas in the book. Martin Wachs, John Pucher, and David Walters reviewed the manuscript for RFF Press, providing important ideas for its improvement. Theodoros Natsinas commented on parts of the draft and helped with the material pertaining to Thessaloniki in the concluding chapter. Yaakov Garb, Daniel Rodriguez, and David Thacher read parts of the draft and served regularly as sounding boards for the arguments presented here. Aseem Inam, Gwo-Wei Torng, and Richard Werbel collaborated on projects referred to in the later chapters. Larry Helfer provided useful feedback as the book proposal went to publishers. Special thanks are due to the Urban and Regional Planning faculty at the University of Michigan for sustaining an environment of friendly collegiality throughout the years.

The professionals of RFF Press—Don Reisman, Meg Keller, and Grace Hill—were a joy to work with from start to finish. Sally Atwater edited the manuscript for RFF Press, offering significant suggestions for improvement. The text also benefited from the critical editing of Julie Steiff and Ana Jovanovic. Ana provided important research assistance as well. My parents, Hillie and Rose Levine, read and commented on the entire draft. Their engagement and support have been a constant over the decades.

Most of all, the book is a product of my twenty-five year partnership with my wife, Noga Morag-Levine. The ideas presented here developed intertwined with hers, deriving nourishment from near-constant dialogue. No one has been a greater source of encouragement for this book, and for my academic career in general. *Zoned Out* is dedicated to her, with love.

Jonathan Levine
Ann Arbor, Michigan

CHAPTER ONE

MARKET FAILURES
AND PLANNING FAILURES

The low-density, car-dependent development that characterizes most U.S. metropolitan areas—"urban sprawl"—has been implicated in a host of societal ills. These have included pollution, congestion, greenhouse gas emissions, traffic crashes, and excess energy consumption because of the intensive automobile use that this urban form demands. Poor physical fitness has recently been added to this list, along with an obesity epidemic stemming from the inactivity of a car-reliant lifestyle. Sprawl's territorial appetites have been linked to loss of habitat, wetlands, prime agricultural land, and the beauty of open spaces. A stunted community life is the ostensible product of the lack of casual, face-to-face interactions in lively public spaces. And this organization of our metropolitan areas has been accused of leaving low-income carless households isolated in job-poor central cities. The literature arguing for the presence of these impacts is immense, matched only by the countervailing studies questioning the causal link between metropolitan form and any particular set of outcomes.

Underpinning this debate are notions about markets, regulation, and the conditions that justify governmental intervention. According to a story broadly accepted on both sides of the debate, urban sprawl is primarily a product of free markets in land development. The scarcity of compact, mixed-use, walkable and transit-friendly neighborhoods (termed here "alternative" development forms) in areas developed or redeveloped since the mid-20th century is a function of market disinterest or inability to provide such alternatives. Since most Americans prefer low-density living, the free market offers few profits for those who would build compact, mixed-use, transit-accessible neighborhoods. Urban planning interventions seek to constrain the market's sprawling tendencies through regulatory tools aimed at fostering development forms that the market is otherwise incapable of providing.

To some observers, these interventions are warranted as responses to the market failures of sprawl. To others, they are unjustified impositions on households' freedom of choice, with scarce evidence of benefit in reducing pollution or congestion. Yet for both camps, the justification for planning interventions rests on the quality of the evidence of benefits of the alternative development forms. Scientific confidence that the alternatives to sprawl reduce driving, increase walking, spur transit use, curb obesity, promote cleaner air, or demonstrate other benefits tends to justify planning interventions into the workings of the market. By contrast, ambiguity in the scientific findings tends to undermine the rationale for planning intervention; if we do not yet know enough about the relationship between land use and transportation, public health, or other policy realms, we ought to refrain from seeking gains in these areas through land-use interventions.

There is an internal inconsistency with that account of U.S. metropolitan development, however. It supposes that planning interventions tend to counter any sprawling tendencies of the land-development market. Yet empirical social science research into the impact of land-use regulation on metropolitan development patterns (Chapter 3) suggests that zoning and other municipal interventions actually do the opposite: they lead both to development that is lower in density and to communities that are more exclusive than would arise in the absence of such regulation. This should hardly be surprising; zoning ordinances typically limit building heights and lot coverage and set minimum parking space requirements for a development, and engineering standards determine roadway-width minima. Empirical research suggests that rather than mitigating the market's sprawling tendencies, the ubiquitous interventions of municipal land-use regulation actually exacerbate them. Current regulatory approaches are certainly not the sole cause of urban sprawl; the interaction of household preferences and developer tendencies would almost certainly generate vast areas of low-density, auto-oriented development even if municipal regulation did not compel these development forms. But the empirical evidence suggests that the "American way of zoning" truly does make the suburbs of U.S. metropolitan areas more spread out than they might otherwise be (Fischel 1999a). If this is the case, land-development markets are capable of producing more compact development than is currently observed but are thwarted by municipal regulation.

That finding would suggest an entirely different paradigm regarding the relationship between urban sprawl and the free market. In this alternative story, although the private market may well have sprawling tendencies of its own, it is capable of producing alternatives but is impeded by municipal regulations that lower development densities, separate land uses, specify wide roadways, and mandate large parking areas. Under these circumstances, an easing of some governmental interventions is a prerequisite—a necessary though perhaps not sufficient condition—to the flourishing of the alternative development forms. The thrust of policy reform on behalf of compact development would not be market forcing but market enabling; it would seek to overcome regulatory impediments to compact, mixed-use development so that these neighborhood forms can be provided where they are economically feasible.

This framework also suggests an entirely different rationale for land-use policy reform, justified on the basis of increased individual and household choice in transportation and land-use. Where compact, mixed-use development is no longer zoned out, people who prefer these alternatives would be able to get more of what they want in their transportation and land-use environment. Compact development may well have benefits in travel behavior, public health, or other realms, but policy reform would not hinge on scientific proof of these effects. Ambiguity in the scientific data would not undermine the rationale for reform, since policy change would be based on removing obstacles to choice, rather than on scientifically proven benefits of alternative development forms.

It matters greatly which of the two competing paradigms governs our policy environment; it influences both our planning prescriptions and the degree to which metropolitan areas provide alternatives to low-density, auto-oriented development. Within the first paradigm, the burden of proof of benefit falls on those who favor compact, mixed-use alternatives to

Table 1-1. Alternative Paradigms of Metropolitan Land-Use Policy

	Paradigm 1	Paradigm 2
Explanation for scarcity of alternatives to sprawl	Market disinterest	Regulatory barriers that exacerbate market tendencies toward sprawl
Thrust of regulatory reform	Market-forcing regulations	Lowering of regulatory barriers to alternative development forms
Justification for regulatory reform	Scientific proof of benefit of alternative development forms	Expansion of household choice

sprawl; proponents must establish the transportation, environmental, or public health advantages of compact development. Within the second, ambiguity of scientific data would not be an obstacle to the promotion of alternative development forms. (See Table 1-1).

Under the first paradigm, only where proof of benefit is reasonably conclusive are the alternatives to sprawl justified. Where proof of benefit is lacking, metropolitan development reverts to the default condition—the sprawling status quo. In other words, the current degree of sprawl is a default choice, the way in which development proceeds if alternatives lack sufficient basis in science. Within this paradigm, scientific uncertainty regarding the benefits of compact development forms becomes a reason for maintaining the status quo. If it were easy to figure out the relationship between land-use patterns and travel behavior, this might be of little consequence. But in fact the relationship is notoriously complex and has resisted precise quantification over decades of research. Travel behavior and public health benefits of compact, mixed-use development forms are not amenable to laboratory experimentation: researchers cannot assign control and experimental groups randomly to different neighborhood types in order to assess their impact on people's behavior. Instead, research in these realms rests on quasi-experimental designs that use statistical controls to account for real-world variability. These studies are given to more varied interpretations, and as a consequence, the benefits of alternatives to sprawl remain controversial. In this scientific environment, the question for urban planning and transportation policy will remain the identification of desirable institutional arrangements in the face of continued uncertainty.

If uncertainty is indeed pervasive, policies built on the assumptions of the first paradigm will tend to replicate the status quo of sprawl with relatively few alternatives. Many land-use and transportation alternatives may never arise because science is incapable of proving them superior to sprawl. By contrast, policies under the second paradigm—linked to choice expansion rather than proven travel behavior modification—could introduce transportation and land-use solutions that are needed or desired by significant sectors of the population, even in the face of scientific ambiguity. To the extent that municipal regulatory requirements limit the development of more affordable housing forms (Chapter 4), such policy reform could improve housing affordability as well.

Which of the two paradigms better captures development reality in the United States? The empirical research on the impact of land-use regulation seems to point toward the second paradigm. And many of the reforms proposed—such as those allowing denser or mixed-use development—seem to be market-enabling rather than market-forcing, since they lower the barriers to alternative development forms. Even land-use regulations specifying *minimum* densities cannot compel development in line with their prescriptions; if private developers are not interested in developing compactly on a particular site, they will simply shun the area and invest elsewhere. Yet in policy debates, the land-use status quo is often treated as the product of a more or less free market. Policy reform to facilitate more compact and mixed-use development forms is similarly construed as a market intervention requiring justification in scientifically proven benefits (Chapter 2).

How could such a disjuncture arise? One explanation might be lack of awareness of land-use regulatory processes and their tendency to exclude more compact development forms from close-in areas and to compel a sprawling metropolitan form. This is the simplest equation between sprawl and markets. This hardly seems plausible, however, since observers on all sides of the debate refer extensively to these exclusionary processes, often under the "not-in-my-backyard" (NIMBY) label. Instead, a much more fundamental reinterpretation is taking place in transportation and land-use policy debates and scholarship. Municipal land-use regulation is itself interpreted as a market force, or at least as something other than governmental intervention into the workings of the private market. Where this reinterpretation occurs—and it pervades the debate—the American status quo of extensive municipal regulatory prerogative in land use is treated as a "free-market" state of affairs.

The view that municipal control of land use is more akin to a market force than to governmental regulation of economic activity finds considerable basis in both economic models (Chapter 3) and legal scholarship (Chapter 5). Moreover, once municipal land-use regulation is reinterpreted in this way an important redefinition has taken place: even if land-use regulations are understood to exacerbate sprawl, action at the metropolitan or state level to limit the capacity of local governments to enact these regulations can still be considered intervention into the workings of the free market. In other words, the reinterpretation of local regulation as a market force puts policymaking squarely in the first paradigm, even if zoning spurs sprawl and suppresses its alternatives. Unsurprisingly, the reinterpretation is broadly accepted by those who would defend the status quo against what they see as the draconian interventions of proponents of smart growth.

It is somewhat more surprising that proponents of compact, mixed-use development alternatives often appear to accept the same reinterpretation. At times they do so explicitly (Chapter 2). More commonly, they accept the framework implicitly with research that seeks to justify compact, mixed-use development by proving that it causes people to reduce their driving and increase their walking, cycling, and transit use. The very framework—justifying a certain development form through travel behavior benefits— implies the existence of a default development form, should their evidence fall short. The statement that policy reform is warranted because compact development reduces vehicle miles traveled appears to imply its converse: if compact development does not reduce vehicle miles traveled, policy reform is unwarranted. But the latter statement is meaningful only within the policy assumptions of the first paradigm. Researchers within this tradition see their work as a relatively straightforward application of objective social science to a current policy issue. But this construction implies acceptance of the first paradigm, which is actually quite hostile to the very reforms they propose.

This book argues for the second paradigm. Despite its pervasiveness and academic pedigree, the reinterpretation of municipal land-use regulation as a kind of market force is unwarranted. In part, this is because the reinterpretation fails the classic "duck" test of the late Cardinal Cushing: "When I see a bird that walks like a duck and swims like a duck and quacks like a duck, I call that bird a duck" (Bartlett 2002). Municipal land-use regulation constrains outcomes that the free market would otherwise have produced and employs the power of the state to this end—a virtual textbook definition of governmental regulation. This book develops this simple observation further, examining the bases for economic and legal reinterpretation of municipal land-use regulation as a kind of market force, and finds them wanting.

None of this is to suggest that municipal regulation of land uses is undesirable, or that a laissez-faire approach is called for (or even possible) in metropolitan land-use policy. It does argue, however, for recognizing that municipal regulation that zones out the alternatives to sprawl is neither a preordained state of nature nor the free market's invisible hand, but a governmental decision to constrain market processes. As such, it does not deserve the "default" status it has attained in debates over transportation, land use, and metropolitan development.

THE POLITICS OF TRAVEL BEHAVIOR RESEARCH

Implicit to the social scientific debate over the transportation impacts of land use is a compound question that fuses scientific and policy dimensions: "Do alternative forms of development improve travel behavior with sufficient magnitude and certainty to justify the policy interventions required to bring these forms about?" In evidence of reduced automobile use and increases in the nonmotorized modes associated with particular urban designs, analysts supportive of land-use alternatives find justification for such planning interventions. Others question these findings, pointing out that people's self-selection into neighborhoods may affect observed differences in travel behavior more than physical variables like density, mixing of land uses, or accessibility. This uncertainty is construed as evidence against policy interventions on behalf of these alternative development forms.

The differences may extend beyond assessment of the scientific evidence to competing philosophical conceptions of the conditions justifying government intervention. An assessment that planning for alternative development lacks sufficient transportation rationale can stem from a perception of weak or ambiguous travel behavior effects, a determination of a high threshold before policy intervention is justified, or both; the inverse is true for positive conclusions. An analyst inclined to governmental intervention into markets may conclude that available scientific evidence is sufficient to justify such action; another less inclined towards public action may reach the opposite conclusion even from an identical reading of the evidence. In some cases, these questions may even fuse, such that the perception of the quality of the data is colored by the policy conclusions observers hope to draw.

Although researchers split sharply over the answer to the question, they write largely as if they agree on the framework for the debate. Equating the status quo in metropolitan development with market ordering, both proponents and skeptics of alternative development forms seem to agree that these options require planning intervention into land-development markets.

If urban sprawl is the product of market ordering, then any negative by-products might represent market failures. Congestion and pollution are classic externalities often associated with a low-density, auto-oriented development pattern; other negative effects may include energy consumption, surface water pollution, traffic accidents, and others. Under a market-driven view of sprawl, policies for compact development might be a justified response to these market failures if their effects on travel behavior can be shown to be sufficiently beneficial. A search for evidence on the transportation impact of alternative development forms, then, amounts to a test of whether intervention on behalf of these forms remedies a market failure. Conversely, absence of evidence of beneficial impacts—for example, ambiguity in the link between land use and travel behavior—would tend to undermine the claim that these policies are a remedy for the market failures of sprawl.

The view of sprawl as a potential market failure was articulated by Brueckner (2000, 163):

> The confluence of an expanding national population, rising incomes, and falling commuting costs makes the rapid expansion of cities in recent decades unsurprising. The real question is whether this expansion has been too rapid. In other words, does the invisible hand, which guides the conversion of land to urban use, push too hard in the direction of bigger cities?
>
> Economists use the term *market failure* to describe a situation in which the invisible hand fails to allocate resources in a socially desirable manner so as to maximize aggregate economic well-being. Is a...market failure involved in the spatial expansion of cities? If so, the criticism of urban sprawl is justified, and measures are needed to restrict urban expansion.

Viewed in this way, the question is strictly whether the invisible hand of the market does or does not lead to economic inefficiencies in land development. Yet another hand is at work in metropolitan development, one that is highly visible to people who interact with the messy reality of planning: the regulation of land uses by local governments through tools like zoning, subdivision controls, and roadway and parking standards. When the problem is by definition a search for possible inefficiencies of the "invisible hand" in metropolitan expansion, an alternative view connecting sprawl to the visible hand of municipal land-use regulation is unlikely to surface. Yet the ubiquity of this form of governmental regulation—and the extent to which it fundamentally alters the outline of the public policy problem—is clear to some observers. Downs (1999, 963) expresses the precise antithesis of the market-failure formulation of the problem above:

[T]he belief that sprawl is caused primarily by market failures is based on the false assumption that there is a freely operating land use market in U.S. metropolitan areas. *No metropolitan area has anything remotely approaching a free land use market* because of local regulations adopted for parochial political, social and fiscal purposes. Most suburban land use markets are dominated by local zoning and other regulations that are aimed at excluding low-income households and that distort what would occur in a truly free market. (emphasis added)

The debate regarding whether scientific evidence warrants policy reform makes sense only within a market-failure definition of sprawl—the first of the two paradigms described above. A view that sprawl is primarily caused by market failures puts the burden of proof on those who would seek to remedy those failures through market interventions. The status quo of auto-oriented development then becomes a neutral choice, deviation from which is or is not justified by scientific evidence.

Construction of such a neutral default fits social science-based policy analysis well. Statistical studies are structured around a null hypothesis—the hypothesis that an independent variable has no effect on an outcome of interest—and an alternative hypothesis that a cause-and-effect relationship exists. A failure to reject the null hypothesis—scientific code for "no conclusive effect found"—is often construed as supporting a policy of "no governmental intervention" into market processes. In this way, the results of science are mapped—often too neatly—onto policy recommendations.

By contrast, the alternative, nonmarket-failure view of sprawl—that *no metropolitan area has anything remotely approaching a free land-use market*—implies something very different regarding both the action required for promoting alternative development and the rationale for this reform. There is a near-universal acknowledgment among transportation and land-use researchers that municipalities regularly employ their land-use regulatory powers to exclude denser development (e.g., Gordon and Richardson 2001; Boarnet and Crane 1997; Cervero 1989). Thus a prerequisite to the development of alternatives is the *liberalization* of restrictive regulations that compel a low-density development pattern. If municipal regulations constrain development to this pattern despite market interest in alternatives, a paucity of these options is not a market failure but a product of regulatory policy, a "planning failure" (Cervero 1996). Sprawl's claim to being the market—and hence default—solution from which deviations demand justification in science would be undermined. Quite independent of travel behavior benefits, the immediate payoff of such policies would be the expansion of transportation and land-use choice—that is, the ability of households to find the environments that fit their needs and preferences in housing type, neighborhood characteristics, and travel options.

Although many compact development policies facilitate market-driven development in areas targeted for growth, others rest on market-constraining regulation. As an example, urban growth boundaries that specify a perimeter beyond which metropolitan expansion is prohibited clearly constrain markets. But if the U.S. status quo of development is driven largely by density-lowering municipal regulation, the choice to switch to growth management and urban growth boundaries would amount to a choice of "planning versus planning," not "planning versus the market." When the choice is understood as one between alternative planning arrangements, it becomes clear that no particular option inherently deserves the "default" designation.

Where restrictive regulations are proposed to encourage compact development, travel behavior impacts of alternative development may be needed to justify these interventions. Many countries do not promote low-density development with land-use regulatory tools to the extent that the U.S. planning system does. Where such counties take action to channel metropolitan development into more compact and transit-oriented forms (Chapman 1998), debates over these policies may sensibly hinge in part on the quality of evidence regarding the influence of land use on travel behavior. But imposition of restrictions such as urban-growth boundaries while maintaining U.S.-styled low-density land-use regulations can hardly lead to compact development. Where municipal policies significantly constrain compact development, reform of the sprawl-inducing regulations is the first order of business in a smart-growth agenda. Here, the question of whether science justifies interventions becomes vacuous.

Although strong evidence for the link between land use and travel behavior can be viewed as a rationale for regulatory reform, relying on this claim is not necessarily a good strategy for proponents of relaxation of exclusionary municipal policies. When a scientific finding is brought forth in *support* of a controversial policy, it is inevitable that doubts about the finding's reliability will be construed to be evidence *against* the policy. These counterarguments may not be based in logic; the finding may be sufficient but not necessary evidence for implementing the policy. But having used the scientific finding in this way, proponents predictably expose themselves to this vulnerability.

The argument presented here is not restricted to transportation policy. Consider claims pertaining to obesity, physical activity, and public health;

claims about the influence of neighborhood form on community formation; and assertions about the water quality impact of sprawl. Wherever the legitimacy of alternatives is seen to hinge on the quality of scientific data, research is effectively engaged with the "market failure" question: does sprawl present a market failure that is remediable through governmental intervention into land use? If sprawl is exacerbated by current policy interventions, lack of conclusively demonstrated effects ceases to be a reason to continue the status quo, since the present state is not a neutral free-market condition but one created and maintained by municipal land-use regulations.

PLANNING INTERVENTION FOR LOW-DENSITY DEVELOPMENT

Questions of whether planners ought or ought not to intervene in land markets—and worries about whether intervention is justified by travel behavior science—are likely to puzzle those who have interacted with land-use planning in suburban municipalities. At the municipal level, not only is intervention pervasive, but its legitimacy is largely taken for granted. Municipalities in the United States zone their territory in a detailed and prescriptive fashion, as anyone who has ever attempted to start a business or add an apartment unit in a single-family zone will readily attest. The interventions of local zoning are legion and include regulations on lot coverage, floor-area ratio, number of unrelated persons who may live together, and restrictions on buildings' architectural details. In economically successful suburban areas, planning conflicts frequently arise between developers who seek to develop more densely than regulations allow, and neighbors who want their municipalities to keep development densities low with land-use regulation. The effort required to stave off higher densities hardly squares with one popular image of New Urbanism, as expressed by Ronald Utt of the Heritage Foundation:

> Since the 1960s, there has been this effort at urban revitalization; when expensive projects have not been enough to get people to go back into the cities, a movement has risen up that says we should simply force people to live in what certain others have decided is good. That's the main idea of New Urbanism. (Lehrer 1998, 18)

This image—forcing people to live in alternatives they do not want—is a mismatch with reality. Proposals for compact development are made by profit-seeking developers on the basis of perceived market interest but are

Figure 1-1. Townhouse Development Excluded from Fruit Heights Site

Source: Garbett Homes

frequently rejected by local planning authorities, as in the following example from Fruit Heights, Utah, 20 miles north of Salt Lake City:

> After months of dispute and adding the threat of litigation, the city has taken a hard hand against a developer's proposal to build 150 condominium units and continues to reject The Springs preliminary plan. A recent City Council meeting came to a screeching halt when Councilman Dan Phelps moved to table action on The Springs, a planned residential unit development, until January. The city has strongly opposed a proposal to develop the high-density housing project on 46.61 acres for sale by Richard Harvey because it could increase the city's population by 20 percent. (*Ogden Standard-Examiner*, December 10, 2003)

Units in the proposed development were to be priced at $140,000 to $190,000 (Figure 1-1) (Garbett 2005). The townhouses were ultimately zoned out not to preserve open space, but rather to ensure lower-density development. To be built instead on the site is a development with exclusively single-family homes advertised by their developer, Richmond American Homes, from $298,000 to $363,000 (Figure 1-2). A passerby in Fruit Heights would observe a low-density single-family neighborhood, and might naturally assume that it arose because of market demand for housing of this type. Invisible to this observer would be the more compact and affordable neighborhood that the market would have provided but for

Elevation A

Elevation B

Elevation C

Floorplans, exteriors, features, specifications and plans may change without notice.
All floorplans and renderings are artist's conceptions. Square footages are approximate and may vary.
Plan, options and elevation features vary by community.

Figure 1-2. Single-Family Homes to be Built on Fruit Heights Site

Source: Richmond American Homes

municipal regulatory exclusion. If this story is typical—and indeed a perusal of planning reports in the domestic press suggests that it is ubiquitous—then whether travel behavior science offers sufficient certainty to justify policy interventions is beside the point. Backers of compact developments may articulate a social or environmental agenda—in fact, a lawsuit over the Fruit Heights case was joined by both the NAACP and the Disability Rights Action Committee (*Ogden Standard-Examiner*, September 17, 2004)—yet their products ultimately succeed or fail on their capacity to generate profits for investors. Observed conflicts between municipal planning officials and developers seeking permission for denser development would logically represent only the tip of the iceberg of potential market-driven densification in land-use patterns. This is because savvy developers would be expected to refrain from the costly process of proposing development that stands little chance of approval by local planning authorities.

In more limited instances, however, municipalities have become interested in promoting alternatives to auto-oriented development. For example, in 1999, the Denver suburb of Westminster sought a New Urbanist approach to development on a 120-acre site:

> The city wants to build a "test" development project that includes a mix of residential housing with retail and commercial uses. The idea is called "new urbanism" because it harkens back to the old mixed-use neighborhood...On Monday the city council gave the go-ahead to seek proposals from developers for a mixed-use project. One developer has expressed an interest to do such a project. (*Denver Rocky Mountain News*, October 4, 1999)

Notwithstanding journalistic shorthand, the city was never considering "building" such a project, but rather seeking proposals from developers. Interested developers would presumably include only those who viewed such a project's profitability as equal or superior to that of other development opportunities. Nearly two years later a related story appeared regarding the same site:

> In late April the Westminster City Council agreed to revamp its zoning rules to let Continuum build its brand of denser, more urban-style development... (*Denver Post*, June 10, 2001)

Thus, enabling the project required liberalizing the restrictive zoning rules that had previously applied. Despite its proactive stance, Westminster City Council could at best accommodate and facilitate market forces; bringing about alternative development by regulatory fiat was never an option, since developers would shun opportunities they viewed as unprofitable. Where markets exist for alternative development forms—as they apparently did in Westminster—uncertainty in travel behavior science is hardly the appropriate basis for their regulatory exclusion. And where no markets for such developments exist, regulatory exclusion would be unnecessary; the absence of profits would be at least as effective in keeping the development out. Proactive policies toward alternative development can bear fruit only in an environment of sufficient demand; for this reason, they amount to market facilitation, rather than market forcing.

Figure 1-3. Bradburn Row House Apartments, Westminster, Colorado

Photo by Andrea Mrzlak

In other cases, regional bodies have actively encouraged transit-oriented development; in many of these cases, policy reform is geared at reducing regulatory obstacles to market-driven densification. For example, the Bay Area Rapid Transit (BART) District (1999) considers the willingness of a municipality to accept higher-density, transit-oriented development near proposed station sites in determining routing and location of new service extensions. The policy is controversial not because municipal officials doubt the economic feasibility of high-density development but for precisely the opposite reason: they are convinced that permitting such development will in fact bring the density they prefer to zone out. One city council member from an outlying community said of this policy that Orinda, a wealthy suburb, wouldn't tolerate four-story apartment buildings near its BART station, "so why should we?" (*Contra Costa Valley Times*, October 11, 2003). The district is thus employing the lever of transit extensions to induce less restrictive zoning than the municipality might otherwise enact. Although such policies may challenge municipal regulatory prerogative, the reform of low-density regulation, when successful, leads to expansion of market choice.

Smart-growth policies in Maryland have trigged concerns similar to those expressed in the San Francisco area:

"Smart growth is inconsistent with the American dream of a big home on a five-acre lot," said David Bliden, executive director of the Maryland Association of Counties, which opposed [former Maryland Governor] Glendening's effort as an unreasonable intrusion into counties' power to regulate building. "The concept of a higher authority, of a Big Brother, is inconsistent with the democratic principles that have to be intertwined with land use management." (*Washington Post*, August 10, 2004)

Here the objection is made explicit: rather than an intrusion into free land-development markets, smart-growth policies are reviled as interference into local regulatory powers. Municipal prerogative in land-use regulation is equated with an impressive list of desiderata: democracy, freedom from Big Brother, and the American dream of a big home on five acres. Of course, if this particular American dream were universally held—and could be afforded by all—it would hardly need county-level regulatory protection against denser building forms. Promulgating low-density land-use regulation because of an ostensible American dream of a big home on a five-acre lot is akin to banning the Geo Metro because of Americans' big-car reveries; the fact that a pricier good may be the ultimate object of desire hardly justifies regulation against the more attainable alternative. Moreover, the implicit belief in monolithic preferences is both implausible and unsupported; it should come as no surprise that different people want different things in transportation and housing, as in so many other realms. In the end, the high-flying rhetoric of the above quote legitimates regulatory preference for one particular American dream over others, an outcome quite at odds with its invocation of market-imbued freedom.

There is much to be said on behalf of strong land-use regulatory powers. Preemptive separation to stave off land-use conflicts—such as barring industry from residential districts and vice versa—remains as good an idea today as when late-19th-century reformers employed it to address unhealthful urban conditions. But market-driven residential and commercial densification and integration can hardly be called hazardous threats to the quality of life to the point that regulatory zoning is inherently justified when it excludes them. Whereas local governments now seek to ensure quality of life by limiting development densities, this book advocates a planning practice that supports a high quality of life at a full range of metropolitan densities, some of which will support greater transportation alternatives than are currently offered.

Over the longer term, one can reasonably hope that such an altered planning practice would in fact mitigate the harms associated with current development patterns; this book is motivated by just such a hope. But metropolitan areas change slowly: each year's development is tiny compared with the established stock of buildings in a region. For alternative developments to moderate a region's dependence on the automobile, they cannot remain isolated pockets but must benefit over time from aggregation and contiguity. Although the urgency of the policy imperatives makes a certain impatience understandable, advocates of reformed land-use practices ought not to hang their hopes on environmental, energy, societal, or health improvements that are measurable from one year to the next. In contrast, the short-run goal of expanding household choice by removing regulatory obstacles to alternative development can have immediate benefits.

IS MUNICIPAL REGULATION "THE MARKET?"

The book's argument begins by considering how research testing the link between urban form and travel behavior has proceeded. The establishment of travel behavior benefits through scientific research is generally taken as the foundation of the legitimacy of policy intervention. Chapter 2 argues that by proceeding in this fashion, the literature has constructed the status quo as a more or less free market and viewed any needed policy reforms as governmental interventions. This construction is not monolithic, however, and several variations are identifiable. The simplest version is the view that unconstrained markets tend toward sprawl, and that planning intervenes on behalf of compact development. Given the prevalence of municipal regulations geared at low-density development and land-use separation, this view is difficult to sustain. A related view acknowledges the centrality of municipal regulation in shaping metropolitan form but holds that regulation is itself tantamount to the market, or else treats the extent of municipal regulatory powers in the United States as an immutable fact—almost a state of nature—rather than one institutional arrangement among alternatives. A similar view acknowledges the impact of municipal regulation in fostering a low-density, auto-oriented metropolitan form but sees stricter regional regulations as the only alternative; the possibility of liberalizing exclusionary local regulations is not acknowledged.

Those understandings of the development of metropolitan areas square poorly with empirical research that largely finds municipal land-use regulation to be a binding constraint that lowers development densities and creates more exclusive communities than would arise under a free market. But even though many economists freely acknowledge the density-lowering impact of municipal regulations—and hence the connection between these

regulations and metropolitan sprawl—economics-based interpretations of
the status quo are surprisingly sanguine. Chapter 3 describes how a line of
thinking based in Tiebout's (1956) work concludes that a municipal ability
to exclude by regulation is a necessary element of the marketlike process of
"voting with one's feet" for residential communities. Notwithstanding the
regulatory nature of municipal exclusionary zoning, the intervention is
broadly viewed as essential to the efficient supply of publicly provided
goods. This idea evolved, with the work of William Fischel (1985), into a
concept of zoning as a collective property right held by the municipality as
fiduciary for its citizens.

Chapter 4 challenges that sanguine view of the impact of municipal
zoning practices on metropolitan form. As a regulatory constraint on economic activity, zoning creates a loss among households excluded from
what would otherwise be their first-choice residential communities. If this
loss were outweighed by the efficiency gains associated with a decentralized
supply of publicly provided goods, the equation of municipal decentralization with economic efficiency might be warranted. But rather than balancing these costs against other benefits, research in the Tiebout tradition
explicitly assumes away the costs imposed on excluded households. The
"zoning as a collective property right" framework seeks to correct that view.
Although its prescriptions can modify some of the extremes of exclusionary
municipal practices, they remain significant obstacles to the development
of alternatives to low-density, auto-oriented development.

The economics-based views of municipal zoning function—whether as
governmental regulation or as a collective property right—have notable
parallels within legal scholarship and judicial reasoning. In a formal legal
sense, the zoning function is a delegation of the state's police power to
municipalities. But legal scholars have argued that some courts (including
the U.S. Supreme Court) have ruled as if the zoning power inhered in the
rights of local citizens to protect their private property. This ambiguity
reflects historical ambivalence within the Anglo-American legal tradition
over the status of municipalities as intermediaries between the individual
and the state. In general, Chapter 5 argues, the deference that U.S. courts
have accorded municipal zoning places it in a category apart from other
instances of regulation, treating zoning fundamentally as protection of private property rather than as governmental regulation of economic activity.
In this way, judicial rulings both bolster and reflect a view that current metropolitan development is governed by a more or less free market. When the
status quo is defined in that fashion, the question of whether intervention

in land-use development and policy is justified by proven travel behavior benefits appears to make sense. By contrast, when zoning is recognized as a form of governmental regulation, the burden of proof for land-use reform shifts.

When the current state of metropolitan development is defined as a more or less free market, the task for compact-development planning becomes employing regulatory tools to produce alternatives that the market is incapable of providing. This is simultaneously the aspiration of smart-growth proponents and the fear of its critics. Chapter 6 argues that under most circumstances, regulations are incapable of forcing land-development markets to develop at above-market densities: any minimum-density regulations are ultimately unenforceable because of the mobility of capital. Because developers have numerous alternative investment opportunities, the choice to develop in a zone that is subject to minimum-density or other requirements is evidence that profits expected from such development are at least the equal of those associated with the best alternative site. That regulations cannot compel compactness may be sobering to some advocates of transportation-land integration. It should not be. If regulatory reform cannot usually compel compact growth but can only allow or facilitate it where markets are sufficient for its support, the ostensible threat of forcing people to live in ways they do not want is revealed as chimerical. This view ought to inform and invigorate planning efforts for compact development and integration of transportation and land use.

The arguments above lead to families of empirically testable hypotheses. To the extent that the contentions are valid, one would expect a number of outcomes. Land developers would be expected to seek to develop more compactly than regulations allow. Metropolitan areas whose neighborhood alternatives include transit- and pedestrian-friendly neighborhoods should support a closer match between households' transportation and land-use preferences and actual neighborhood choices than their more uniformly auto-oriented counterparts. States whose planning regimes limit municipalities' prerogative to exclude denser housing forms ought to witness accelerated growth in these forms. Chapters 7 and 8 report on empirical investigations into these issues from the supply side and the demand side, respectively, finding strong and consistent effects.

Chapter 9 concludes by calling for a change in the terms of debate in transportation and land use as a necessary prerequisite to policy reform. As long as the status quo in metropolitan development is accorded default status—as long as it is viewed as a virtual state of nature rather than one set of institutional arrangements among many—the transportation and land-use debate will hinge on the quality of scientific evidence linking travel behavior to metropolitan form. Recognition that the status quo is intensely regulated at the municipal level ought to alter the debate fundamentally, changing the rationale for policy reform, the goals of reform, and the manner in which scientific evidence is linked to policy implications.

CHAPTER TWO

TRAVEL BEHAVIOR RESEARCH AND THE "MARKET"

"I think people generally assume that whatever you have right now *is* the 'free market system,'" reports an interviewee quoted in Lewis (1996, *211*). Implicitly or explicitly, research on the link between land use and travel behavior has largely accepted this interpretation of the status quo. When investigations in this tradition assess the impacts on driving, walking, or transit use as the test of smart growth, New Urbanism, or transit-oriented development, they automatically set up a default: if scientific proof of beneficial impacts falls short, the conclusion is that there is no legitimate transportation reason to alter auto-oriented development patterns.

The construction of a default development choice is not a single perspective. Rather, it has been based on a range of supporting assumptions, many of which are shared by both advocates and skeptics of land-use approaches to transportation. The simplest of these is that markets tend toward low-density development but planning intervention seeks to compel more compact communities. This assertion does not withstand cursory scrutiny, however, when one notes that in the vast majority of cases, planning regulations impose caps rather than floors on density and intensity of development. In rare instances planning regulations specify minimum densities, but without developers who are interested in building at the specified densities, the regulations are powerless to compel such growth, since the developers can seek more favorable investment opportunities elsewhere.

A second view equates decentralized municipal regulation with market forces. This interpretation enjoys significant basis in economics, where zoning is viewed as a foundation of the efficient supply of publicly provided goods; the idea will be considered in the planning context here and in its economics incarnation in the following chapter. A related assertion, considered in the next chapter, is that municipal regulations follow or replicate market results. Under this view, the metropolitan form that emerges under a zoning regime differs little from what a less regulated market might have produced.

A third perspective acknowledges the regulatory character of municipal land-use controls, together with their capacity to restrict transportation and land-use alternatives, but views it as an inherent and inexorable outcome of the preferences of established residents. Land-use policy may be made at the local, regional, or state level, but in the U.S. system of land-use governance, a high level of deference is granted to municipal authorities. Rather than being one institutional arrangement among alternatives, municipal prerogative in land use is taken to be a natural outgrowth of the will of local electorates. According to this view, which enjoys some grounding in common-law jurisprudence (Chapter 5), the powers of a municipality to regulate land uses derive not from the state's regulatory power but directly from the inherent rights protecting home and family from nuisance. Just as householders have the right to choose whom they allow into their home, municipalities have the right—independent of the state—to determine what kind of development they will host and, by extension, what kinds of people will become community members. The view that land-use regulation is fundamentally a property right implies a broad municipal prerogative to act on local sentiment. By contrast, if cities derive their power strictly from the state, they are more accountable to public purposes beyond their borders, and less able to regulate on the basis of parochial interests alone. Thus development proposals are said to fail because of "neighborhood opposition"—as if this sentiment were a force independent of the regulatory authority required to operationalize it.

A fourth perspective acknowledges the local regulatory component of the status quo but considers regional regulation the only alternative, thus overlooking another possible antithesis: the liberalization of restrictive municipal regulations. Even increasing authority of higher-level administrative or judicial bodies overseeing local land-use planning does not necessarily amount to ever-stricter interventions into land markets. In fact, one focus of regional planning is overcoming parochial local sentiments for exclusion by regulation (Lewis 1996).

Finally, a relatively small subset of research into travel behavior and land use explicitly acknowledges the role of municipal regulation in creating a low-density, auto-oriented metropolitan form. But even though these studies may consider the possibility of "planning failure" in creating jobs-housing imbalances or excluding New Urbanist developments, the test of policy reform remains unchanged. Whether an auto-intensive metropolitan form is seen as largely a market product or as a result of municipal regulation, the question remains unchanged: would planning for alternatives increase walking or transit use, or reduce vehicle miles traveled (VMT) or congestion? That is, proof of beneficial impacts on travel remains the rationale for regulatory reform regardless of whether the status quo represents a market failure or a planning failure.

Even as the core problem definition has remained constant over decades, the specific policy goals to which transportation and land-use research is addressed have evolved over the decades. Work in this tradition in the 1960s tended to be concerned with the quality of life in communities. The energy crises of the 1970s sparked interest in the potential fuel-saving impacts of alternatives to auto-oriented development. Air quality concerns grew over the same era and continue unabated. The 1980s saw a growth in research motivated by the hope that alternative land-use arrangements might mitigate congestion. All of these issues received newly focused attention in the 1990s with the prominence of the New Urbanist and smart-growth movements in urban design and planning. The turn of the century saw a rapid rise in public health concerns regarding the relationship of neighborhood form to a person's level of physical activity, especially walking and cycling.

Throughout this period, increasingly sophisticated social science methodologies have been applied to ever-finer datasets in search of an understanding of the relationship between land use and travel behavior. Yet improved methods have hardly produced consensus. Researchers remain sharply divided on the usefulness of alternative development forms for domestic transportation policy. These divisions run largely between proponents, who assert significant travel-behavior benefits, and skeptics, who find these outcomes to be ambiguous or illusory. But improved scientific understandings of the relationship between land use and travel behavior will not resolve the controversy because travel behavior studies are not designed to shed light on the more fundamental question of why there is so little alternative development to begin with.

This chapter examines some of the early research in this field and then considers the implicit and explicit views of current transportation literature on the relationship between municipal regulation and "the market."

EARLY STUDIES OF URBAN FORM AND TRAVEL BEHAVIOR

The methods of quantitative social science have been applied to the impact of land use on travel behavior since the middle of the 20th century. Mitchell and Rapkin (1954) revolutionized transportation planning by establishing that the best way to understand traffic flows was through analysis of the patterns of land use that determined the origins and destinations of trips. This understanding served as the basis of transportation demand models, whose forecasts are a lynchpin of the professional practice of transportation planning and engineering. Although much of the research endeavor was motivated by the straightforward prospect of forecasting travel demand given some future arrangement of land use, a distinct alternative motivation emerged in the late 1960s. During that era, some researchers began to examine the link between land use and travel behavior with an eye toward reducing the need for automotive travel, rather than merely predicting it.

Transportation and land-use research in the early 1960s was largely oriented toward gauging future transportation requirements; the work from this time does not consider land use as a potential policy lever that might be applied consciously to reduce the need for some travel. Levinson and Wynn (1963) wrote in this vein, taking future land-use patterns to be a given and extensively cataloguing their anticipated connection to car use, transit ridership, and highway needs. John Lansing and his colleagues extensively applied survey research methods to people's travel behavior. Their 1964 report, "Residential Location and Urban Mobility," studied variations in travel behavior by land-use category, primarily considering the planning of transportation facilities; the potential for policies altering the status quo in land use was not explicitly examined. Considerable emphasis was placed on households' location preferences and how these are likely to evolve; consistent with transportation planning methodology of that era, land uses and their change were largely taken as external inputs into the transportation planning process.

By 1970, however, the emphasis had shifted. *Planned Residential Environments* (Lansing et al. 1970) was an explicit evaluation of the potential for alternative development practices to alter transportation (and other) outcomes. The study, prepared for the Bureau of Public Roads, focused on the master-planned communities of Reston, Virginia; Columbia, Maryland; and Radburn, New Jersey; in-town redevelopments in Washington, D.C. and Detroit, Michigan were also evaluated. These master-planned environments were compared with a series of "less planned" communities. Though the study was strictly a postoccupancy evaluation of different types of communities, its identification of its subjects as "planned" or "less planned" implied a policy agenda for transportation planning. Land use did not need to be viewed strictly as an external input into the planning process for transportation facilities: it could be the product of conscious foresight. The authors were circumspect about this agenda, however, explaining their motivations with cautious statements like "[a] transportation planner who knew what the future density of residential development was to be in an area could be more confident of his plans than one who did not" (3).

The study recognized a core definitional difficulty in characterizing environments as "more" or "less" planned—a difficulty that would follow the land-use and travel behavior literature for the next three decades. "Unfortunately (for the purposes of a neat dichotomy)," they wrote, "virtually *any* individual or developer must address himself to these basic questions of 'planning' when deciding to locate in a particular place whatever the size of the land parcel to be developed. Since zoning regulations in this country were initiated and upheld in the 1920s, residential development usually has been based on plans and regulations controlling land use, lot coverage, setback, and street and utility layout. When such controls exist, 'unplanned' seems a misnomer" (4–5).

Thus, more than many of its successors in travel behavior research, this work understood that the ubiquity of municipal regulation implies that policy issue is not one of "planned" versus "market-driven" development. Instead, the differences observed were between neighborhood environments that were all characterized by extensive planning intervention—albeit under different institutional structures and with different aims.

The project nonetheless characterized the distinguishing hallmarks of planned environments. To accomplish this task, the study implicitly equated physical attributes of the environment with the processes (ostensibly more or less planned) under which these elements developed—a linkage common to research in this field over the next three decades. In some cases the rationale for linking physical product and development process was evident. For example, the separation of incompatible land uses, such as residences and factories, was identified as a hallmark of "planned" environments; most land-use planners would agree that this separation is in fact a foundation of their practice. Similarly, a design harmony among contiguous buildings was seen as an element of the planned environment. A congruity of design is a plausible hallmark of planning, since it is often based on public design standards and site plan review.

By contrast, other indicators of the planned environment bore a looser relationship to actual planned outcomes. For example, a variety of housing types throughout a community (including single-family detached, townhouses, and highrises) was seen as a hallmark of planning. Yet planning processes in many suburban communities seek specifically to restrict housing types by limiting the supply of denser, more affordable, or smaller housing units through land-use regulation, thereby creating less variety than might otherwise arise. The equation between planning and a mix of housing type is unsupported. Similarly, the proximity of commercial, institutional, recreational, and residential uses was taken as an indicator of the planned environment. Yet in many cases, zoning practices explicitly separate these uses and reduce their commingling.

Ultimately, despite its acknowledgment of the ubiquity of planning, the study presaged much future work in the field by conflating process and product; "planned" environments were those that contained elements that the authors liked, even though ordinary municipal planning processes were frequently designed to produce precisely the opposite outcome. Thus auto-oriented suburbia was viewed as the antithesis of planning, despite the ubiquitous interventions of land-use regulation on which it is based. This view continues throughout much of the travel behavior literature to this day. Given the nature of the 1970 study—an expost evaluation of specific residential environments—the report was probably not greatly affected by this problem definition. For example, it could have resolved the definitional issues by comparing "master-planned" and "conventionally planned" environments. By contrast, the literature that came afterward seemed motivated more explicitly by the prospect—some of its authors would say "threat"—that planning would shape metropolitan form. For this later work, confusion over what does and does not count as planned would affect the policy debate fundamentally.

An early research approach to the impact of metropolitan form on travel behavior was based on linear programming methods. The analyses defined as their objective some minimization of travel requirements under various land-use configurations to simulate the sensitivity of travel demand to those alternatives. This framework implied an unrealistically large degree of central planning control over land uses. For example, one study asked, "Is there a best combination of elements of urban form in the sense that this particular combination requires less travel than any other combination of elements?" (Hemmens 1967, 33). The reader gets the feeling that rather than believing that such central control could actually be exerted, researchers were driven to these questions primarily by their linear programming methodology, and any link from research to policy and practice appears to be somewhat of an afterthought.

By contrast, in 1974 Watt and Ayers explicitly offered "down-zoning at the urban periphery" as an approach for decreasing the rate of agricultural-land conversion, with an eye toward potential energy savings from compact development. Much of this current literature also gives explicit clues to its conception of the policy task at hand, by considering auto-oriented suburbia as the default choice for development. The remainder of this chapter analyzes the (sometimes contrasting) components of transportation and land-use research's construction of a neutral default in metropolitan development.

ASSUMPTION 1: THE MARKET WANTS TO SPRAWL, BUT PLANNING ENCOURAGES COMPACT CITIES

The most straightforward articulation of the idea that auto-oriented suburbia is the antithesis of planning is found in an unadorned "markets-versus-regulation" perspective. In this version, land development markets tend toward low-density, auto-oriented forms; when planners intervene, they attempt—with greater or lesser success, and with greater or lesser justification—to generate more compact alternatives through regulatory means. Conventional understandings of the American dream—the single-family home surrounded by a yard in a low-density environment—accord with this view. Even much writing in favor of compact development diagnoses the role of the market in this fashion. "The reason the land is disappearing is simple," according to a *California Journal* (1997) article that frets over the loss of farmland in the Central Valley. "Developers built it, and people came."

Travel behavior researchers rarely express their conception of metropolitan development processes that starkly. But by setting up auto-oriented suburban development as an explicit default, they confer on it "unfettered market" status. For example, Levinson and Kumar (1997, 169–70) write that "[t]he ability of policy-makers in relatively free markets to modify density is clearly marginal compared to the size of cities," an analysis that appears not to consider the demonstrated potential of regulatory policy to lower development densities. Moreover, relationships between urban form and travel behavior "are particularly weak compared with total variation in commuting. Using density as a primary tool influencing commuting behavior seems an expensive approach to the problem" (169). The nature of the expense is not detailed, but the implication is that actively altering what is presumed to be the relatively free market outcome—"*using* density"—entails costs in enforcement or loss of utility for people in denser environments.

Research on the connection between travel behavior and land use frequently characterizes alternative development as seeking actively to control or manipulate travel behavior; this formulation of necessity implies the existence of an unmanipulated situation. Presumably low-density, auto-oriented development represents this default. For example, Boarnet and Sarmiento (1998, 1156) write, "Viewed as transport policy, the New Urbanism and related ideas are the latest steps in a planning tradition which is increasingly arguing that land use can be manipulated to influence travel behavior...Yet the empirical evidence for this claim is often weak." Under this formulation, New Urbanist development represents an artificially engineered shift from the base—or natural—case of low-density, auto-oriented designs.

The conception of sprawl as the market's solution is similarly evident in an equation of processes of densification and rigid planning: "The risk inherent in using long-lived urban designs to manage today's congestion and air quality problems is that if situations change, if new solutions become available, or if urban design policies have unanticipated consequences, it is difficult to readjust something as durable as urban form," write Boarnet and Crane (2001, 14). This equation of redevelopment at higher densities with planning rigidity overlooks the fact that densification in the face of changing economic conditions is one of the prime ways cities have revealed their adaptivity throughout history. It is ironic that these processes are equated here with planning rigidity when the authors elsewhere document the propensity of municipalities to zone out much transit-oriented development.

Advocates for compact development are equally likely to equate sprawl with the unplanned market. For example, in response to critics of compact-city policies, Newman and Kenworthy (1992, 354) ask rhetorically:

> Are there no options for managing cities other than to argue academically for the charging of correct prices? Surely we can choose how to organize our cities other than just by being consumers. Those who reside in and work in our cities are consumers and that is a powerful force in how the city operates. But it is not all, because those people are also citizens who have sensibilities about how their communities ought to be. Both forces involve a role for the physical planner.

The authors thus implicitly yield to the assertion that low-density, auto-oriented development bears no trace of the planner's thumbprint and is the relatively untrammeled product of millions of households' decisions. Ewing (1995, 17) appears to see things similarly: "Governments' ability to affect density, mode choice, and the single-purpose commute may be limited, as the skeptics argue, yet greater accessibility may still be achievable and effective in reducing vehicular travel." This quote suggests that current patterns of suburban development are relatively unaffected by government policy.

Alternative designs are sometimes viewed as a foreign intervention imposed on a landscape that otherwise embodies people's preferences. For example, Crane (1996, 118) writes of New Urbanist approaches that "[h]owever well intentioned, the new designs can thus cause problems when naively applied." It is doubtful that many development forms can avoid the potential for causing problems—particularly when naively applied. Yet those associated with the status quo are seemingly exempted from this litmus test, presumably because they have passed the test of the market. Crane (1998) has been even more explicit, arguing that "[w]e must strive to avoid new urban and suburban developments that, although pretty and ambitious, might unintentionally cause more traffic problems than they solve." Thus development alternatives are judged unidimensionally by their contribution to solution of traffic problems. Only an artificially imposed intervention would logically be judged in this fashion; naturally developing existing neighborhoods are understood to have multiple purposes beyond their impact on roadway congestion. Stopping all new developments that could "cause more traffic problems than they solve" would shut down development entirely in many metropolitan areas.

Neighborhood Self-Selection and the Default Choice

The views of travel behavior research on the "market" nature of low-density, auto-oriented development are revealed particularly clearly through researchers' interpretations of processes of neighborhood self-selection. In social science research, self-selection is a perennial source of bias whereby individual choices mask the true effect of the independent variable of interest. Researchers steeped in social science methods are trained to heed the following admonition and seek to weed out self-selection bias from their research designs:

> If any basis other than chance is used to assign subjects to groups, then subject selection may account for differences on the dependent variable. Any selection procedure that permits subjects themselves to determine to which treatment they will be exposed is particularly hazardous. Such self-selection on the part of the research subjects makes it impossible to tell whether the treatment affected dependent variable scores or whether differences in scores were determined by the personal characteristics of the individuals who chose to expose themselves to the experimental treatment. (Crano and Brewer 1986, 32)

In the case of transportation and land use, researchers worry whether "[u]rban design...might not lure would-be automobile commuters out of their cars as much as the new designs might provide residential neighborhoods for persons who already prefer to drive less" (Boarnet and Crane 2001, 94). An approach to remedying this bias is "to control for the influence of urban design on residential location choice, and then examine any remaining link between land use and travel behavior." In other words, self-selection is a source of bias to be eliminated before the pure effect—the impact of alternative land uses on the travel behavior of randomly selected populations—can be identified. In travel behavior studies, the self-selection effect may be defined as the difference between the impact of urban form on travel behavior of a self-selected group of individuals and a randomly selected group. The self-selection phenomenon complicates any policy inference one might draw from observed differences in travel behavior; if residents of dense, close-in, mixed-use neighborhoods are observed walking more than others, is the behavior difference because of the neighborhood's characteristics or simply because it attracted people who like to walk? In this vein, Boarnet and Greenwald (2001, 32) write, "Another possibility is that some people prefer to travel in certain ways and that those people choose to live in neighborhoods that support their desired travel patterns. For example, people who prefer to walk might live in dense, pedestrian-friendly neighborhoods, while people who prefer driving live in more car-oriented suburbs. Yet it would be shaky to infer from those associations that urban design can be used to get people who prefer driving to forsake their cars."

This would indeed be a shaky inference, but if transit- and pedestrian-oriented neighborhoods are undersupplied because of regulatory obstacles, it would not be the policy task at hand. By way of analogy, consider a hypothetical school district that offered only a single, standard type of elementary school. A new, "open" model of elementary school is established in the district, and parents can choose to send their children to the new school. Assume that the open model improves educational outcomes for some students but not all, and further, that pupils upon whom the alternative model would have a positive effect are significantly more likely than others to select this school. The school would be expected to have a positive impact on educational outcomes in the district, with a large portion of that effect being due to self-selection. Its test is not to improve educational outcomes for pupils who prefer conventional education, but rather to allow children who do better in alternative environments to flourish. In fact, the entire impact of the new school would be the "self-selection" effect if a randomly selected group of students assigned to the new school demonstrated average performance no better—or even worse—than a control group that remained in the conventional educational environment. Most observers would agree, however, that self-selection here is not a source of bias to be controlled for but rather the primary route through which the treatment is effective. Correcting for the self-selection "bias" by modeling the effect of alternative education on a randomly selected group of students would underestimate the impact of the new school on educational outcomes. It would be much better to study the effect of open education on the self-selected students who chose it: how did they do before and after their shift?

It is worth analyzing the elements of self-selection in this case. The treatment—open elementary schools—is most effective on a subpopulation that cannot be fully identified by measured variables such as test scores or previous academic performance. But members of the group on whom the treatment would have beneficial effects—or their parents—are able to identify themselves as potential beneficiaries, at least to some degree. This capacity leads them to self-select into the treatment group at higher than average rates. Under these conditions, self-selection cannot be viewed strictly as a source of bias, but it is at least in part a real effect of the treatment.

If the high academic performance of members of this subpopulation would not have been observed if they were exposed to standard elementary education, then none of the self-selection effect represents "bias" and the entire effect is a real outcome of the availability of the alternative elementary school.

The travel-behavior case is similar to the education policy issue in several respects. Residence in accessible, pedestrian- and transit-oriented neighborhoods is likely to affect the travel behavior of people oriented toward extensive automobile dependence less than that of people who prefer walking, cycling, transit, and short auto trips. Members of the group on which the treatment is effective—people who prefer environments that support reduced car use—are likely to be aware of their preference. For this reason, they can be expected to self-select into amenable neighborhoods at higher than average rates when given the opportunity.

The preferences that lead to this self-selection are not entirely measurable by researchers. Yet unlike the education case above, this process of neighborhood self-selection is viewed by many researchers as a source of bias to be eliminated in search of the pure effect of neighborhood form on the travel behavior of a randomly selected population. This search for the pure effect is pursued even though once developed, these neighborhoods would fill up not with randomly selected individuals but with self-selected residents. The built environment then becomes a mediator, in the sense that it enables the exercise of preferences. In this way, the self-selection effect would be a real impact of policy reform rather than a source of bias by definition to be isolated and discarded.

The view that self-selection is inherently a source of bias to be measured and eliminated presupposes that these market preferences for transit- and pedestrian-oriented neighborhoods have already been satisfied. If regulatory obstacles impede the satisfaction of these preferences, then one would expect significant unmet or latent demand for residence in such neighborhoods. Any new walkable neighborhood would enjoy beneficial self-selection. Its residents' behavior would be expected to resemble that of the self-selected individuals living in similar neighborhoods, rather than the behavior of a hypothetical, randomly selected group of people somehow forced to live in a pedestrian-oriented neighborhood. If these households would otherwise live in more auto-oriented districts and travel like their neighbors, any reductions in their VMT would in fact be attributable to the provision of the new neighborhood. Thus the neighborhood form effect would work partly, or even mostly, *through* the self-selection effect. The dominant view that self-selection represents a source of bias thus implies that the status quo is a reasonably free market in metropolitan development in which all preferences are more or less equally likely to be satisfied.

That view is logically based on one of two assumptions, neither of them particularly supportable. The first is that although residents self-select because of a neighborhood's transportation characteristics, the observed low-VMT lifestyle of self-selected residents of transit- and pedestrian-friendly communities would be similar even if those individuals lived in auto-oriented environments. That is, the effect of these neighborhoods is simply to assemble in a single locale groups of people who would walk, cycle, or use transit even if they happened to live in low-density, auto-oriented environments. This assumption may be reasonable where poverty or other factors limit households' access to a private automobile; households living under those constraints would likely exhibit low VMT per capita regardless of the environment in which they found themselves. But residents of transit- and pedestrian-friendly neighborhoods are not limited to those without access to cars, and a study of people's travel behavior before and after residential relocation demonstrated significant impact of urban form on the travel behavior of the very same individuals (Krizek 2003).

There is a second possible basis for viewing neighborhood self-selection strictly as a source of bias. In the past, pedestrian- and transit-oriented neighborhoods enjoyed beneficial self-selection; that is, they tended to attract people who preferred to walk, cycle, or use transit. Perhaps self-selection has changed, and this beneficial self-selection will not continue into the future; car use among the future self-selected population will be no less than that of the population at large. It is frankly difficult to see why such a shift should occur. If transportation and land-use characteristics are among the bundle of attributes that households consider when choosing a neighborhood, households that do not particularly value a transit- or pedestrian-friendly environment ought not be willing to bid as much for these neighborhoods as households that do. Only if all households with any such preference already reside in these neighborhoods would the neighborhood self-selection be expected to shift from beneficial to neutral. This condition would be unlikely to hold given the regulatory restrictions on denser development.

Even under unconstrained market conditions, existing residents of auto-oriented neighborhoods would be likely to exhibit a continuum of preferences, from those more amenable to transit- and pedestrian-oriented alternatives to dyed-in-the-wool fans of low-density living. Within any given income class, a new transit-oriented neighborhood would likely be occupied disproportionately by the former group. It is therefore difficult to imagine the circumstances under which the self-selection effect would not continue to operate in any new transit- and pedestrian-oriented neighborhoods; if that is the case, modeling the travel-behavior effect of these neighborhoods on a randomly selected group of residents would surely underestimate their impact.

Under the second assumption, pedestrian- and transit-oriented neighborhoods represent an imposed addition to a region's housing stock, unlike existing walkable neighborhoods, which presumably arose through more organic processes. That alternative development forms represent an artificial imposition on otherwise free markets is evident in a scenario presented by Kitamura et al. (1997, 126):

> One could argue that certain types of land use patterns attract residents with certain demographic and socio-economic attributes, attitudes and values, and that these attributes of residents are the true determinants of their travel behavior. Spatial segregation of socio-economic classes and resulting relative homogeneity within each residential neighborhood are consistent with this view. If this is in fact the case, then altering land use characteristics by itself would not affect the residents' travel behavior; travel characteristics would change only after new residents are attracted by the new land use and move into the area while old residents who find the land use unsuitable eventually move out. In the case of new developments, given the increasingly unaffordable cost of single-family dwellings in major metropolitan areas, the demand for higher-density housing may be for many people due to its lower cost, not due to a lifestyle preference for a higher-density environment. If so, then selection of a home in a higher-density neighborhood may not be accompanied by the same travel characteristics that have historically been associated with such residential locations. That is, auto ownership and use may not be as low in the future for these types of developments as has been the case in the past. It is then unclear how effective or desirable it would be to attempt to manage travel demand through land use policy.

The operation of self-selection of walkable neighborhoods of the future is seen as discontinuous with the operation of the process in the past. Why this might be the case is not made explicit; presumably, the denser neighborhoods of the past were a product of ordinary market processes, whereas future such developments would be imposed through regulation and would therefore function entirely differently.

The perspective on self-selection in Kimura et al.'s research is further illustrated by their use of attitudinal variables in explaining travel behavior. Eight factors were extracted from responses to statements with which respondents indicated their agreement or disagreement. These factors gauged attitudes toward transportation issues, such as "pro-environment," "pro transit/ridesharing," "suburbanite," or "urban villager." These attitudes were then used as independent variables jointly with neighborhood characteristics to model travel behavior outcomes. The authors' interpretation follows:

> Land use characteristics as represented by the neighborhood descriptors are associated with mobility and offer some explanation of the variation in the mobility measures in addition to that offered by the attitude factors. Their associations with the mobility measures, however, tend to be weaker compared with the associations shown by the attitude factors. One may conclude that attitudes are at least more strongly, and perhaps more directly, associated with travel than are land use characteristics. (154)

In other words, this project sought to model the effect of neighborhood type on travel behavior *while controlling for* a family of transportation-related attitudes. The fallacy of this view is evident: if my choice of neighborhood type is endogenous to my transportation attitudes (the very essence of neighborhood self-selection), then gauging the impact of neighborhood characteristics while controlling for attitudes leads to downward-biased estimates of the neighborhood effects.[1] For example, if households' "pro-transit" or "urban villager" attitudes spur them to select residence in a transit-oriented neighborhood, then the question of how much of their travel behavior is attributable to their attitudes and how much to their environment makes little sense, since their attitudes influenced their travel behavior at least in part *via* neighborhood choice. Hence, the two factors cannot plausibly be viewed as rival explanations within this research design.[2]

Cervero (2002) acknowledges the role of self-selection in explaining observed travel patterns but seeks to articulate a residual role for urban design factors in shaping travel behavior: "While a household might move near a rail station in order to enjoy a stress-free ride to work each morning, nicely landscaped pathways to retail stores near their residence might very well influence nonwork trips, such as for shopping. That is, self-selection might largely explain variation for some trip purposes, but not for all." The explanation is surprisingly mild given Cervero's (1996) own analysis implicating local regulation as the primary impediment to the provision of affordable housing near suburban job centers. If such housing is undersupplied because of regulatory obstacles to its development, removal of these obstacles would enable people who might otherwise live in auto-oriented areas to choose transit-oriented development. Under these circumstances, the self-selection effect is a real outcome of changes in the built form on travel behavior overall. If the land-use effect works largely via self-selection, then a search for a residual pure effect would underestimate the potential impact of land-use policy reform.

Lansing et al. (1970, 23) expressed this idea in an especially direct fashion: "If a unique group of people have been attracted to Reston, for example, their responses to Reston may be different from those of people who are in some relevant sense different from them and who now live elsewhere. The extreme (and unlikely) possibility is that everybody who would like Reston is already there." If supply of alternatives is limited, there is every reason to believe that the high bidders for housing with few close substitutes would be households that value its unique attributes more highly than others. Thus the view that self-selection is inherently a source of statistical bias reveals an underlying view that the status quo, as a product of a more or less free market, serves a complete range of neighborhood preferences equally well. Under this view, the planning interventions that are presumed to be required for transit- and pedestrian-friendly development come to impose on the market a greater share of such development than the market itself demands. Absent from this view is the perspective offered by economics research (Chapter 3) that acknowledges that land-use regulations in fact lower development densities to below-market levels.

Competing understandings of neighborhood self-selection—as a source of statistical bias or as a way to affect travel behavior through land use— have an additional implication for travel-behavior research. Such research cannot be interpreted in the absence of a theory of production of metropolitan form. If all preferences were equally likely to be satisfied, self-selection would have one interpretation for travel behavior, as a bias inherently to be eliminated; if preferences for transit- and pedestrian-oriented neighborhoods were systematically undersatisfied, the phenomenon would have a different interpretation entirely. Thus without accounting for the processes by which neighborhood options are produced, travel behavior researchers have no means of interpreting their findings. The question of how land use affects travel cannot be answered without asking why so few transit- and pedestrian-friendly neighborhoods get produced to begin with.

Traditional Transportation Planning as Default

A view of current metropolitan development as a neutral base case rests on two principal assumptions. As described in this chapter, the first is a view that land development is guided by a more or less free market. The second is that the practice of transportation planning itself is a reasonably value-free accommodation of people's preferences. Boarnet and Crane (2001, 4) articulate this view of the traditional "predict-and-supply" mode of transportation planning:

> The planners who designed and built these roads were physical, not social, engineers. They saw their task as building street and highway capacity to meet certain precisely specified vehicle flow and circulation objectives. They rarely sought to change urban form to influence travel patterns. Instead, they took existing travel patterns as a given, designed a road system for current and projected demand, and constructed the system.

The characterization of these engineers' self-perception is accurate enough, but it begs the question of whether value-neutral accommodation of travel preferences is possible in the first place; is there a way that physical systems on the scale of the U.S. highway system can be engineered without social engineering as a by-product? If not, then it is logically impossible to identify certain modes of transportation and land-use planning as "travel by design" (Boarnet and Crane 2001) in contrast with others that are driven by value-free technical rationality. The impossibility of value-neutral transportation planning was recognized as early as 1961 by Melvin Webber, and no one has articulated it better since:

> Distrustful of the city planner's judgmental and valuative approaches to land use planning, the engineer has been quick to adopt the positivistic land use models as a means for substituting land use forecasting in the place of land use planning. The attractiveness of these models lies in their promise of a relatively simple and straight-forward method of portraying future land use patterns with the precision and the certainty that good engineering demands. (380)
>
> The value neutrality of transportation planning is clearly impossible. A transportation system does not solely serve traffic demand. Its major effect is to modify and shape time-distance relationships, hence to modify locational decisions, hence to modify over-all land use patterns, hence to modify spatial linkage patterns, hence to modify traffic movement patterns. The effect of a transportation system, then, is to create its own traffic demand. (382)

ASSUMPTION 2: MUNICIPAL REGULATION EQUALS THE MARKET

An alternative view implicit in much of the transportation and land-use literature acknowledges the pervasive municipal regulation of land use but treats it as a market force. One variant of this perspective is that advocated by Fischel and discussed in Chapter 3: zoning is most usefully viewed as a collective property right. Transportation and land-use research is generally less explicit about the reasons for treating municipal regulation as a market force and often treats the subject obliquely.

For example, Cervero (1989) argues that "[t]he principal reason for jobs-housing mismatches is that *ad-hoc market forces* have generally shaped suburban growth in most U.S. metropolitan areas. Localities typically make decisions to accept or reject housing and employment with little regard for the regional consequence of these decisions" (emphasis added). Under this view, the decision of localities to accept or reject housing and employment is an example of a "market force." The article specifies five "powerful economic and demographic forces that have impeded the ability of Americans to reside in the community where they work" (138). Two of these five—fiscal and exclusionary zoning and growth moratoria—rest on the exercise of the state's regulatory power but are combined as "economic and demographic forces" with more autonomous societal processes, like growth in job turnover and two-income households. At the border between regulatory processes and sociodemographic trends in this list is the factor of "worker earning/housing cost mismatches." This is identified as an outcome of municipalities' "restricting housing supplies, fiscal zoning and growth ceilings." Thus of the "economic and demographic forces" identified, three are the regulatory processes of municipal government—underscoring the equation of decentralized local land-use regulation with "the market."

Surprisingly, this view is shared across the spectrum of transportation and land-use policy analysts. Altshuler (1979, 376) wrote, "If consensus is lacking on the objective of high urban density, this is not to suggest that there is any discernable support for deliberate government action to promote low-density development. Rather there is continuing predominant support in virtually all American regions for letting market forces and consumer preferences—constrained by zoning and environmental regulations, to be sure, but not guided in any more positive planning sense—determine the evolution of urban form." In Altshuler's view, then, municipal regulation limiting development density does not amount to "deliberate government action to promote low-density development." By implication, municipal regulation limiting development to one unit per acre must be nondeliberate, nongovernmental, or nonpromoting of low-density development. It is not clear which of these conditions is fulfilled according to this analysis, but in any case the municipal land-use controls are clearly being redefined as something less than regulation.

An equation of municipal regulation and market forces is implicit in Bogart's (1993) study of exclusionary zoning. Four motivations underlie exclusionary zoning, according to this study: fiscal zoning to exclude people who pay less in taxes than they consume in public services; public goods zoning to avoid increases in the costs of public services; consumption zoning to mitigate the negative effects that one land use is likely to impose on another; and political economic zoning to exclude people with preferences for publicly provided goods significantly different from those of established residents. Bogart argues that it is difficult to distinguish among the various motives for exclusionary zoning and concludes that "the existence of exclusionary zoning does not constitute a prima facie case for *any particular intervention* designed to affect the incentives to zone" (1679, emphasis added). Implicit in this view is the belief that municipal regulatory power—including the power to zone in an exclusionary fashion—is the preintervention state. Modifying municipal exclusionary powers would constitute intervention into the workings of the economy, whether justified or not. Unexamined in this formulation is the possibility that zoning itself is the governmental intervention, and that action to reduce municipal exclusionary prerogative can *increase* the role of markets in providing for a variety of land-use forms.

A view that local governmental regulation amounts to a market force is similarly implicit in Gordon and Richardson's (2001) call to "let markets plan." Rather than a prescription for freedom of land development from regulation, the article implies that "markets" means the decentralized control of land use at the municipal level, as opposed to interference by higher levels of government. First, the article sets up a market-based critique of New Urbanism and related initiatives: "Do we progress via a 'spontaneous order' that is essentially 'bottom-up,' or is 'top-down' better? About the time when the latter appeared permanently discredited, it was revived in the guise of growth controls, New Urbanism, and 'smart growth' plans for 'sustainable development'" (138). But within this ostensibly spontaneous order, exclusionary regulatory actions on the part of municipal governments are taken as a given:

If New Urbanist-type developments were demanded by consumers, they would be built. Obviously, we have no objection in principle to the idea that producers should offer consumers what they want, and we favor experiments by builders that provide a market test to see whether households are open to a change in residential lifestyles. An interesting question, especially with regard to infill projects, is whether these alternatives are *acceptable to the community at large,* as opposed to the prospective purchasers. There are many examples of *broader community objections to high-density* projects, usually on traffic-generation grounds." (140, emphasis added)

Objections by the community at large would have little relevance for the prospects of New Urbanist development but for the transformation of these objections into legally binding land-use regulation. The statement above mistakes the *supply* constraint of local regulation for lack of consumer *demand;* high-density projects are indeed demanded by consumers (otherwise there would be no reason for the expression of "community objections") but those demands are unlikely to be satisfied in an environment where these projects are excluded by the "community at large" through regulation.

It is similarly difficult to square the acknowledgment that community objections lead to regulatory exclusion with this statement: "the New Urbanist fall-back position that '...people should be given a choice' is not plausible; there is no acknowledgement of the fact that markets regularly generate the more feasible choices while discarding the infeasible ones, based on opportunity costs compared to consumers' willingness to pay" (138–39). Markets would hardly be expected to generate these feasible choices in the face of their acknowledged exclusion by municipal regulation.

Despite such contradictions, the call to "let markets plan" can be explained if one views municipal regulation of land uses as an element inherent to the market, something akin to governmental establishment of property rights. The authors explicitly say that this is their view: "it is understandable that choice of residence is often influenced by how property rights are secured. Such rights include the very important 'collective neighborhood property rights' that assure that neighboring properties are well maintained. Buyers understandably look for credible commitments by cities and/or developers. These motives underlie the demand for land-use controls and zoning rules" (134). It is notable that the impetus for zoning rules is referred to as a marketlike "demand;" in few other arenas is the desire for governmental regulations referred to in these terms. The position that Gordon and Richardson espouse amounts to a deference not to free markets per se but to municipal regulatory prerogative, even when that prerogative is employed in a fashion that impedes the development of options demanded by some households. The principal threat to markets, under this view, is challenge by state or federal administrative bodies to municipal prerogative, notwithstanding the authors' own acknowledgment of the tendency of local regulation to exclude denser development options.

ASSUMPTION 3: MUNICIPAL REGULATION IS IMMUTABLE

A third view, evident in much of the transportation and land-use literature, takes the current status of municipal regulation—including its exclusionary prerogative—as a given, rather than as one particular set of market-government relations among many potential alternatives. This position rests in part on simple pragmatism; given the entrenchment of municipal prerogative within the U.S. planning system, many analysts would argue for policies that offer progress on land-use issues that do not depend on a challenge to home-rule traditions. But transportation and land-use research frequently appears to go beyond this pragmatic acknowledgment of political realities, treating municipal powers as if they inhered from sources beyond the reach of any policy reform.

For example, Boarnet and Crane (1997) examine land-use plans to assess the willingness of Southern California municipalities to accept transit-oriented development and find pervasive exclusion of such development. One possible policy prescription of this finding would be a reduction of regulatory barriers to transit-oriented development, or even a reduction of the prerogative of municipalities to erect those barriers. Instead, the study views municipal regulatory hostility more as evidence of the "uphill battle" (189) that transit-oriented housing faces than as an argument against the regulatory practices that tilted the battlefield to begin with. The authors' prescription takes municipal prerogative as a given and asks under which circumstances the communities could be offered sufficient compensation to permit such development: "Indeed one measure of the merit of such projects is their ability to generate sufficiently high regional benefits to offset their local opportunity costs. The problem of compensating municipal authorities for those costs is the primary economic and political hurdle that this research lays bare" (191). Systems of compensation for accepting transit-oriented development—or at least rewards for good behavior—are in fact in use. But the problem is not inherently one of compensating municipalities to persuade them to remove obstacles; if this were the case, then the solution for any inefficient regional, state, or federal government regulation would be to compensate the relevant administrative agency enough to persuade it to liberalize.

A variant on the "immutability of local prerogative" theme equates local regulation with simple community will, as if no state-authorized regulatory body were needed to implement that will. Statements like "the developer ran into neighborhood opposition" are true enough but appear to construe that opposition as sufficient to exclude the development. Neighborhood opposition affects development only when translated into the regulatory decisions of bodies like city councils and municipal planning commissions. This shorthand parlance can tend to blur the exercise of the police power involved. For example, Downs (1992, 89) writes that for the transportation–land-use relationship "to bear fruit, local residents must permit previously low-density development near transit stops to be converted to higher density development." The development's neighbors as *residents* are irrelevant to the permitting process; its neighbors as a powerful political interest affecting the decisionmaking of a municipal regulatory body are clearly central.

A frequent assertion presumes that municipal land-use regulation—as opposed to state or federal regulation—is a simple expression of "the people's will." But if regulations enacted through local democratic processes are expressions of the people's will, surely state or federal regulations deserve the same deference. Apparently at issue is the level of geography at which that will is aggregated. Notwithstanding an ostensible American predilection for participatory local governance, any geographic aggregation in a democratic system includes some dimension of the people's will and excludes others. Processes of enactment of regulation at regional, state, or federal levels in the United States are not *a priori* any less democratic, and hence have no inherently weaker claim on the mantle of the people's will.

The position that municipal regulation represents the people's will more than that of higher levels of government reduces to a position about the level of geography at which that will is properly aggregated. Conferring the mantle of the people's will on the local level implies a particular set of interests that will be pursued, and others that will be ignored. Lewis (1996, 213) argues that "under almost no circumstances will neighborhood-sized polities deal with metropolitan issues" because "latent majorities essentially lack political representation in highly fragmented metro areas." Thus elevating neighborhood or municipal concerns to the level of the people's will amounts to a supposition that the people's will does not legitimately pertain to metropolitan-wide concerns.

ASSUMPTION 4: THE OPPOSITE OF MUNICIPAL REGULATION IS REGIONAL REGULATION

In many instances, municipal regulation is identified as a significant barrier to alternative development practices, yet the liberalizing option of limiting municipal regulatory prerogative is not considered as an alternative. Instead, the antidote considered frequently consists of regional regulation in the form of specified targets and imposed goals. For example, Cervero (1989, 148) offers as remedies for jobs-housing imbalances a set of alternative governmental interventions: "[i]nclusionary zoning, growth phasing, fiscal disparity programs, and fair-share housing laws." Boarnet and Crane (1997) considered three possible remedies to municipalities' practices of zoning out transit-oriented development: compensation to municipalities for accepting transit-based housing, education about the circumstances under which transit-based housing can benefit local communities, and regional mandates of local shares of transit-based housing. Although the problem to be treated was municipal-level regulation, regulatory liberalization was never considered as an alternative. The third option, that of regional-level regulation, was rejected for its potential to induce distortions in the local land market. That the pervasive interventions of local-level regulations documented by the research did not constitute such a threat further underscores a view of the "market" quality of local land-use regulation.

Seeing municipal regulation as tantamount to the market in this fashion leads to a paradox: regional or state rules that are designed to overcome local regulatory barriers to denser development would be seen as "market interference" even when geared toward *reducing* regulatory barriers to development. For example, the Oregon Transportation Planning Rule specifies, among other elements, the following: "In MPO [Metropolitan Planning Organization] areas, local governments shall adopt land use and subdivision regulations to reduce reliance on the automobile which: (a) Allow transit-oriented developments (TODs) on lands along transit routes" (Section 660-012-0045(5)(a)) and "...[O]n sites at major transit stops provide the following: ...(e) Existing development shall be allowed to redevelop a portion of existing parking areas for transit-oriented uses, include bus stops and pullouts, bus shelters, park and ride stations, transit-oriented developments, and similar facilities, where appropriate..." (Section 660-012-0045(4)(C)(e)). Although the language of much of the rest of the Oregon Transportation Planning Rule is highly prescriptive, the key provisions require the municipalities to *permit* land uses in the vicinity of transit lines that might not otherwise be allowed. These uses are not required; local government is simply enjoined from preventing the development that may arise through the initiative of other parties.

A critical element of statewide growth management programs is overcoming local opposition to compact development in appropriate locations. When this antigrowth sentiment is translated into exclusionary land-use regulations, it does not stop growth within the region, but rather compels a low-density pattern of development. These state regulations, rather than further restricting private development, seek to increase the role of markets in the face of local exclusion. In this vein, Lewis (1996) writes that where some land-use authority is vested in a geographic aggregation larger than the municipality, "[l]ocalized opposition to certain land uses may be overwhelmed by a more widespread, if less intense, preference for other goals in the rest of the city: economic vitality, for example, or regional transportation mobility, or an equalization of living conditions" (34). Thus a major role of regional or state involvement in land regulation is to counter, or neutralize, exclusionary local regulations.

Policy analysis in market economies—certainly in the United States—generally proceeds along the logic that market ordering is the default arrangement, and that governments intervene where justified through market failure or other rationales. Although there is little agreement over the criteria or standards of proof that justify such intervention—this is the stuff of most domestic political disputes—there exists a broad consensus that it is the *intervention* that needs to be explained, not the reliance on market ordering. If this principle is followed with any consistency, policy prescriptions based on regulatory liberalization would be analyzed differently from those based on increased restrictiveness. Markets would be evaluated on their capacity to satisfy preferences without generating undue spillover harms, rather than on any proven capacity to generate spillover benefits.

But the conventional equation of municipal regulation with "the market" or "the people's will" precludes a distinction between state or regional regulations that expand the role of the market in guiding development and those that constrain it. Although market-constraining regulations are supportable in many circumstances, discerning between them and market-expanding regulations is central to a sensible policy debate; without such a distinction, the debate becomes hopelessly muddled as both regulatory and liberalizing policy positions are subjected illogically to the same burden-of-proof tests.

ASSUMPTION 5: TRAVEL BEHAVIOR IS THE TEST OF POLICY REFORM EVEN IF THE PROBLEM IS PLANNING FAILURE

Sometimes the policy issue is acknowledged to stem from planning failure, rather than market failure. Yet even under this problem definition, the test remains largely unchanged: does compact, walkable, transit-friendly development reduce VMT or provide other provable benefits? For example, whereas in 1989 Cervero faulted "ad-hoc market forces" for systematic jobs-housing imbalances (138), by 1996 he had updated his problem definition: "When developers are prevented from building housing near employment centers that is targeted at the local workforce, as recently happened in Pleasanton, California and Hunt Valley, Maryland, there are, I believe, grounds for some degree of policy intervention—to correct planning, not market failure" (508). Yet despite this appropriate redefinition of the problem, the burden of proving VMT impacts within this framework remains. This may stem in part from the 1996 article's halting adoption of the "planning failure" problem definition: elsewhere it argues that '[s]ince the San Francisco Bay Region has not embarked on any significant regional programs to balance employment and residential development, it represents a context where *market forces alone have shaped metropolitan growth*" (494, emphasis added). Clearly where local regulations impede the potential for market-driven co-location of jobs and housing, metropolitan growth is not shaped by market forces alone; yet the older problem definition—too much market, too little planning—is surprisingly persistent, as is the burden of proof that it implies.

If ill-advised regulations—rather than market disinterest—impede alternative development, then scientific confidence regarding the benefits of compact or mixed-use neighborhoods would not be a logical prerequisite to policy reform. But for the most part, even when the impact of restrictive municipal regulations is acknowledged, the questions posed revert to impacts on travel behavior. For example, Boarnet and Crane (2001) acknowledge that "local incentives can at times work against the development of the new urban designs" (116). Yet the relevance of this finding to transportation policy is discounted, since "the travel impacts of building more neighborhoods that are less car dependent are in important respects still incompletely understood," and "there might not be enough [latent demand] to result in the large-scale changes in urban form needed to have a sizeable impact on metropolitan travel patterns" (116). Notwithstanding changing views of the underlying processes of relationships between markets and planning, the relevant policy outcome to be measured remains tightly circumscribed around travel behavior.

THE SCIENTIFIC DEFAULT AND THE POLICY STATUS QUO

An argument for shifting the burden of proof in transportation and land use issues may appear somewhat arcane. As a practical matter, the status quo carries the weight of the political default, and deviations from its trajectory tend to demand some manner of justification. But the idea that transportation and land-use policy reform hinges on proven benefits is more than a pragmatic adaptation to the political reality that change, not continuity, demands justification. Instead, this formulation demonstrates the relationship between policy and scientific definitions of the transportation and land-use policy problem. Scientific inquiry proceeds with the construction of a "null" and an alternative hypothesis. The former is generally the hypothesis of "no effect" or "no difference." In research linking travel behavior to land-use patterns, the conventional null hypothesis is that land use has no impact on travel behavior, when the effect of extraneous variables is controlled. Scientific research, by convention, grants the benefit of the doubt to this null hypothesis; that is, under conditions of significant uncertainty, the null hypothesis of "no effect" is provisionally accepted. This process—essentially the basis for scientific skepticism—has served scientific inquiry well: with an infinite number of potential hypotheses about the natural and social world, the burden of proof properly falls on those putting forward a new notion.

The problem comes when the scientific conclusion—"fail to reject the null hypothesis," which in the case of transportation and land-use research is "no proven impact of urban form on travel behavior"—gets mapped onto a policy stance. The debate, among both proponents and skeptics of the land-use approaches, has largely equated that scientific outcome with a policy position supporting the status quo of reliance on low-density, auto-oriented development forms. This formulation of the problem would be more appropriate if these development forms were themselves free of policy intervention as the product of an unconstrained market. Yet because metropolitan development is shaped largely by municipal regulatory policy, there is little justification for equating a failure to reject the null hypothesis with the conclusion that policy reform is unwarranted. An unexamined default to the status quo stifles debate because it treats current municipal regulatory prerogative as a state of nature rather than as a policy choice.

Many authors cited here explicitly say that although there may be no *transportation* rationale for alternative development, there may be other perfectly good reasons to pursue policy reform. For example, Downs (1992, *111*) argues against the centrality of jobs-housing balancing policies to traffic congestion but concludes that "[t]his does not mean that improving the jobs-housing balance in a region is a bad idea or that it would produce no social benefits...[I]t could help provide greater justice and equality of housing opportunities for low- and moderate-income households, improve the availability of the local labor force in suburban communities, increase socioeconomic and cultural diversity in such communities, and enable both old and young members of families living there to remain residents of those communities." Giuliano (1989, *311*) concurs and emphasizes the role of municipal regulatory barriers:

> Jobs-housing balance has emerged from concerns about the lack of affordable housing both in central cities and suburbs, the desire to maintain the economic viability of downtowns, the prevalence of exclusionary zoning practices that have restricted the supply and variety of housing available in suburban areas, and the emergence of employment centers in suburban areas. All of these issues are made more complex by the more generalized concern over growing traffic congestion. Jobs-housing balance puts these problems together and attempts to solve all of them.

If the academic debate that has swirled around travel behavior and land use would focus sequentially on each of the purported benefits that Downs and Giuliano listed, the result would likely still be indeterminacy and controversy. For example, one might hypothesize that areas of plentiful housing supplies near suburban job centers improve labor-force availability in those centers; yet scientific tests of this hypothesis may well generate the same controversy that has surrounded travel-behavior research. By contrast, considering the regulatory roots of jobs-housing imbalances or the paucity of alternative development changes the analysis fundamentally: the indeterminacy of any particular benefit considered in isolation loses policy relevance. When governmental interventions like low-density zoning cause multiple—though sometimes uncertain—market distortions, the assertion that problems are best "separated and dealt with directly" (Giuliano 1989, *311*) is not self-evidently true.

Uncertainty is pervasive in policy realms whose subject matter is not amenable to controlled experimentation, and travel behavior and land use fit squarely into this category. Imagining that policymaking can be put on hold until some future date when such uncertainty is eliminated or reduced presupposes that transportation and land-use policy is not being made constantly—that there actually exists a "no policy" or "no intervention" alternative. On the continuing uncertainty in this realm, consider the following two quotes, separated by nearly three decades of transportation and land-use research. In 1974, Gilbert and Dajani concluded,

> [T]he extent to which urban form influences transportation energy usage and the possibilities for using transportation policy as a land use control...are complicated and perhaps not subject to definitive answers, and thus we are led to the all-too-common conclusion that more research is needed.
> In the case of the impact of urban form on travel demand, research is needed to: (a) identify and define the relevant dimensions of urban form; and (b) systematically relate these dimensions to travel demands....Only then can the variations in predicted travel demands be understood in terms of specific urban form dimensions as opposed to variations in analytical methodologies. (Gilbert and Dajani 1974, *275*)

In 2001, Boarnet and Crane wrote in a nearly identical vein:

> Our conclusion is not that urban design and transportation behavior are not linked, or that urban design should never be used as transportation policy. Rather, we conclude that we know too little about the transportation aspects of the built environment... (Boarnet and Crane 2001, *14*)

This uncertainty, spanning nearly three decades of transportation and land-use research, leads to a question: what will be published on the pages of transportation and urban planning journals in 2030? Will researchers announce that the ambiguities of the land use–travel behavior relationship have been settled once and for all, and that the new consensus will finally allow us to begin making sensible development and transportation policy?

Improved data, software, and analytic methods will no doubt help, and the fresh insights will shed light on public questions surrounding transportation, metropolitan form, and the environment. But imagining that public policy regarding transportation and urban form can wait for future consensus requires us to ignore the ubiquitous policymaking that currently occurs in the form of municipal regulations. These interventions lower densities, separate land uses, mandate land-intensive roadway and parking investments, and zone out affordable housing in locations where it is needed most. Nevertheless, much travel behavior research persists in constructing the current regime as a fundamentally free market. Persistent uncertainty is a fact of policy life. But this reality hardly justifies the maintenance of exclusionary barriers that limit the capacity of metropolitan areas to adapt to changing economic and demographic circumstances and restrict the ability of households to fulfill preferences that may support less auto-intensive lives.

CHAPTER THREE

MARKETLIKE INTERPRETATIONS OF LAND-USE CONTROLS

Municipal land-use policy turns the discipline of economics inside out. Terms like "liberal" and "conservative" lose their meaning as economists oriented toward free-market policies tolerate or even endorse governmental intervention in the form of municipal zoning. On the other side, declarations that "[w]e must free the land of unnecessary restrictions" and condemnations of "employing the police power to protect [people's] own interest in the land" are not the libertarian's call to arms but the social-equity appeals of the advocacy planner (Paul Davidoff, quoted in Aumente 1971, 56).

These normative positions are distinct from views on the effect of land-use regulations on municipal development patterns. Concluding that zoning lowers densities inherently implies neither support for nor opposition to current land-use regulation. In fact, even though most economists tend to reject urban sprawl as a problem definition per se, the preponderance of their empirical research concludes that municipal regulatory practices underpin American patterns of low-density settlement.

The conclusion that municipal zoning lowers development densities should hardly come as a surprise. Among zoning's original stated purposes was to "prevent the overcrowding of land [and] avoid undue concentration of population" (Standard Zoning Enabling Act, 1926, Section 3). *Euclid v. Ambler*, which established the constitutionality of municipal zoning, was clear in defining dense housing as part of the problem to be treated. It declares that "the development of detached house sections is greatly retarded by the coming of apartment houses, which has sometimes resulted in destroying the entire section for private house purposes; that in such sections very often the apartment house is a mere parasite, constructed in order to take advantage of the open spaces and attractive surroundings created by the residential character of the district" (394). *Euclid* later softened this disparaging characterization of denser housing with an "everything in its place" argument but left the conclusion clear: public action to stem the spread of multifamily housing in single-family districts was inherently legitimate.

In practice, tiny shares of developable land in U.S. metropolitan areas are zoned for multifamily housing, suggesting regulatory limitations on its growth.[1] Although multifamily housing is often allowed in commercial and manufacturing zones, municipalities have demonstrated a willingness to use their regulatory powers to limit it where it might be most in demand, such as near transit stations (Boarnet and Crane 1997). Even where higher-density development is permitted on land zoned industrial or commercial, the planning function—often driven by residential neighbors of the site—can still be employed to reduce densities to a level lower than those desired by developers (Chapter 7). And, denser residential development zoned out of one location does not necessarily translate into similarly compact forms elsewhere; rather, development shifted to more remote, lower-accessibility areas would be expected to adopt lower-density forms (Alonso 1964).

The problem is not that local governments lack the tools to allow for greater land-use flexibility. Planned-unit developments are a widespread approach to reducing the rigidity of standard zoning codes, and rezoning to denser or mixed-use development is nearly always within the municipal purview. The issue is rather that many jurisdictions are motivated to exclude more compact and more affordable developments for a variety of often overlapping reasons (Bogart 1993). In a study of land-use regulation in Illinois, Talen and Knaap (2003) found scant evidence of zoning codes informed by smart-growth principles but a preponderance of municipal regulations effectively excluding such development. Moreover, with a surfeit of motives to constrain compact and affordable development, municipalities may limit growth through ad hoc controls (Landis 1992). These can take the form of regulations that are more or less malleable (Shlay and Rossi 1981) and can be based on negotiated agreements between planners and private developers (Field 1997). For all these reasons, the presence of zones nominally equipped to accommodate denser development forms hardly ensures a welcoming regulatory environment to entrepreneurs who might propose them.

Transportation and land-use planning often asks whether policy ought to intervene on behalf of *higher* densities. By contrast, large body of empirical research concludes that current interventions in the form of municipal regulation *lower* densities below market levels and create more exclusivity in suburban municipalities (e.g., White 1988; Moss 1977; Pasha 1996; Fischel 1999a; Shlay and Rossi 1981; McMillen and McDonald 1991; Thorson 1994, 1997; Peiser 1989). The question amounts to whether municipal land-use regulations specifying maximum development densities (via such requirements as lot-size minima and floor-area ratio maxima) impose a binding constraint on development. If these are set in a fashion that permits development densities that the private market would seek in any case, they would not appreciably affect development outcomes. If they are set for lower-than-market densities, they would alter development patterns. One test is in the price differential between land zoned and not yet zoned for development. If municipal land-use regulations were not a binding constraint on development, one would not expect large price differences between these two categories of land. The market would be confident that the permission to develop at desired densities would be forthcoming. Instead, land zoned for development commands a significant price premium (Brownstone and DeVany 1991), suggesting that zoning is a binding constraint. Noting that rezoning to allow denser development can lead to huge increases in the value of a parcel, Fischel (2001, 56) reasons that "[i]f zoning were a will-o'-the wisp, malleable at the mere request of developers, it is difficult to see why zoning classifications should contribute to differences in the value of otherwise similar properties."

Another test of the binding nature of land-use controls is in the price of housing. If zoning replicated the results that markets would produce in its absence, one would not expect it to induce housing price increases. Yet "characteristics" zoning—for example, minimum lot size and setback requirements—has been found to raise housing prices significantly. This suggests that zoning represents a binding constraint on development rather than a duplication of land-development markets (Podgodzinski and Sass

1994; Green 1999). Even the most widely cited article arguing the contrary position—that zoning follows the market—concludes that zoning led to an oversupply of large-lot residential development in the area studied (Wallace 1988).

Thus the view that municipal land-use regulations lower development densities is broadly held among economists who study the topic.[2] Yet many view this finding relatively benignly (Wheaton 1993; Calabrese et al. 2004). For example, Gyourko (1991, 246–47) writes,

> The desire to avoid capital losses underlines the situation...in which the local government (assumed to act on behalf of existing residents) has an incentive to zone out the high-density demanders. As those authors note, existing residents could in theory band together and outbid potential residents who might want to subdivide into less expensive, smaller lot size developments. Nevertheless, the evidence appears consistent with the hypothesis that the cheapest way to prevent entry is to zone out the demanders of high density development.

This quote is an apt description of the exclusionary process. But the normative position regarding the process is surprising: "[E]xclusionary zoning is optimal if high density demanders' willingness to pay is not sufficient to cover the cost of the required publicly provided goods" (251). This chapter considers the basis for this view. If municipal zoning lowers development densities below those the unconstrained market would generate—and thereby spurs more sprawl than would otherwise arise—why does mainstream economics seem relatively tolerant of the status quo in metropolitan development?

One candidate explanation is the external costs that neighboring land uses can impose on one another. Traffic, pollution, and visual blight are among the chief concerns of local planning. One of the land-use planning functions is to define compatible and incompatible land uses; another is to enforce public policies that treat this tendency of development to impose external costs. Yet the economics literature seems to place little stock in the capacity of proactive standards-based regulation to treat these kinds of externalities efficiently. Fischel (1999b, 404) refers to this notion as "an idea even planners have given up." The assessment is at least partly correct, as a growing recognition of the inherently political nature of the planning process is inconsistent with a view of planning as a profession whose legitimacy rests on the technical expertise of disinterested practitioners. The tolerance that much of the economics profession extends toward extensive municipal powers of land-use regulation has its roots elsewhere.

ZONING AND MARKETS FOR PUBLICLY PROVIDED GOODS

The economist who most influenced his profession's views on land-use regulation did not especially set out to study zoning at all. Charles Tiebout (1956) developed a model of efficient allocation of publicly provided goods in a regime of decentralized municipal jurisdictions. He was primarily concerned with the varying bundles of services that communities provide and the varying taxes that they choose to levy to finance those services. Tiebout showed that given certain restrictive assumptions, a household's choice of residential location amounts to a shopping trip for publicly provided[3] goods. In this he demonstrated that households actually did reveal their preferences for these goods—a subject that had previously worried economists—thus rendering efficient public sector provision theoretically possible through a marketlike mechanism.

Tiebout's treatment of land-use regulation was oblique. He argued that communities required a mechanism for regulating their total growth and touched on the potential of zoning practices to accomplish this goal:

> For every pattern of community services set by, say, a city manager who follows the preferences of the older residents of the community, there is an optimal community size...The assumption that some factor is fixed explains why it is not possible for the community to double its size by growth. The factor may be the limited land area of a suburban community, combined with a set of zoning laws against apartment buildings. It may be the local beach, whose capacity is limited. Anything of this nature will provide a restraint. (419)

The land-use policy implications of the "Tiebout model" were worked out nearly two decades later by Hamilton (1975). Hamilton saw the potential for efficiency-reducing "free rides" within the original Tiebout formulation: households would seek to locate in communities with average housing consumption higher than their own and, by keeping their property tax burden lower than that of their neighbors, would effectively enjoy a subsidy—high-level schools, police protection, and the like at a discount. Unchecked, Hamilton reasoned, this would lead to "musical suburbs, with the poor following the rich in a never-ending quest for a tax base" (205). For Hamilton, the route out of this bind ran via exclusionary zoning policies. His main assumption was that "each community is authorized to enact a 'zoning ordinance' which states, 'No household may reside in this community unless it consumes at least some minimum amount of housing'" (206). With this, zoning gained a foothold among many economists not merely as a tool to control local externalities, such those that a polluting factory might impose on a residential neighborhood, but as a necessary condition for household sorting into communities sufficiently homogeneous to support an efficient supply of publicly provided goods. Hamilton (1976) modified his view a year later to accommodate heterogeneous communities, but the economic role of zoning to prevent unforeseen growth in populations of below-average income remained.

BARGAINING OVER ZONING RIGHTS

Thus the marketlike efficiencies that Tiebout asserted with decentralized provision of publicly supplied goods are based on the ability of individual municipalities to exclude through land-use regulation. The concept of "exclusionary zoning" is not unambiguously negative within this framework, as some manner of exclusion is needed for the system of decentralized governance to generate its putative efficiencies.

A relatively sanguine view of apparent municipal exclusion is further abetted by the analysis of Coase (1960), under which the possibility of inefficient or "too much" exclusion by land-use regulation is theoretically eliminated as long as certain assumptions are met. Coase considered the situation of parties whose actions cause harmful effects on their neighbors, such as environmental pollution, intrusion of livestock, or—in an explicitly urban land-use example—shadows cast by buildings on neighboring property. His analysis incorporated both the initial regulatory assignment of rights and the possibility of negotiated outcomes, including compensation or merger. Given the restrictive assumptions of fully assigned and transferable rights and zero transaction costs, the analysis demonstrated a surprising result: parties would negotiate themselves to the same efficient outcome, regardless of the initial assignment of rights. For example, in the case of environmental pollution, rights to pollute may be assigned to a firm; alternatively, rights to freedom from pollution may be assigned to the firm's neighbors. Where the firm initially holds the right to pollute, its neighbors would be expected to negotiate for the purchase of those rights up to the point where their marginal benefit from saving an additional increment of pollution just equals the firm's marginal benefit from emitting an additional increment of pollution. Conversely, where the neighbors hold the right to clean air initially, the firm is predicted to purchase those rights to allow some pollution—and the negotiations will end at the same solution regardless of their regulatory starting point.

Fischel (1985) considered the applicability of the Coase model to the case of municipal zoning and land-use conflicts in general. He presumed that local residents, acting through their municipal government, tend to prefer more rather than fewer restrictions on the development of vacant land. The owner of the land is assumed to be interested in developing it with as few restrictions as possible and would tend toward greater density or intensity of development than the residents of the community would otherwise prefer.

With land-use disputes framed in this fashion, the applicability of the bargaining model becomes apparent. Rights to prevent or control development can reside with the municipality; alternatively, rights to develop could reside with the landowner or developer. In either case, if those rights are fully assigned and transferable, and if transaction costs are zero, Coase's analysis would suggest that the initial assignment of rights is merely the starting point for processes of bargaining between the landowner and the municipality. A landowner may secure development rights from the municipality through voluntary exchange involving cash, in-kind contributions, or other valuable considerations. Conversely, if the landowner initially holds the rights to develop at will, the municipality can control development by purchasing some or all of those rights. As long as the zero-transaction-costs restriction is fulfilled, the Coase model predicts that the outcome will be unaffected by the initial assignment of development rights, since the parties bargain themselves to the same efficient outcome under either scenario.

Thus the danger of rigid and inefficient exclusion through zoning would be eliminated. Where a proposed development would generate sufficient profits, the landowner would be able to purchase rights for its construction even in the face of nominal regulatory exclusion. If the municipality rejects the proffered payment, this would be a signal that the development does not offer sufficient societal benefits to outweigh the local costs that it imposes, such as traffic congestion or school overcrowding.

For that reason, the Coase framework became another basis for many economists' relatively sympathetic stance toward municipal regulations that limit density and intensity of development. If dense development that *should* happen *does* happen regardless of local zoning against it, then there is little reason to worry about zoning's effect on land markets: developers, acting effectively as agents of future residents or tenants, will purchase the rights to develop up to the point where the marginal benefit to them of an additional increment of development is equal to the marginal benefit to the community of an additional increment of restrictiveness (Maser et al. 1977). Where there is a net social benefit to development denser than initially permitted by regulation, such development will occur regardless of the nominal initial prohibition, under the assumptions of the Coase model. Even residents of single-family zones, the reasoning goes, would agree not to oppose development if sufficiently compensated by developers. Conversely, if the developers cannot afford to offer sufficient compensation to induce relaxation of a community's strict zoning rules, the development does not offer sufficient societal benefit and should therefore not happen.

In fact, there is some evidence of that kind of bargaining. Tools that urban planners might consider innovations of their profession—such as exactions, impact fees, or transfer of development rights—would be seen by many economists as evidence of bargaining (Levinson 1997). Ellickson (1973, *708*) writes that "[f]lexibility devices prominent in the zoning field in the last decade, like conditional use permits, contract zoning, and planned unit development (PUD), are actually vehicles by which local governments agree to waive inefficient standards when offered a sufficiently attractive package of donations and preventative measures." The possibility of Coase-type bargaining between developers and municipalities has led some observers to conclude that zoning follows the market—that is, municipal zoning is not a binding constraint on overall patterns of development—and that the outcome of an unzoned world would not be especially different from the status quo (Wallace 1988; Podgodzinski and Sass 1994). But the evidence from economics suggests that zoning rights are highly consequential to the final development outcomes and, in particular, tend to lower development densities. Reasons why this might be the case are considered later in this chapter.

(LACK OF) FAITH IN BARGAINING PROCESSES

The Coasean argument about the irrelevance of initial rights assignment, if consistently applied, would lead to conclusions that would sit uncomfortably with most economists. If this bargaining in fact renders the nominal strictures of municipal zoning irrelevant, then under Coasean reasoning, the opposite assignment of rights could be enacted with no difference in development forms. Specifically, the right to develop at will could be assigned wholesale to the landowner. Should the municipality wish to limit the height, building footprint, or floor-area ratio, it would seek their voluntary sale by the landowner. The position that zoning follows the market because of Coasean bargaining implies that development would be no different under this scenario than under the previous. Yet economics researchers have rarely taken this policy prescription, largely preferring instead to endorse municipal regulatory prerogatives and saying that when regulations need to be changed, they will.

Faith in the capacity of Coasean bargaining appears limited. Another example is found in the selective endorsement of some land-use interventions and criticism of others. For example, many economists are comfortable with low-density zoning but criticize urban growth boundaries as inefficient market interferences (Turnbull 2004). But if Coasean bargaining works in the former case, it ought to operate in the latter as well. A growth boundary represents, in Coasean terms, an initial assignment of rights: landowners within the boundary possess the rights to develop, while their counterparts outside do not. If Coasean bargaining holds, then presence or absence of a growth boundary should be immaterial; development that *should* happen outside it would in fact occur. Development that has sufficient societal value would enable the landowner-developer to compensate the community or regional government for its permission to build outside; development that fails to generate such profits would not cover the cost of the local harm it imposes.

It may be that the geographic scale of the implementing government makes the difference, with more presumption of economic rationality extended toward local government than toward regional or state bodies. But as long as the implementing body has the legal authority to make decisions on boundary adjustments, there is no theoretical reason to presume that the bargaining model cannot apply. The costs perceived are different, to be sure. Metropolitan government can weigh the value of development proposals (together with their proffered cash or in-kind payments) against the goal of regional containment, a question that municipal governments acting in isolation are unable to consider. But an a priori exclusion of regional-level land-use considerations receives no particular justification within the Coasean framework. The larger geographic aggregations could even claim greater latitude to make appropriate tradeoffs regarding development decisions, as greater shares of the costs and benefits of their development decisions would be internal to their constituencies. By contrast, smaller jurisdictions have a greater tendency to impose external costs on their neighbors.

Moreover, deference to local government does not explain opposition to municipal, as opposed to metropolitan, urban-growth boundaries. It would be inconsistent to advocate deference to municipal prerogative in the case of low-density zoning but not in the case of municipal growth boundaries. Under Coasean logic, in both cases, easing of the regulations would be expected when a development proposal offers sufficient surpluses to compensate the community for its negative impacts.

By imagining a world where initial assignment of rights is not consequential to final outcomes, the Coase framework provides a theoretical basis for a view that zoning follows the market—that is, that it more or less replicates the development patterns that would have held in the absence of municipal land-use regulation. But the empirical evidence suggests otherwise: zoning in fact lowers development densities and generates greater exclusivity in settlement patterns than would otherwise hold. The most comprehensive economics framework on municipal zoning is that of Fischel (1985), who builds on the reasoning of Coase but also demonstrates why zoning is consequential and how it, in fact, inefficiently lowers development densities.

ZONING AS COLLECTIVE PROPERTY RIGHT

Fischel (1985) analyzes zoning as a collective property right that is at least potentially tradable between municipalities and landowner-developers. This framework has been extensively adopted in the economics literature, to the extent that it can be identified as a mainstream-economics view of the zoning question. One way of explaining a property-rights view of zoning is by contrasting it with its two primary alternatives.

One alternative begins with the observation that neighboring land uses can confer on each other both external benefits, such as visual amenity, and (more notably) external costs, including congestion, pollution, crowding, and noise. Many urban planners, but fewer economists, tend to explain zoning primarily as a regulatory response to localized externalities (Crone 1983). Remedying the situation requires cadres of technically trained planners who can identify both the costs and the benefits of proximity or separation of various land uses, and who then apply reasonably objective judgments regarding which uses are compatible and which ought to be separated by regulation.

A second alternative views zoning as a set of "irrational rules that impose arbitrary constraints on the land market" (Fischel 1985, *xiii*). Policy prescriptions emerging from this view frequently include replacing zoning with devices from contract and nuisance law (e.g., Ellickson 1973). Ellickson's view of zoning is in line with most economists' skeptical views toward standards-based governmental regulation at the state and particularly federal levels. Yet few economists write in this vein, perhaps because of the influence of the Tiebout-Hamilton view of municipal zoning as a necessary underpinning of efficient decentralized allocation of publicly provided goods.

The property-rights view sees zoning fundamentally as something other than governmental regulation. Under this view, the harm that one land use imposes on another does not inherently demand elimination, and the planning function is poorly described as a technocratically driven regulatory separation of incompatible land uses. At the same time, economic efficiency does not demand that local government remain neutral regarding these land-use conflicts, since the municipality is the institution that is best positioned to act on behalf of the collective interest of landowners in its jurisdiction. Rather than all the development rights being held by individual landowners, some are held collectively. The municipality is the body best able to act on those rights, and it embodies them in municipal zoning rules.

Within this framework, the municipal government becomes a device to lower transaction costs. Rather than negotiating with landowners individually, developers interact with a single point of contact for development proposals. Zoning rules represent neither an arbitrary governmental imposition nor a fixed requirement regarding maximum building densities, but instead, property rights held by the municipality, which can relinquish or trade them when such modification would be to the community's benefit.

But development rights are not traded easily. Institutional and legal impediments that render zoning untradable include restrictions against buying zoning rights outright and prohibitions against "spot zoning" of single properties. Political and cultural barriers exist as well: buying and selling of zoning rights is thought to be unseemly, and many in the planning profession would see the practice as undermining their claim to technical expertise. Under these circumstances, developers seeking to build medium-density housing in a single-family suburb currently face the barrier of single-family zoning and have insufficient opportunities to bargain for its modification. Even such development that should happen—that is, development whose societal benefits exceed its local costs—may not happen because significant impediments to the trading of development rights remain. Thus the situation precludes many possible gains through voluntary exchange.

Fischel's policy prescription under this property-rights view is to create institutions to increase the tradability of development rights: housing developers would be able to offer cash for development rights, which the municipality would be free to accept or reject. For zoning to become such a fungible property right, several reforms would be required. Legal restrictions against the sale of zoning rights—including restrictions on "spot zoning"—would need to be eliminated, and the municipality would need to become a legitimate fiduciary agent acting on behalf of its citizens. The former reform would render the relevant rights fully defined and tradable; the latter would overcome transaction costs and collective action problems by designating an institution empowered to act on behalf of multiple individual households.

If those reforms were to be implemented, it might be argued that the restrictive assumptions of the Coase model would have been met. Regardless of where the formal legal rights lie, the developers and municipality would bargain themselves to the same density and intensity of development. (Of course, the developers would end up considerably richer if they held development rights than if they had to pay for them, but the Coase model predicts no impact of the initial assignment of rights on physical form.) In contrast to this view, Fischel suggests that assignment of development rights will continue to matter, even where institutions support trades in development rights. Chief among these factors is an "endowment" effect, under which the very ownership of property (in this case, the development rights) affects one's willingness to exchange. From proprietary pride or habit, or from doubts about the very legitimacy of exchange or simple sloth, I may become attached to my property, such that the minimum price I would accept for its sale is considerably greater than the maximum price I would offer to purchase it if I did not already own it. In other words, willingness to pay can diverge markedly from willingness to accept (Miceli and Minkler 1995).

The endowment effect has been demonstrated in other realms. For instance, in a now-famous experiment, university students were offered coffee mugs that they could keep or sell at any mutually agreed price to those who had not been offered the gift. To demonstrate the relevance of initial endowments, the experiment showed that students who were given the mugs systematically valued them more highly than those who would have needed to purchase them (Kahneman et al. 1990). If this effect has been demonstrated for items as prosaic as a coffee mug, it is difficult to imagine that rights to develop in one's community—with all the emotionally fraught attachment to the status quo in one's neighborhood—would escape this phenomenon. If the endowment effect is in fact influential in the willingness to trade development rights, then their initial assignment would be consequential (contrary to expectations of the Coase theorem); whether the developers had the right to develop densely or the community had the right to exclude such development would in fact matter to the final outcome.

One difference between development rights and coffee mugs is the share of a household's wealth that each represents. Since a substantial share of households' wealth is in their homes, increases in the value of homes makes people measurably wealthier (in contrast to proportionally equal increases in the value of coffee mugs). Wealthier people demand more of most goods and services. Logically, among the services demanded would be regulatory protection over one's neighborhood. Under this reasoning, wealthier people would be expected to be willing to pay for greater exclusivity in their neighborhoods than their poorer counterparts. If the initial homeowners in a community were made wealthier by the unpriced right to enact zoning in their community, the very fact of this windfall might increase their wealth and hence the price they would demand for development rights. This is known as the "wealth effect."

Many economists have preferred to explain the endowment effect through the wealth effect. That is, where initial endowments are relevant to one's willingness to trade, the wealth effect explains the behavior with no resort to irrational notions, such as attachment to one's property, that would be contrary to a calculated self-interest. Yet the wealth effect would be associated only with the first generation of homeowners; for the second generation, any value of zoning would have been capitalized into home prices, and the new homeowner would enjoy no windfall (Fischel 1999b). Thus over the long term, any endowment effect in zoning would need to be understood as something apart from the wealth effect.

A final reason to assume the relevance of initial endowments in development rights pertains to matters of scale. Consider a suburban community, developed largely in a single-family development pattern that has transformed into a significant job center. Developers are interested in acquiring older single-family properties and vacant parcels in order to build multifamily townhouses or apartments. Such a proposal might be well received by individual homeowners, but their neighbors would be virtually certain to oppose the rezoning needed to allow the denser development. The developer could seek to overcome this by offering either to purchase or to compensate the entire neighborhood for the contemplated construction. This possibility would run into several obstacles, however. First, holdouts who refuse either to sell or to assent to the neighborhood's transformation could prevent or significantly raise the cost. Second, few developers have sufficient capacity to buy up an entire neighborhood, and the costs of assembling consortia of smaller developers would themselves constitute barriers to action. Finally, even if an entire neighborhood were bought out, residents from adjoining neighborhoods who viewed themselves as harmed by the contemplated change would fight the development at the planning commission and city council. The relevant unit for such change may in fact be the municipality as a whole: as long as a majority of community residents believe they will be harmed, their representatives in city government are likely to share in this opposition.

For all those reasons, initial endowments of development rights matter to final outcomes, even where property rights are defined and fungible and transaction costs are low. This view is hardly new to practicing urban planners, who understand the political power of neighborhood opposition. Under the view of zoning as a property right, free exchange of development rights is a desirable goal that will never be achieved, and such rights will tend to stick to the party to whom they are assigned. If landowners are assigned the rights to develop at will, too few of those rights will be bought back by municipalities in the form of development restrictions. Similarly, if neighbors are assigned the rights to exclude development, too few of those rights will be purchased by developers, and too little development will occur.

Granting extensive prerogative to municipalities to exclude development (Choppin 1994) therefore leads to inefficiently low development densities. Fischel's approach to this problem is to establish a "normal" development standard to guide the initial assignment of development rights. Development that matches current land uses in a community—for example, single-family houses on quarter-acre lots—may be considered "normal" for that community. Development that holds greater potential for land-use conflict than "normal" development may be considered subnormal. For example, high-density apartments in a single-family community would match this description. Conversely, regulations that expose developable land in a community to more stringent control than that which is already developed would be considered above-normal standards.

In Fischel's scheme, rights to "normal" development would be initially vested with the landowner-developer, and rights to keep out subnormal development would be vested with the community. Thus a community of single-family homes on quarter-acre lots that wished to exclude proposed development of similar character would need to buy the rights from the landowner, who could choose to sell or not to sell. In contrast, a landowner who wished to develop an apartment building in the same community would need first to bargain with the city for the purchase of development rights. Although such trading in rights is desirable under this view, it is understood that the initial assignment of rights remains important as a default choice.

ZONING AS A MARKET FORCE

In contrast to a view of zoning as regulation to treat the externalities of land use, much of the economics profession sees municipal land-use controls as an element of the market among competing jurisdictions in a metropolitan system. The Tiebout-Hamilton framework emphasizes potential efficiencies of supply of publicly provided goods through multiple decentralized municipalities. At the same time, it requires an exclusionary zoning capacity to prevent the free-rider effect, whereby lower-income individuals seek the benefits of residence in higher-income communities. In this way, it both presumes and endorses the capacity of zoning to exclude more compact housing forms.

The Coase model envisions processes of bargaining over rights that lead, under certain restrictive conditions, to efficient levels of development regardless of where those rights were initially assigned. This view raises the theoretical possibility that zoning may not be consequential to development patterns. Regardless of the initial assignment of development rights, bargaining and exchange between municipalities and landowner-developers might lead to the same development outcome. This theoretical basis underpins the view that zoning follows the market, yet empirical evidence suggests that zoning makes a great deal of difference by lowering densities and creating more exclusive municipalities than would otherwise arise.

Fischel's view of zoning as a collective property right helps identify the gap between the theoretical predictions of the Coase model and the realities of municipal development. Zoning is best viewed as a right to develop that is collectively held by the community, but the right is alienable, meaning that it can—in principle—be traded, bought, or sold. The principal problem with zoning is not that municipalities wield too much regulatory prerogative but that zoning rights are insufficiently fungible, leading to more exclusion than is efficient, and to a U.S. metropolitan development pattern that is too spread out (Fischel 1999a). In addition, the assignment of rights to the municipality to exclude development is not the correct assignment in all cases. In this model, the rights to develop "normally" ought to be vested with landowner-developers.

The theoretical views, and the empirical investigations that have built on them, are central to transportation and land-use research and policy in several ways. First, empirical findings show that municipal regulations lower metropolitan development densities compared with a hypothetical unzoned situation. If regulations impede the ability of land-development markets to generate more compact development, then their liberalization is a prerequisite to alternative development forms. As long as the first order of business is the elimination of regulatory obstacles to compact development, a search for the travel behavior benefits that would justify governmental intervention is poorly matched with the policy task at hand.

Second, findings reported here imply that municipal land-use controls lower development densities inefficiently. Compact development that would generate more benefits than costs is frequently excluded under current regulations. This is a product of both legal and institutional limitations on trade in zoning rights, and of the endowment effect: when rights to exclude development are vested with the municipality, they tend to be valued by residents more highly than if the rights had to be purchased. This suggests that the common belief that U.S. development is too sprawling, with too few compact alternatives, is quite consistent with economic theory.

Nevertheless, much of the economics profession views zoning considerably more favorably than other forms of standards-based regulation. Ultimately, much of the field has interpreted municipal zoning in terms that render it a kind of market force, rather than the local cousin to state- or federal-level command-and-control regulation. This redefinition serves to confer upon current institutional arrangements in metropolitan development the status of a default, intervention-free choice: since municipal low-density zoning is truly an element of "the market," then its reform must be "planning intervention," at least if that reform rests on actions from higher governmental levels. By contrast, the following chapter argues that municipal regulation is, in fact, regulation. Any redefinition of local zoning as a "market force" rests either on a set of implausible assumptions regarding metropolitan development, or on predefined notions regarding municipal exclusion of compact development, or both.

CHAPTER FOUR

THE HARMS OF REGULATORY EXCLUSION

The notion that municipal land-use regulation may cause urban sprawl is, for smart-growth observers, ample basis for reform of current policies. Many economists aren't so sure. Rather than focusing on the regulatory inducement of sprawl as a problem, they tend to see the benefits in the current regime—the decentralized provision of publicly supplied goods and services—and thus consider the exclusionary effects of zoning benign. This chapter argues that these economists systematically neglect the costs of this regulation. Research in affordable housing has long focused on the role of municipal exclusion in creating artificial scarcities of housing in certain locations. These same processes also impede the ability of many households to choose the kind of transportation or land-use environments they prefer. These costs are unaccounted for in economics models that equate decentralized municipal regulation with the market.

Economists' surprisingly sanguine views are mostly grounded in Tiebout's (1956) study. In his framework, decentralized governments can supply publicly provided goods efficiently if their stable income mix is ensured by land-use regulation. This school of thought readily acknowledges that the metropolitan status quo is in large measure the product of local zoning, but tends not to view this outcome as a problem. Under this framework, interventions that some might decry as "exclusionary zoning" are necessary underpinnings for the efficient sorting of households into communities.

THE SELECTIVE VISION OF ECONOMICS-BASED VIEWS

The Tiebout-Hamilton justification for exclusionary land-use regulations defines "efficiency" overly narrowly and systematically neglects issues of concern to transportation and land-use planning. Tiebout (1956) demonstrated the potential efficiency of decentralized supply of publicly provided goods, and Hamilton (1975, 176) showed that a community's ability to zone out—or at least control the increase in—populations that consume less housing than average was a necessary element of the Tiebout model. The policy conclusion that such a system yields economic efficiencies rests on the assumption that a household excluded from what might otherwise have been its first-choice community can select an alternative location without incurring or causing harm. Yet to believe that no harm is incurred in such exclusion, one would have to assume that households excluded by regulation suffer no negative impacts in transportation, housing, or neighborhood preference. For example, one would need to assume that employed households excluded from what would otherwise be their first-choice residential location do not, as a consequence, commute longer distances or suffer other harms to their accessibility. Tiebout (1956, 419) dispensed with this problem by heroically assuming that "[r]estrictions due to employment opportunities are not considered. It may be assumed that all persons are living on dividend income." Hamilton (1975) develops this assumption further, suggesting that excluded households can costlessly choose alternative municipalities (with the usual caveat that he is dealing in "pure theory"):

> [C]lassify all households in the urban area by demand for housing, and cross-classify them by public service demand...Each doubly-classified cell is what we have referred to as a community. We can now cross-classify everybody again by location preference and call each triply-classified cell a community. Again, the required number of communities may expand with each cross-classification since each resident must now find a community which satisfied three requirements rather than one or two. But we say that if the variables used to cross-classify households are highly correlated with one

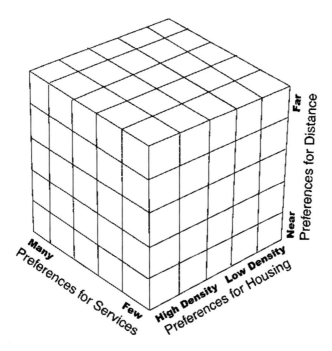

Figure 4-1. Hamilton's Three-Way Classification of Municipalites

another, then the number of communities required to satisfy three requirements is not much greater than the number required to satisfy one or two.
And it can, on theoretical grounds, be argued rather strongly that location
preference (as measured by most preferred distance to [the central business
district]) is highly correlated with housing demand. (209)

In other words, Hamilton envisioned a full set of community types—
classified in the three dimensions, based on preference for housing, public
service, and location (Figure 4-1). Exclusion from one would merely channel the household into an alternative that was a probably a better fit in the
first place. Moreover, the range of community types would be distributed
spatially throughout the metropolitan area, implying that a household's
accessibility would not suffer through the process of regulatory exclusion.
While the Tiebout-Hamilton model thus envisions exclusion of households from communities where they would pay lower-than-average taxes, it
imagines that these households select alternative communities whose mix
of housing type, public services, and accessibility character match their
preferences and pocketbooks.

Absent from that framework is the possibility that this regulatory exclusion may systematically separate the excluded households from their actual

preferences. Where travel behavior research focuses solely on the external costs of transportation—such as the pollution and congestion imposed on others—it erroneously assumes that households are able to choose their optimal location, within budget constraints. But such optimization would be impossible if a community that would otherwise be desirable to a household were closed because local regulations excluded the kind of housing the household desired or could afford. Thus this research systematically neglects the internal costs of exclusion—the gap in benefits from a household's actual location and the location it might have chosen in the absence of exclusionary regulations.

Regardless of the magnitude of these costs, they are disposed of by assumption in the Tiebout-Hamilton view of the world. This model does not balance these costs against asserted efficiency benefits of decentralized provision of governmental services. "With each of the many local governments in a region zoning on the basis of its own interests, what guarantee is there that land uses and land users displaced from one community will find a place elsewhere in the region?" asks Briffault (1990a, *104*). And even if a place is found, what assurance is there that a choice of the alternative location would not entail costs, both to the individual and to society? The answers that the Tiebout-Hamilton model provides for these questions are especially unconvincing and will be discussed in the next section.

EXCLUSION'S COSTS, INTERNAL AND EXTERNAL

A land-use regime predicated on regulatory exclusion opens a gap between the preferences and actual neighborhood choices of excluded households. Low-density land-use regulations tend to be put in place by the first-comers to suburban territory at the metropolitan fringe (Fischel 1985). For a mix of reasons, including insufficient fungibility of development rights and the endowment effect described in the previous chapter, these land-use regulations are ultimately too restrictive from the standpoint of economic efficiency. That is, they compel development whose density is inefficiently low even after conditions change and development pressures on the community grow. The initial low-density development pattern, which might have been altered by the market as metropolitan conditions changed, becomes locked in by regulation.

Households excluded from these areas are hardly a potent political force, since they are not likely to be voters in the municipality in question.

Even more importantly, they are probably not even aware of the processes by which they were excluded from their first-choice residential location; all they perceive is high housing prices. Even if these households are aware of the processes of exclusion, the Supreme Court has ruled that they have no standing to sue even if the municipality's exclusionary motives were improper, since any harm to them is a generalized "consequence of the economics of the area housing market" rather than a specific outcome of an exclusionary act of municipal regulation (*Warth v. Seldin* 1975).

The prevalence of disputes between developers and moderate-income communities over density of development suggests that exclusion by land use is not the exclusive domain of the wealthy. If the excluded households now support low-density land-use regulations in their current locale, the cycle of exclusion is complete; other households who might choose denser living in those communities would now be excluded from that choice by regulation.

Land-use regulation that systematically imposes overly-low-density development patterns would thin or even empty some of the cells of Hamilton's three-dimensional matrix, since compact housing would be systematically undersupplied in suburban areas. Hamilton deals with this problem by invoking the model of monocentric cities. Monocentric models of urban areas, following Alonso (1964), begin with a single point at the center of the city where all economic activity happens. Since access to that central point matters to every household—yet not all can live there— households need to arrange themselves throughout the city with reference to that metropolitan center. Some have longer commutes but are compensated with lower-cost housing at the metropolitan periphery; others occupy expensive housing at the center but are compensated through their short commutes. In this framework, the trade-off between housing cost and travel time to a metropolitan center drives households' locational choice, with the size and land area associated with housing units increasing regularly from the center to the periphery.

That assumption regarding the structure of metropolitan areas underpins Hamilton's (1975) statement that "[i]n most models of urban structure, households with strong demand for housing (this is generally taken to mean households with relatively high income) are induced to endure the cost of commuting a relatively long distance to the [central business district, CBD] by the fact that land rents, and thus housing prices, are lower as one gets farther from the CBD. The stronger a household's housing demand, the more commuting he will endure to live where housing prices are low. It can be seen that we should expect a very high correlation between housing demand and location preference" (209). In other words, it is misguided to worry about community types that are absent from Hamilton's three-way cross-classification. There is no need for denser housing forms in suburbia since the whole point of living in the suburbs, with the commute that lifestyle entails, is having a detached, single-family house on a larger lot.

The tautology of this statement should be immediately apparent. It purports to explain that denser housing can be zoned out of suburban municipalities without social cost, since the monocentric model predicts larger houses in such communities anyway. Yet if there were in fact no demand for denser housing forms, the municipalities would hardly need an exclusionary zoning regime to ensure that they are not built. The error comes in confusing the monocentric model with a highly polycentric metropolitan reality. In a metropolitan region with multiple suburban employment centers, processes of development are not as simple as those envisioned under the assumption of monocentricity. When the central business district of the region is just one center among many, accessibility varies not only with distance from the metropolitan center but also from subcenters. In these circumstances, one might expect the development of denser housing close to suburban employment centers. Thus housing density would not decrease smoothly with distance from the central business district, but would have local peaks in suburban high-accessibility zones. By imagining a single metropolitan center, Hamilton is excluding the possibility that households might actually have preferences or needs for denser suburban housing; his assumption is then used axiomatically to justify regulatory exclusion of such housing from suburban centers.

Even in the absence of polycentric development, sheer growth in metropolitan population could put pressure for denser-than-original development on accessible suburban locales. If such development were excluded by land-use regulation, the households that might otherwise have occupied it will be rendered worse off. For example, they may end up in communities farther from their destinations, or in housing stock that is less appropriate for them. By assuming away this outcome, the Tiebout-Hamilton policy prescription becomes a self-fulfilling prophecy: zoning out denser development in suburban areas imposes no costs, because suburban densities are low.

In this way, the cost side of the model is unexamined. The model instead focuses on publicly provided goods and services, finding economic efficiencies in their decentralized supply as long as individuals choose the kind of community they want. For a finding of economic efficiency to hold, however, the benefits of decentralized public service provision would need to be balanced against the costs of municipal exclusion described above. But nowhere does this model take account of costs imposed on households excluded from what would otherwise be their desired location within the metropolitan region. Nowhere does the Tiebout-Hamilton model even show awareness of these costs, or demonstrate that they are smaller than the asserted efficiencies of decentralized supply of publicly provided goods. In place of this balancing—an essential element to the conclusion of economic efficiency—is the unsupportable presumption that all community types demanded by the market are available at a range of locales, and that individuals excluded from one community select another without individual or social cost.

UNVERIFIABLE THEORY VERSUS UNCERTAIN EMPIRICS

The idea that decentralized supply of publicly provided goods leads to economic efficiencies is not an empirical observation but a theoretical construct. Empirical research can test the extent to which the model's assumptions and predictions hold in the real world, but cannot measure efficiency directly. For example, the Tiebout model would predict that larger numbers of competing jurisdictions are associated with greater homogeneity in each one. This hypothesis can be tested empirically (Dowding et al. 1994), but the economic efficiency of that circumstance is established through theoretical reasoning.

By contrast, the notion that municipal regulations push densities to a below-market level, thereby accelerating metropolitan sprawl, is empirically testable. Studies cited in Chapter 3 provide considerable empirical evidence for this finding. If this process is at work, then there must be a class of households which would have been willing to live at higher densities in locations different from their current neighborhoods; this group bears costs of exclusionary regulations. Part of these costs can be observed in travel behavior, especially if this group ends up driving more than it otherwise might have. Other studies call this idea into question, suggesting that the land-use–travel behavior relationships involved are not understood with sufficient confidence to be used as a basis for regulatory policy. But what if the policy reform involved the loosening of restrictive regulations? Some observers would view such liberalization as desirable, even if it required limiting the regulatory prerogative of local governments. Others, arguing within the Tiebout-Hamilton tradition, would suggest that limiting suburban communities' ability to establish minimum housing standards within their borders would interfere with the efficient supply of publicly provided goods. Yet these efficiencies are themselves a theoretical construct given, at best, to indirect empirical investigation. Rather than a debate over "the market" versus "planning," this policy argument hinges on preferences for unverifiable theory based in part on implausible assumptions (the Tiebout-Hamilton model) versus preferences for uncertain evidence on the land-use–travel behavior link.

This point deserves particular emphasis. On complex policy matters, empirical evidence tends to be mixed and open to conflicting interpretation. In fact, almost by definition, if an issue comes under the rubric of "policy" (as opposed to "professionalism," or "technical expertise"), differing scientific interpretations remain regarding the implications of alternative approaches. In this kind of environment, the clarity of a theoretical argument (such as that of the Tiebout-Hamilton model) may appear to lift it above competing empirical claims. But dealing forthrightly with uncertainty demands treating both theory and empirics with skepticism and according *a priori* primacy to neither. Adhering to exclusionary policies rooted in the Tiebout "marketplace" because of ambiguity in travel behavior research amounts to a position that elegant theory trumps uncertain evidence, notwithstanding the implausibility of the theory's cornerstone assumptions.

ALTERNATIVES TO EXCLUSION

Given the internal and probable external costs of zoning households out of their first-choice communities, one might expect research in the Tiebout-Hamilton tradition to seek less exclusionary solutions to the theoretical problem of "the poor following the rich in a never-ending quest for a tax base" (Hamilton 1975, *205*). For example, tax-base sharing policies, in which multiple jurisdictions agree to share the revenues from new development, would remove some of the incentives both for pursuit on the part of the poor and for flight on the part of the wealthy. Accepting provision or financing of services at higher levels of geographic aggregation—as when states act to equalize school financing—would similarly limit the incentive for games of "musical suburbs." These modifications would be deviations from a strictly decentralized supply of publicly provided goods, but given the costs associated with exclusionary land-use practices, they should be natural candidates for analysis.

According to Hamilton, households that consume less housing than the community average are a "free-rider problem" (1975, *211*) in that they pay less in tax for their public services than their wealthier neighbors. They may also pay less in tax for those services than the services cost the community. Yet one person's free-rider problem is another's system of progressive taxation. It is not at all self-evident that solving this free-rider problem is desirable policy in the first place. Hamilton himself offered the disclaimer that "I am not prepared to argue, on equity grounds, that local public services 'ought' to be distributed in accordance with market criteria" (211). Whereas a single community accepting large numbers of households with below-average income would find itself an untenable competitive disadvantage (Peterson 1981), general policies that limit municipal exclusion could increase progressivity in municipal-government finance without unduly burdening certain communities. Exclusionary zoning is not the only solution to the problem that Hamilton describes.

Moreover, in the absence of municipalities' ability to exclude households with lower-than-average housing consumption, it is uncertain that the musical suburbs game would ever be initiated. If wealthy householders were certain that their lower-income neighbors could follow them to new locales, the incentive to move might actually be reduced, since few long-term fiscal gains could be had. In contrast, under the status quo, migration into homogeneous communities at the metropolitan fringe is rational at least in part because of the protection from other income groups that zoning offers. Moreover, the sequential impoverishment of older suburbs described by Orfield (2002) suggests that the game of musical suburbs is already in full swing, even (or especially) with municipal exclusionary land-use powers firmly established.

THE LIMITATIONS OF THE PROPERTY-RIGHTS VIEW

The view of zoning as a collective property right as articulated by Fischel (1985) is a partial answer to the problems of exclusion. In a land-use regime designed to facilitate trade in property rights, communities that currently have little incentive to allow alternatives to the large-lot, single-family home may become open to alternatives. At least some of the societal value of those alternatives will translate into landowners' and developers' profits; developers can use these anticipated profits to purchase zoning rights. Zoning as a collective property right is still a far cry from a strict laissez-faire view; the municipality retains rights to accept or reject deals.

A Diamond Is Forever, a Suburban R-1 Zone Nearly So

Fischel's "normal behavior" standard envisions a system that initially assigns rights according to the "normal" or "subnormal" status of a development proposal. A normal proposal is one that seeks to develop in a community in a fashion no more dense or intense than current development; a subnormal development is one that goes beyond what has been typically developed in the community, as when a developer proposes an apartment building in a community of single-family homes. Under Fischel's scheme, the rights to develop normally would be vested with the developer; the right to exclude subnormal development would be vested with the community. The initial assignment of rights should not inevitably determine physical development outcomes, since they would be subject to bargaining between landowner-developers and municipalities. But Fischel acknowledges that even where development rights are fungible, their tendency toward inertia renders that assignment consequential.

That standard of normal behavior could, however, preclude precisely the kinds of urban transformation that land-use and transportation planners seek to facilitate. Consider, for example, a suburb of predominantly single-family homes on quarter-acre lots. Years after its initial development, economic conditions in the community change significantly: a rapid-transit station opens and leads to development pressures in the vicinity, say, or the community becomes a significant suburban job center. Developers who would now redevelop land—or develop passed-over land—in the community may seek to increase development densities over those that held in the community's earlier era. In Fischel's terms, this development would be subnormal and the right to preclude it would be vested with the municipality. Aspiring landowner-developers could attempt to purchase the rights to develop but, as described above, development rights will tend to remain with the party to whom they are initially assigned.

The normal standard for development appears to be geared at facilitating new development on the metropolitan fringe, rather than redevelopment or infill in built-up areas. In fact, the very evolution of cities necessarily entails the permitting of subnormal behavior. In almost all cases, cities begin as villages. Following the normal behavior standard would demand that the low-density, single-family land-use pattern as established by initial settlers remain; restricting development to such a standard would have precluded the development of most of the world's cities by compelling them to adopt a low-density form. To be sure, the normal behavior standard is not intended as a rigid development template, merely as a guide to the initial assignment of development rights. But the view that initial assignment of rights matters implies that it is relevant to final development outcomes.

Regulation obviously did not preclude the historical transformation of New York, Chicago, Amsterdam, or Zurich from villages to cities. But suburban zoning may be precluding similar transformations today. Territory that is zoned and built as single family in U.S. suburbs is rarely changed to higher-density residential uses, regardless of the change in the economic circumstances of the community. In some cases, those changes can be very dramatic. Few areas have transformed as thoroughly in recent decades as California's Santa Clara County, where areas that had suburbanized in the 1960s and 1970s as the far fringes of the San Francisco Bay Area were transformed later in the 1970s and 1980s into Silicon Valley, the global center of high-technology industry. This shift pushed housing prices to among the highest in the nation; median single-family home prices in the county reached $587,000 in 2003 (U.S. Census). If developed under today's economic conditions without low-density zoning constraints, many of the 1960s ranch homes and split-levels would probably give way to higher-density development forms, including multifamily developments, attached homes, and single-family homes on smaller lots. Yet the physical form that developed under an earlier economic environment is preserved by the R-1 residential zone; only a tiny portion of the neighborhoods zoned for and developed as single-family neighborhoods are ever redeveloped for other, higher-intensity land uses, according to local planners.[1] It is difficult to reconcile the Coasean view of bargaining over development rights with the fact that nearly every developed single-family residential zone remains intact throughout the massive transformation of this region and the development pressures that it engendered. If the single-family zone is adequate to resist the massive transformation of a suburban backwater into the global high-technology center, it appears more than adequate to resist more run-of-the-mill urban transformations. The Coasean notion that final outcomes are unaffected by the initial assignment of rights does not seem to fit metropolitan development processes well at all.

The impressions of Silicon Valley city planners—that there is a lack of transformations in single-family neighborhoods—are strongly supported by data from Massachusetts, a state that has detailed data on land supply over several decades. Between 1970 and 1999, of 351 monitored communities, only three—Cambridge, Chelsea, and Lawrence—experienced a net loss of acres developed as single-family (Massachusetts Executive Office of Environmental Affairs 2002). These three communities saw a net decline of only 21 acres of single-family in the intervening 29 years. Throughout the state, 640,000 acres were in single-family in 1970; thus the single-family transformation that occurred in these three communities amounted to 3/1000 of a percent of the existing 1970 single-family base. These figures may understate the change in single-family neighborhoods, however, since they report the data on the basis of municipalities, not parcels. Thus, if a single-family neighborhood was transformed to another use but equivalent single-family growth occurred elsewhere in the municipality, no net loss would be evident.

That can be partly corrected by analyzing the various categories of single-family in the Massachusetts data: low-density (no more than two single-family units per acre), medium-density (between two and four units per acre), and high-density (more than four units per acre). Over the 29-year period, transformations occurred as follows: 1,906 acres of low-density, 8 acres of medium-density, and 208 acres of high-density single-family units were transformed. Even if one makes the maximalist assumption that all of these losses of single-family acreage were conversions to non-single-family uses, only three-tenths of 1 percent of the 1970 single-family acreage would have changed by 1999. In fact, this is likely to be an overstatement of transformation of single-family areas to other uses. Over 80 percent of the transformation of low-density single-family acreage occurred in a single suburban municipality: Sudbury, 22 miles west of Boston. All of the "lost" low-density single-family development in this community was developed as medium-density single-family. These data strongly suggest that the single-family zone is impervious to economic and demographic changes and tends to keep its form even over a period of several decades.

The preceding discussion focuses on urban transformation through processes of redevelopment, as opposed to construction on open sites. American planners frequently use the term "buildout" to refer to a condition under which all developable sites in a community have been built upon. Although the concept is an adequate descriptor, it also connotes something of a final form, after which the community is expected to remain physically constant. This view precludes the kind of redevelopment-based transformations that have kept cities vital and responsive to changing times. For example, Downs (2004, *201*) considers the potential of land-densification strategies to affect traffic significantly, concluding that "[a]ll strategies that raise residential densities suffer from one major drawback: they might influence additional future settlement patterns, but they would leave existing settlements largely unchanged." The presumption is that once a neighborhood is developed, its form is set, and future transformations are largely precluded. This view, which seems true enough under the current land-use regime, is a major break with centuries of urban history, during which cities grew through both territorial expansion and densifying redevelopment. But with current land-use regulations constraining this manner of growth, the capacity of already-developed areas to respond to economic changes through densification is severely limited.

The Surprising Mildness of Proposals for Zoning Reform

Given the dominance of the single-family zone in U.S. metropolitan development,[2] the normal standard proposed by Fischel, if adopted, would likely replicate current development forms while precluding significant transportation and land-use innovation. Large cities would continue to allow dense development, while the metropolitan fringe would develop at low densities because of low development pressures there (and the establishment of this pattern in the relevant municipal jurisdictions). High-employment suburbs that developed primarily along an auto-oriented, low-density development model would continue to resist the pressures for more compact development, since such development would be subnormal and rights to exclude it would be vested with the municipality. Similarly, municipalities inclined to maintain low-density zoning in the vicinity of transit stations would have little difficulty in asserting the subnormal character of transit-oriented development proposals; their ability to zone these developments out would be unaffected. To be sure, under Fischel's scheme, development rights would be more easily exchanged, so higher-density development proposals could seek approval through purchase of or barter over development rights. But the reason for assigning development rights according to the normal or subnormal character of the proposals to begin with is that such rights tend to remain with the party to whom they are initially assigned.

For that reason, Fischel's normal-development standard is more oriented to status-quo development patterns than to market ordering of land use. His standard is certainly less market oriented than the Oregon Transportation Planning Rule, which requires local governments to allow transit-oriented developments on lands along transit routes, in that the Oregon law challenges the ability of local regulation to exclude such development; Fischel's proposal would leave that exclusionary ability in place. Similarly, the proposals are less geared toward market ordering than the antiexclusionary zoning policies of the Pennsylvania Supreme Court, which require municipalities to zone adequately for a full range of housing forms (Mitchell 2004). In the realm of transportation and land use, the rallying cry of "let the market decide" amounts in many instances to a call to avoid altering the current degree of municipal regulatory prerogative.

Property Rights and Public Purposes

With single-family development covering the largest share of developed territory in U.S. metropolitan areas, the normal-behavior standard proposed by Fischel would preclude much growth through densification. As with the status quo, the metropolitan periphery would remain the reservoir for new development, since the capacity to accommodate growth through denser redevelopment would be severely limited. This argument does not fundamentally challenge the view of zoning as a collective property right; it merely questions the value judgment regarding where to assign property rights initially.

In contrast, the very meaning of zoning as a collective property right—a view now broadly adopted by the economics profession—is worth reexamining. Analyzing zoning as a collective property right puts it in a class with property rights generally; by implication, these may be used, traded, or sold at their owner's pleasure (subject to restrictions of legal trade). If I choose to buy the house next door, my purchase needs no justification. I may want the property for the use of elderly family members, or I may have bought it to prevent its occupancy by a household whom I consider an undesirable neighbor for reasons of race or religion. Since my transactions in property rights are voluntary—I lack the power to compel or forbid action—they demand no justification beyond my idiosyncratic preference, at least under free-market systems. Similarly, defining zoning as a collective property right tends to legitimate any manner of regulation that the municipality, acting as the agent of its citizens, desires. Land-use regulation would remain subject to legal "takings" limits and scrutiny over racial or religious discrimination. But the property-rights formulation implies that no link to any larger public purpose is needed.

If zoning is a collective property right, the mere fact that community residents prefer this intervention is ample reason for its promulgation and legitimation. If the community is merely exercising a property right, one would not need to ask whether the regulation's benefits exceed its costs, or whether the interests of the population of the state (from which the regulatory power derived) are being served. This is because property rights are disposed of with no greater accountability than their owners' (legal) pleasure. But in contrast to the voluntary exchange that characterizes the individual exercise of property rights, zoning entails the power to prevent private market action. Few economists would legitimate such idiosyncratic use of governmental regulatory power as a "collective property right" if the venue of this exercise were state or federal government; at the larger geographic scale, they tend to demand that regulation be subjected to the bright lights of economic analysis and scientific proof. Treating regulation differently when it gets down to the local level amounts to granting small groups of individuals the right to use public power for essentially unchecked private purposes.

THE AFFORDABLE HOUSING–TRANSPORTATION CONTINUUM

Tensions between municipal exclusionary prerogative and households' freedom to choose has clearest relevance in debates over affordable housing. Observers from a range of disciplinary and political perspectives have long implicated suburban zoning practices in raising the cost of housing beyond the reach of low- to moderate-income households. Jack Kemp, President George H.W. Bush's conservative secretary of Housing and Urban Development, introduced a report on barriers to affordable housing by charging that "exclusionary, discriminatory, and unnecessary regulations constitute formidable barriers to affordable housing, raising cost by 20 to 35 percent in some communities" (Advisory Commission on Barriers to Affordable Housing 1991).

The report provided background to Secretary Kemp's diagnosis. "In some places," the report explained, "single-family homes are chosen as the standard for preserving neighborhood homogeneity, and desires for intangibles such as community ambiance influence the zoning process. The more affordable housing types, including multifamily housing, manufactured housing, accessory apartments, and single-room-occupancy dwellings are often cited as incompatible uses" (2-6).

This is one policy formulation on which some conservatives and liberals can apparently agree. Paul Davidoff, credited as being the founder of "advocacy planning," said 20 years earlier, "Suburban populations which are generally conservative—and one would suspect believers in permitting the free market to operate—don't trust the free market to operate to serve their own interests. They have employed the power of the state to protect their own very selfish desire to create a community that is amenable to themselves, but to prohibit the large mass of the population from sharing in those amenities. They have not bought the land, but instead have done the cheap and nasty thing of employing the police power to protect their own interest in the land and to exclude the largest part of the population" (Aumente 1971, 56).

These policy positions are well founded in recent research as well. Pendall (2000) demonstrated that exclusionary zoning reduces the presence of both rental housing and ethnic minorities in a community. Glaeser and Gyourko (2002) find land-use regulation to be a determinant of high housing prices but focus more on "classic impact fees or more Byzantine approval processes that slow construction and put up costly hurdles to construction" (11) than on low-density development regulations. The authors suggest that "[o]ne implication of this analysis is that the affordable housing debate should be broadened to encompass zoning reform, not just public or subsidized construction programs" (6), a position well articulated 30 years early by Davidoff (Aumente 1971) and subsequent researchers.

Housing research has focused not only on the question of affordability to low-income households, but also on the development of housing choices throughout the metropolitan region. Myers and Gearin (2001) forecast significant growth in alternative development forms, based on U.S. demographic trends. Danielson et al. (1999) equate "smart growth" with the lowering of regulatory barriers to housing development. "The politics of smart growth, as it now stands," they write, "favor just one part of the equation—limiting greenfield development. Yet the far tougher political fight awaits those who attempt to redress the NIMBYism and regulatory opposition that now face most infill projects" (519).

Municipal regulatory barriers, which underpin the asserted efficiencies in the Tiebout model, are broadly understood by housing researchers to impose costs on excluded households, including expensive housing and mismatch between neighborhood choices and household needs. By contrast, transportation policy researchers tend to assess the current land-use regime only in terms of travel behavior: can we or can we not reduce congestion or vehicle miles traveled through alternative land-use policies? This problem definition represents an overly narrow criterion by which to judge the transportation relevance of land-use policy.

Notwithstanding the tendency of researchers to circumscribe problems tightly in order to isolate them for analysis, policymakers need to recognize the transportation–land-use and affordable housing problems as portions of a continuum. "The fact that jobs-housing balance is unlikely to solve transportation problems does not imply that such policies cannot play a role in solving other urban problems," writes Giuliano (1989, *311*). "Rather, the point is that these problems are more likely to be solved if separated and dealt with directly." Downs (1992, *111*), writes similarly, "Why focus scarce resources on altering an area's jobs-housing imbalances when other institutional changes would be much more effective at cutting traffic congestion?"

The statement implicitly presumes both that congestion relief is the ultimate goal of transportation and land-use policy and that increasing affordable housing supplies in job-rich areas entails expenditures of "scarce resources." This view is hard to square with the observation that municipal regulation causes shortages of affordable housing in many areas. If "[m]ost suburban land use markets are dominated by local zoning and other regulations that are aimed at excluding low-income households and that distort what would occur in a truly free market" (Downs 1999, 963), then the main resource needed to expand housing supplies in job-rich suburban areas is the political will for the reform of exclusionary land-use regulations.

Viewed in this fashion, a precise demarcation of the transportation and land-use problem from the affordable housing problem is impossible. The major expression of housing unaffordability is not homelessness but an inability to afford adequate housing in an area where one's needs are met, imposing on individuals and society the costs of either extra transportation or, worse, inaccessibility. If municipal exclusion underpins the affordability problem, it underpins this transportation and land-use problem in equal measure.

In his introduction to the report on regulatory barriers to affordable housing, Housing and Urban Development Secretary Jack Kemp conveyed the transportation dimension of the affordable housing problem well: "As a result [of exclusionary, discriminatory and unnecessary regulations], many lower-income young families cannot find housing *near* their places of work, and elderly couples cannot afford to live *close to* their children" (Advisory Commission on Regulatory Barriers to Affordable Housing 1991; emphasis added). When municipal exclusion prevents households from being able to afford housing where they want, it creates a systematic gap between their needs and preferences on the one hand and their actual choices on the other. Transportation is an element of that gap, whether the above-mentioned young families travel additional distance to get to their workplace or drop out of the workforce entirely, or whether elderly couples drive further to visit their children or curtail their visits because of the distance.

ACKNOWLEDGING REGULATORY EXCLUSION

Because they enable municipal governments to sort out the population by levels of housing consumption, land-use regulations find significant theoretical justification in the Tiebout-Hamilton model. Within this framework, municipal decentralization offers potential efficiencies in the provision of publicly supplied goods but requires local governments to restrict the influx of lower-income outsiders who might "free-ride" on the tax payments of their more affluent neighbors. Yet nothing in the model evidences awareness of the costs that land-use regulations impose on excluded households; rather, it is explicitly assumed that excluded households can costlessly sort themselves out into other municipalities in the same region.

Despite broad acceptance of the Tiebout model's policy implications, observers have offered devices to soften the sometimes rigid exclusion of municipal land-use regulation. For example, within Fischel's property-rights view, zoning ought to be rendered as fungible as possible to enable developers, landowners, and municipalities to bargain explicitly over development rights. Notwithstanding the Coase theorem, however, the initial assignment of these rights matters a great deal to final development outcomes. For this reason, Fischel offers a standard that vests rights to exclude denser-than-current development with the municipality, which threatens to continue the exclusion of significant transportation and land-use innovation, such as transit-oriented developments or improved supplies of housing in the vicinity of suburban job centers. The normal-development standard thus appears better suited to ensuring continued development in the current model than opening the regulatory door to significant modifications.

Ultimately, any assertion of economic efficiency in a land-use regime must account not only for the benefits of decentralized public service provision, but also for the costs imposed on households excluded from their first choice of residential location. Studies of affordable housing have found that a range of impacts accrue from the current regime, including overcrowding, excessive shares of household budgets spent on housing, or living in inadequate or unsafe units or neighborhoods. But a major affordability impact—the inability to afford adequate housing close to one's work and nonwork destinations—incorporates the transportation and land-use problem. Viewed in this way, transportation and housing concerns merge, since affordability is gauged not by housing costs alone but by the sum of housing and transportation costs—together with the costs of inaccessibility—associated with a particular residential location.

In addition to exacting costs on the excluded low- to moderate-income households, a land-use regime that lowers development densities imposes costs on households who prefer alternatives to auto-oriented environments. Significant minorities of U.S. households consistently report preferences for walkable, transit-oriented, mixed-use residential environments (Malizia and Exline 2000). By restricting the supply of alternatives to auto-oriented development, suburban low-density zoning regulations constitute an impediment to these households' preference satisfaction (Chapter 7). In this way, housing affordability and transportation and land-use policy represent a continuum of concerns.

Can we solve transportation problems with land-use policy? That depends on how we define transportation problems. When the focus is on congestion, vehicle miles traveled, and emissions, observers differ on the utility of land-use tools. But these outcomes, however vital, hardly exhaust the domain of transportation policy concerns. Where municipal regulatory policies constitute an impediment to people's getting what they prefer in transportation and land use, or where they prevent low- to moderate-income households from finding affordable housing close to their work and nonwork destinations, their reform is properly viewed as a central concern of transportation policy.

CHAPTER FIVE

IS ZONING STATE REGULATION OR
A LOCAL PROPERTY RIGHT?

"The single most important characteristic of the newer forms of social intervention," writes Charles Schultze (1977, 12), "is that their success or failure depends upon affecting the skills, attitudes, consumption habits or production patterns of hundreds of millions of individuals, millions of business firms, and *thousands of units of local government*. The tasks are difficult not so much because they deal with technologically complicated matters as because they aim ultimately at modifying the behavior of *private producers and consumers*" (emphasis added). Within this scheme, local government is taken to be an autonomous actor in the marketplace, more akin to consumers and firms than to state or federal government. It is not seen as a governmental agency to which the police power of the state is delegated in certain realms. Notwithstanding the apparent regulatory nature of zoning interventions, municipal land-use regulation is often seen as something very akin to a "market force" by many observers of metropolitan policy and politics.

Any exploration into the roots of this view would be incomplete without the writings of legal scholars and judges, who have debated the nature and source of municipal regulatory power for decades, if not centuries. Economists and other social scientists have split on the nature of zoning—with some viewing it as governmental regulation and others viewing it as more akin to a "collective property right." Similarly, lawyers and judges have at times viewed municipal land-use powers as a delegation of the police power of the state, and at times as a right inherent to home, family, and neighborhood. Since well before *Village of Euclid v. Ambler Realty* established the fundamental constitutionality of municipal land-use zoning in 1926, debate has swirled around the proper limits of this exercise of governmental authority. The broader debate seeks to define when land-use regulation becomes an unconstitutional deprivation of property under the Fourteenth Amendment. This chapter does not engage that issue but rather explores the related question of the differences between legal treatment of municipal land-use regulations and other forms of governmental intervention into the economy.

In its early years in the United States, zoning was accorded much more deference than other forms of governmental regulation. With changing legal doctrines over the decades, differences in judicial treatment of zoning and other forms of regulation have become muted, but remain evident. This chapter argues that zoning's relative "free ride"—i.e., legal acceptability with little judicial scrutiny regarding its broader public purpose—stems from its identification with the protection of private property rather than governmental intervention into market processes. As such, judges have viewed it in terms very close to Fischel's (1985) "collective property right." A view of zoning as a property right locates its source in something other than police-power state regulation; rather, the framework suggests that the right to regulate land use is an inherent prerogative of municipal government. This view, which has been identified by Briffault (1990a, 1990b) and Frug (1999), has far-reaching implications regarding the ends to which the zoning power may be put. A distancing of zoning from the state's police power tends to legitimate more parochial uses of the land-use authority than would hold if zoning were strictly a delegated state regulation.

CITIES' HISTORICAL STATUS

Municipal governments occupy an ambiguous middle ground between the individual and the state. Frug (1999) describes how the medieval town arose as an organic grouping of residents, notably the merchant classes, with powers independent of any larger political entity. In the 16th and 17th centuries, however, this view of the city as an autonomous corporation began to come under attack, with central governments asserting control over municipal authorities; such control was seen as "necessary to protect...the vital interests of individual liberty and of the emerging nation-state" (Frug 1999, 32). This rationale underscores the ambiguous relationship of the municipality to the individual. Are the municipalities minigovernments their own right, the "long arm" of central government power, or something more akin to a voluntary association, like a commercial corporation? When they were viewed as organic associations of individuals, municpal action was traditionally understood as inherently consistent with the freedoms associated with voluntary association and contract. When they were viewed as their own centers of governmental power, they held the potential to restrict individual liberties; then the assertion of central state sovereignty over local action could be seen as protecting the individuals subject to municipal control.

Prior to the 19th century, no legal distinctions existed in the United States or England between municipalities and what we would now identify as private corporations; all were seen as groupings through which individuals associate to pursue their interests. Beginning in the 19th century, newly distinguished private corporations were granted protection from the state; by contrast, the public corporations were brought under state domination. Private corporations became more like individuals in their legal rights; public corporations—municipalities—became identified with the state itself (Frug 1999, 39). Because of their voluntary nature, the private corporations became benignly associated with enhanced individual freedom; after all, these were the means by which individuals banded together to pursue collective goals. By contrast, municipal governments, because they wielded the power of the state, required strict delineation of powers lest they impinge unduly on the freedom of those subject to their control.

Yet even these public corporations continued to perform privatelike functions. They owned property directly, and they had interests in the protection of the private property of their constituents. To the extent that these municipal governments acted on these private interests, they tended to receive legal treatment more akin to that of private corporations; they were viewed as having inherent rights independent of state delegation and were worthy of protection from state domination. Whereas within the public realm of governance cities were brought under state authority, their functions that were more private in nature were viewed as inherent to their status as associations of individuals.

One of those actions was the regulation of development. In his "Report on the Sanitary Condition of the Labouring Population of Gt. Britain," British sanitation reformer Edwin Chadwick (1842, 347) wrote, "Regulations of the *sites* of town buildings have comparatively little effect on the cost of construction, and it may in general be said that a Building Act would effect what any enlightened owner of a district would effect for himself...or what the separate owners would effect for themselves if they had the power or co-operation..." In other words, public regulation of land uses was privatelike in character because it would merely add a cooperative tool to landowners' private property-rights bundle.

This view has colored perceptions about municipal action to the current day. Frug (1999, 7) explains the relationship between municipalities' privatelike functions and the broad autonomy they are granted over these realms:

> In America today, suburban power is usually not seen as a threat to local residents or outsiders but as a vehicle for the protection of home and family and of private property. This privatized picture of suburban life not only has helped convince the states to grant these cities significant power over zoning, education and resource allocation, but has helped persuade the courts to defend their power against attacks by insiders and outsiders alike.

PROPERTY RIGHTS AND DEFERENCE TO MUNICIPAL ZONING

Land-use regulatory power fits squarely within this tradition. Formally a grant of the states' police power, municipal zoning nonetheless is frequently taken as the protection of property rights by groupings more akin to homeowners' associations than agencies of the state. The history of the legal treatment accorded to zoning in the United States frequently begins with *Village of Euclid v. Ambler Realty*, the 1926 Supreme Court case that established zoning's fundamental constitutionality. But starting at the turn of the 19th century, the Supreme Court decided several challenges to municipal land-use regulation. In nearly all cases, the court ruled the regulations in question to be permissible, even when they inflicted significant economic losses on the affected landowner. The decisions—which set the stage for *Euclid*—may be seen as paradoxical, given the ostensible property-rights orientation of the court at the time (Hylton 2000). Yet a mismatch between fealty to property rights and deference to municipal regulations impinging on those rights continues in various forms in zoning decisions to the present day. In the realm of governmental regulation of economic activity in the United States, zoning seems to receive exceptional treatment.

At no time was that clearer than with the ruling of the landmark *Village of Euclid et al. v. Ambler Realty Company* (1926). The case was brought by a landowner in Euclid, a suburb of Cleveland, who sought to develop his land with industrial uses. These uses were prohibited in the two of the three zones in which the plaintiff's land fell, which were reserved primarily for duplexes and multifamily structures. The plaintiff's case was based on the constitutional claim that the regulations deprived him of liberty and property without due process of law, and that they denied him the equal protection of law.

The court found the basis for municipal zoning in a delegation of the state's police power, or legal capacity to regulate. At the same time, already in *Euclid* the court hinted at an alternative, more locally rooted source for the legitimacy of land-use regulation. "[T]he village, though physically a suburb of Cleveland," wrote the Court, "is politically a separate municipality, with powers of its own and authority to govern itself as it sees fit within the organic law of its creation and the State and Federal Constitutions" (389). Although the regulatory power was nominally being exercised on behalf of the state of Ohio, no reference to a statewide public purpose was called for, since the zoning ordinance in question had been enacted by the democratically elected authorities in the municipality, "presumably representing a majority of its inhabitants and voicing their will." The court did acknowledge that "the general public interest" might at times "so far outweigh the interest of the municipality" that local regulation could be overturned. Nonetheless it was quite clear that despite the state origin of the police power, the legitimacy of the zoning ordinance would be assessed with regard to a local public purpose.

Such power is not unlimited. The regulations would have been found invalid if they were "arbitrary and unreasonable, having no substantial relation to the public health, safety, morals or general welfare" (395). The standard employed was highly deferential to the regulating municipality; a relation of any substance to one of the three public purposes would be sufficient to legitimate the zoning intervention. The village did not need to affirmatively demonstrate that the ordinance would be likely to further some public purpose; rather, any challenger would have to demonstrate utter lack of relationship to one of the legitimate purposes listed above.

If the issue considered by the court were strictly limited to the separation of industry from residential neighborhoods, the ordinance would undoubtedly have withstood even more rigorous scrutiny. In fact, the landowner was seeking to develop his largely residentially zoned land for industry, and the court could easily have restricted its consideration to such separation. The court took pains to proclaim the ostensible narrowness of its ruling, stating that "in the realm of constitutional law, especially, this Court has perceived the embarrassment which is likely to result from an attempt to formulate rules or decide questions beyond the necessities of the immediate issue. It has preferred to follow the method of a gradual approach to the general by a systematically guarded application and extension of constitutional princi- ples to particular cases as they arise, rather than by out of hand attempts to establish general rules to which future cases must be fitted" (397). Despite its declared preference for narrow rulings—and the fact that the plaintiff was seeking permission only for industrial development—the Court nonetheless extended its ruling to the issue of regulatory exclusion of apartments from single-family neighborhoods, revealing its eagerness to establish the propri- ety of this aspect of land-use regulation.

Euclid established the public purpose involved with the exclusion of multifamily housing in an indirect fashion. Without the obvious threat that industry—with its pollution, vibration and noise—posed to residential districts, the legitimacy of exclusion of multifamily housing needed to be established differently. The Court justified this manner of zoning, a relative newcomer to the U.S. scene, through reference to nuisance, a centuries-old element of Anglo-American common law:

> With particular reference to apartment houses, it is pointed out that the development of detached house sections is greatly retarded by the coming of apartment houses, which has sometimes resulted in destroying the entire sec- tion for private house purposes; that in such sections very often the apart- ment house is a mere parasite, constructed in order to take advantage of the open spaces and attractive surroundings created by the residential character of the district. Moreover, the coming of one apartment house is followed by others, interfering by their height and bulk with the free circulation of air and monopolizing the rays of the sun which otherwise would fall upon the smaller homes, and bringing, as their necessary accompaniments, the dis- turbing noises incident to increased traffic and business, and the occupation, by means of moving and parked automobiles, of larger portions of the streets, thus detracting from their safety and depriving children of the privi- lege of quiet and open spaces for play, enjoyed by those in more favored localities, — until, finally, the residential character of the neighborhood and its desirability as a place of detached residences are utterly destroyed. Under these circumstances, apartment houses, which in a different environment would be not only entirely unobjectionable but highly desirable, *come very near to being nuisances.* (395, emphasis added)

A nuisance-based rationale for zoning hints at a source of legitimacy for zoning other than the state's regulatory power. An element of property law, nuisance protection is strictly a reactive tool; aggrieved property owners must bring offending land users to court for redress. Zoning, by contrast, is a form of proactive regulation. The Court's opinion casts municipal zoning as merely a proactive embodiment of age-old reactive nuisance law, as if to say that the harm of apartment buildings in single-family districts is so self-evident that even when the municipality acts against it with regulation, it more or less acts within the tradition of the common law of nuisance.

Why was it important for zoning to be construed as tantamount to rulings against nuisances, rather than proactive governmental regulation? It may be that this construction assisted in highlighting the aspect of zoning that protects private property, rather than its governmental-regulatory nature. Kennedy (1978–1979) refers to "a system of thought that identifies some forms of collective intervention, such as the defense of private property and enforcement of contracts, with the protection of individual freedom." As a perceived defense of private property, nuisance law is traditionally understood as consistent with the expansion of these individual liberties, as opposed to a tool of the state's will. The latter would have been seen as far more suspect, since proactive enforcement of a governmental interest carries the threat of unwarranted limitation on liberties—a threat against which courts are supposed to be a bulwark. This threat feels reassuringly absent from a nuisance framework that is based on the traditional principle, "Use your own property so as not to harm that of another." This principle also seems inherent in the very definition of the institution of property: no one's property rights are limitless, and mine end where yours begin. The Court's decision in *Euclid* both continued and solidified a tradition that equated zoning more with the protection of private property than with its proactive regulation by government.

Equally importantly, the grounding of a novel form of governmental intervention in ancient common law principles conferred on the new status quo the valuable aura of policy neutrality. Referring to the Supreme Court at the time of *Lochner v. New York* (1905), Sunstein (1987, 874) writes,

> For the Lochner Court, neutrality, understood in a particular way, was a constitutional requirement. The key concepts here are threefold: government inaction, the existing distribution of wealth and entitlements, and the baseline set by the common law. Governmental intervention was constitutionally troublesome, whereas inaction was not; and both neutrality and inaction were defined as respect for the behavior of private actors pursuant to the

common law, in light of the existing distribution of wealth and entitlements. Whether there was a departure from the requirement of neutrality, in short, depended on whether the government had altered the common law distribution of entitlements. *Market ordering under the common law was understood to be a part of nature rather than a legal construct,* and it formed the baseline from which to measure the constitutionally critical lines that distinguished action from inaction and neutrality from impermissible partisanship. (emphasis added)

Allying municipal zoning with a body of the common law quickly established it as the neutral default option, even "a part of nature." This remarkable feat simultaneously conferred inevitability on municipal land-use prerogative and shifted the onus to those who would call for limitations on such regulation. Although legal and political reasoning has transformed much since 1905, the impact of this thinking is felt to this day. Notwithstanding municipal zoning's omnipresent intervention into metropolitan development, advocates of land-use reform bear the burden of proof that this neutral default state of "nature" ought to be altered, even when such change takes the form of regulatory liberalization. When transportation and land-use researchers assess development alternatives by the extent to which they reduce vehicle miles traveled (VMT), they are acting squarely in line with this traditional view.

LOCHNER AND EUCLID

The endorsement of municipal zoning by the Supreme Court in *Euclid* may be seen as paradoxical given the ideology of the court at the time. The *Euclid* decision was written by Justice Sutherland, a man deeply imbued with a property-rights orientation (Siegan 1997), in apparent contravention of a ruling of his from three years earlier. In *New Skate Ice Company v. Liebmann* Sutherland had held that "a regulation which has the effect of denying or unreasonably curtailing a lawful business...cannot be consistent with the Fourteenth Amendment. Under that amendment, nothing is more clearly settled than that it is beyond the power of a state 'under the guise of protecting the public, arbitrarily [to] interfere with private business or prohibit lawful occupations or impose unreasonable and unnecessary restrictions upon them'" (*New Skate Ice Company v. Liebmann* 1923, quoted in Siegan 1997). Although separation of residence and industry under *Euclid's* zoning might well pass that exacting test, it is difficult to see how *Euclid's* endorsement of regulatory separation of residences by density could be supported.

The exceptional treatment accorded to zoning is further highlighted by the contrast between the *Euclid* decision and the other landmark case of the era pertaining to governmental regulation of economic activity. *Lochner v. New York* (1905) considered the constitutionality of a New York State statute limiting employees of bakeries to 60 hours of work per week and 10 hours per day; the Court ultimately deemed the law unconstitutional. In enacting this regulation, New York was employing its police power—at least nominally the identical source as the power that the Village of Euclid, in zoning its territory, exercised on behalf of Ohio. In *Lochner*, however, the Court emphasized not the scope of the police power but its limitation:

> It must, of course, be conceded that there is a limit to the valid exercise of the police power by the State. There is no dispute concerning this general proposition. Otherwise the Fourteenth Amendment would have no efficacy and the legislatures of the States would have unbounded power, and it would be enough to say that any piece of legislation was enacted to conserve the morals, the health or the safety of the people; such legislation would be valid, no matter how absolutely without foundation the claim might be. (56)

In contrast to *Euclid*, under which a finding that apartment buildings in single-family neighborhoods are inherently "very near" to being nuisances was sufficient to justify police-power regulation, the *Lochner* Court famously applied a much stricter level of scrutiny to the work-limitation statute. From the vantage point of the current day, the potential for long hours to harm bakery workers' health does not inherently appear lower than the chance that apartments constitute nuisance to their neighbors. Nonetheless, none of the presumption of validity that was accorded to municipal zoning under *Euclid* was extended to this state-level regulation:

> The mere assertion that the subject relates though but in a remote degree to the public health does not necessarily render the enactment valid. The act must have a more direct relation, as a means to an end, and the end itself must be appropriate and legitimate, before an act can be held to be valid which interferes with the general right of an individual to be free in his person and in his power to contract in relation to his own labor. (58)

In contrast to *Euclid*'s generalized sense that apartments tended to harm their single-family surroundings, in *Lochner* the Court required specific proof of harm before the bakery regulation would qualify as a valid police-power exercise:

Statutes...limiting the hours in which grown and intelligent men may labor to earn their living, are mere meddlesome interferences with the rights of the individual, and they are not saved from condemnation by the claim that they are passed in the exercise of the police power and upon the subject of the health of the individual whose rights are interfered with, unless there be some fair ground, reasonable in and of itself, to say that there is material danger to the public health or to the health of the employees, if the hours of labor are not curtailed. (61)

In absence of such convincing evidence, the Court expressed suspicion that the motives were not health at all but some more economically motivated consideration.

When assertions such as we have adverted to become necessary in order to give, if possible, a plausible foundation for the contention that the law is a "health law," it gives rise to at least a suspicion that there was some other motive dominating the legislature than the purpose to subserve the public health or welfare. (62)

This suspicion stands in marked contrast to the deference accorded to zoning, regardless of any economic motive for municipal land-use regulation. A finding in *Euclid* consistent with *Lochner* principles might have commented that in the absence of conclusive evidence of apartments' harm to public health, safety, morals, or general welfare, the Court was led to the suspicion that the village of Euclid was attempting to use the police power to justify regulations improperly to protect the values of individuals' private property. But far from being improper, governmental protection of these private property values from the vagaries of the market was seen as an inherently legitimate goal of local government.

The thinking continues to the present. The criticism of "rent-seeking" (the use of political power to improve the marketplace returns on one's property rights) is rarely leveled against homeowners in the context of municipal zoning; rather, in the case of land-use regulation, "protection of property values" is self-evident in its validity as a public purpose. Far from being suspect, this motive was celebrated in Fischel's (2001) book, *The Homevoter Hypothesis: How Home Values Influence Local Government Taxation, School Finance, and Land-Use Policies*. While actions to use state or federal government to better one's market position are broadly condemned as "rent seeking," municipal regulation—perhaps the largest venue for rent seeking in the U.S. economy—is largely exempt from the critique as action that is something other than fully governmental.

"HARD LOOK" DOCTRINES AND *BELLE TERRE V. BORAAS*

The New Deal era witnessed a shift away from *Lochner* and its confinement of governmental regulation to interventions for which the benefit in public health, safety, morals, or general welfare could be clearly demonstrated. Judges appointed during this era generally accorded deference to administrative agencies, without demands for scientific or other evidence that the agencies' interventions were acting effectively against proven risks. For a time, then, the deference accorded to municipalities with regard to land-use regulation became less unusual and more squarely within the mainstream of judicial practice.

The New Deal, however, was hardly the end of the line for searching judicial review of the bases for governmental regulation. Morag-Levine (2003, 82) describes the aftermath:

> [A]fter the enactment of the federal health and safety risk-control mandates of the 1960s and 1970s, courts abandoned their early deference in favor of rigorous review of administrative rules. Making regulatory interventions legally contingent upon proof of risk, these statutory mandates paralleled long-standing nuisance doctrines and gave judges a similar veto power to that which they had always possessed under common law. As such, the "hard look" doctrines of the 1970s are better seen not as a novel mode of judicial scrutiny suggestive of a radically new regulatory regime, but as an extension of courts' traditional role under nuisance law.

Thus the 1970s saw some reversion to common law–inspired standards of judicial review of administrative actions. Under the "hard look" doctrine, judges would assess scientific evidence regarding the proof of the harm that the administrative intervention was supposed to treat. Against this backdrop, it is instructive to consider one of the principal zoning cases of the era, *Village of Belle Terre et al. v. Boraas et al.*, which the Supreme Court decided in 1974.

Belle Terre is a village on Long Island's north shore, 60 miles northeast of New York City. Its zoning ordinance restricted single-family occupancy to families of no more than two unrelated individuals. The owners of a house in the village were ordered to remedy violations of the ordinance, since their property was being leased to six unrelated students at the nearby State University of New York at Stony Brook. The case differed from *Euclid* in that neither the structure type nor the residential land use was at issue; similarly, no occupancy standards were being violated. The ordinance was challenged on a number of grounds, including the right to travel, the right to migrate, and the impropriety of social homogeneity as a goal of government.

The Court determined the zoning ordinance to be permissible, finding,

> With regard to the validity of zoning ordinances, a quiet place where yards are wide, people few, and motor vehicles restricted are legitimate guidelines in a land use project addressed to family needs; the police power is not confined to elimination of filth, stench, and unhealthy places, but is ample to lay out zones where family values, youth values, and the blessings of quiet seclusion and clean air make the area a sanctuary for people. (*Village of Belle Terre v. Boraas* 1974, 9)

The reasoning outlined above bears little imprint of this "hard look" doctrine of the era, appearing instead to treat the community's desire for social homogeneity as self-justifying. Evidence of specific harms associated with unrelated people living together—such as traffic, noise, or sanitary conditions—was not relevant to the decision, which hinged more on culture than on the traditional bases for exercise of the police power.

Like *Euclid* fifty years earlier, *Belle Terre* appeared to view zoning as exceptional among governmental interventions into market ordering. Rather than delving into the specific harms caused by the cohabitation of unrelated people, the Court asserted the sufficiency of the police power to bolster a particular suburban ideal, should that be the manner in which the municipality chooses to employ it.

THE EXCEPTIONAL TREATMENT OF ZONING

In both 1926 and 1974, the Supreme Court decided pivotal zoning cases in a fashion that appears, on the surface, at odds with its reigning worldview of either era. These two decisions hint at an exceptional treatment accorded zoning in the United States compared with other forms of governmental intervention. Whether one views landmark Supreme Court decisions as reflecting or leading popular views, an examination of the underpinnings of zoning's exceptional treatment at the hand of the legal system may offer clues to the view implicitly held by many observers of metropolitan planning— including many transportation and land-use researchers (Chapter 2)—that municipal regulatory actions constitute some manner of "market force."

The analysis of Briffault (1990a and 1990b) is especially instructive in this regard. Local governments formally are subject to the hegemony of their states. As creatures of the state, they lack powers except those specifically delegated to them and, in contrast to individuals and private corporations, are not afforded constitutional protection against the actions of their state. Formally, the municipality is "like a state administrative agency, serving the state in its narrow area of expertise, but instead of being functional specialists, localities are given jurisdictions primarily by territory, although certain local units are specialized by function as well as territory" (Briffault 1990a, 8).

That formal analysis of the power of municipalities and their relationship to the state is only part of the story, however. Municipal powers in the form of school funding and land-use zoning have often come before state supreme courts. Although the courts have at times found for plaintiffs, Briffault writes that "these victories were not typical. Despite the evidence of profound interlocal inequalities and the asserted tradition of legal powerlessness, state judges were often moved to vindicate local autonomy and were frequently unwilling to disturb the education funding and zoning responsibilities of local governments" (1990a, 24). Despite evident and ample claims for curtailment of local prerogative—and the fact that that local powers formally derive from the states—judges asserted and reasserted the rights of municipalities to continue to pursue a localized, and even privatized, vision of the public interest, and the desires of municipal governments to maintain the status quo were repeatedly legitimated. Courts called for a balancing of interests between current and prospective residents likely to be kept out through exclusionary zoning regulations. But the bodies they entrusted to carry out this balancing were municipal planning commissions and councils, whose electorate led to the parochial regulatory impulse in the first place (44).

Briffault shows that notwithstanding the formal view that the powers of municipalities are strictly delegated, judges regularly rule as if municipalities' powers emanated from the municipalities' action as the agent of local families. Normatively accepting the suburban-community model, judges—like the Supreme Court in *Village of Belle Terre*—endorse the rights of communities to replicate and maintain single-family suburban environments by regulation. The municipality, under this view, is acting not on behalf of the state but on the inherent collective rights of the residents—chiefly homeowners—in the community. At the individual level, property rights entail the right to exclude others from one's property; the collectively held right of zoning serves a similar function at the municipal level and stems similarly from inherent property rights, under this view.

The implications of this *de facto* redefinition of local powers are far reaching. To the extent that municipal land-use regulation is allied with property rights rather than with governmental intervention into markets, it shifts the nature of requirements regarding the proper exercise of the police power. When the zoning power is seen as originating with local families, it does not need to answer to any state-level public purpose. In fact, those few state supreme courts that have ruled to limit local land-use prerogative have done so through a reassertion of the delegation of the state's police power, which implies demands that local regulation respond to a valid state purpose (Brener 1999).

Briffault's notion that courts treat local zoning powers as emanating from local families rather than the state is consistent with Frug's (1999) view regarding the private and public functions of government. In public realms relating to governance, municipalities' power is strictly checked by the state; unique among collective bodies in the United States, cities require formal delegation of authority to take action—unlike private corporations, which are permitted to take any action that is not prohibited. By contrast, when acting in privatelike capacities, municipal governments enjoy a latitude of action consistent with the analysis of Briffault above. This affects cities and suburbs differently; since cites tend to be large, diverse, and open, their actions are seen as more public, governance-related, and hence checked by state authority. When suburbs act in privatized ways—notably in the protection of their homeowners' private property—their powers are more expansive and are viewed as inherent in the municipality as a creature of its constituent members, rather than of the state. Zoning fits squarely within the privatelike powers of municipalities and as a consequence is treated—at least implicitly— as an inherent power, rather than a state delegation.

Briffault's view that municipalities are seen as acting on behalf of local families rather than on the basis of a state delegation of the police power also matches Fischel's formulation, broadly accepted in economics, of zoning as a collective property right (Chapter 3). Whereas Siegan (1997), Ellickson (1973), and other zoning critics with market orientations identify zoning with police-power regulatory intervention, Fischel (1985) views zoning as a property right held collectively by local residents. The municipality in this view is the institution in the best position to take action with these rights, including enforcement, modification, and (under Fischel's policy prescription) even trade and sale.

The legal frameworks discussed in this chapter are explicitly normative. Judicial reasoning implying that land-use controls are an inherent right of municipalities amounts to a value-laden statement regarding the way in which municipalities should be allowed to act. Similarly, the contrary assertion—that local governments act strictly via a delegation of the state's police power—implies the normative position that municipalities ought to be accountable to a broader, state-level public interest. Although the discipline of economics hardly shies away from policy prescriptions, it aspires to base those recommendations on objective analysis.

Yet the parallels between the legal and economic frameworks demonstrate the inherently normative nature of the "zoning as collective property right" framework. Fischel (1985, *xii*) argues that "zoning and other local land use controls are most usefully viewed as collective property rights controlled and exchanged by economic agents." The "most usefully viewed" formulation is sensible given one of two assumptions:

1. as a consequence of the rights they have implicitly been granted by judges *de facto*, municipalities behave as if zoning were a collective property right; or
2. municipalities ought to be empowered to act as if zoning were a collective property right.

Either position rests, first and foremost, on a normative view of how zoning ought to work: it ought to offer current residents of a municipality, acting on their own, broad powers to control local land use according to their perceived self-interest. The manner in which this control is to be deployed is to be determined by local preferences checked only by restrictions on legality, such as overt racial discrimination. And the far-reaching interventions of local zoning are accepted because it is not really governmental regulation in the first place. This view has ramifications for transportation and land-use alternatives. If the exclusion of compact growth by municipalities is a marketlike action, then regional- or state-level action to curtail that prerogative is a market interference, which is presumably justified in large measure on the basis of proven travel behavior modification. But if municipal zoning is governmental regulation, ambiguous travel behavior findings would present no particular impediment to its reform.

WHAT IS LOCAL ZONING, AFTER ALL?

Ought municipal zoning be viewed as a collective property right, whose exercise is inherent to the municipality? Or should it be viewed as an exercise in governmental regulation, based on a delegation of the state's police power?

Local zoning cannot with consistency be viewed as a collective property right without accepting a redefinition of many—if not most—governmental interventions as collective exercises of property rights. Thus a metropolitan growth boundary, viewed as clearly regulatory in nature by most observers, can be seen as an exercise of the property rights of current residents of the region. If regulations against unrelated people living together are a locally held collective property right, it is difficult to argue why mandated transit-oriented development design guidelines are not a *regionally* held collective property right. The designation of certain governmental restrictions as "property rights" and others as "regulations" can hardly be accomplished without an arbitrary border between the two.

In support of the property-rights view, it may be argued that property rights themselves are by nature limited; my property rights do not confer a right to use my property to harm you or yours. Under this view, municipal zoning is merely a collective and proactive expression of that inherently limited right. But it is worth considering the manner in which property rights are in fact limited. Clearly the threat of criminal prosecution serves to limit property rights, as does the threat of civil litigation. Sometimes property rights can be limited by custom, as when the historic grant of access limits one's rights to prevent trespass. Regulation is the final method by which property rights are limited, and zoning fits squarely into this category. The fact that property rights may be limited by the presence of others' rights does not negate the regulatory nature of the property-right limitation; instead, the regulatory intervention is the means by which the property rights are in fact limited.

For example, my property rights in my automobile clearly do not confer on me the right to drive at 70 miles per hour within the Ann Arbor city limits, nor to operate as a taxicab in New York City. But the tools by which those rights are limited are unquestionably regulatory: the municipal traffic code in the first case and New York's regulations requiring taxi medallions in the second. As such, these regulations are subject to scrutiny regarding their costs and benefits and the legitimacy of the public purpose they are said to serve. In-town speed regulations are hardly controversial; the same is not true of New York taxi regulations. "There is virtually unanimous agreement among economists," reads a Federal Trade Commission (1984, 99) report, "that existing combinations of restrictions into the taxi market, minimum fares, and ride sharing are inefficient and the source of significant welfare loss, including consumer injury." And since the regulatory authority that is being exercised in this case originates with the state, it is reasonable to ask whether a state public purpose is being served.

My property rights in my automobile are thus limited by regulations, the legitimacy of which may be fairly debated. By contrast, a redefinition of a regulatory intervention as an exercise of a collective property right is an end-run around public scrutiny; when a municipality is merely exercising such a collective right, its (legal) preference alone constitutes ample justification. A view of zoning as an expression of the inherent limitation of one's property rights in no way negates the fact that the means by which those rights are restricted is the exercise of the state's regulatory power. One could readily construe New York's limitation of taxi medallions as a property right held municipally on behalf of current taxi drivers. But this view would be unlikely to lead to the economists' critique above, since inherent to a "property rights" formulation is the notion that rights may be held, traded, sold, or otherwise disposed of at will. Viewing land-use regulation as a property right held by the municipality serves to legitimate parochial ends as long as these are the preferences of the locals; by contrast, a forthright acknowledgment of their origin in the state's police power calls for broader purposes.

Why is the state-regulatory nature of zoning so easily masked, and land-use regulation taken to be an inherent power, a collective property right, or a market force? The immobility of land may play a role in this blurring. The limitations on my rights as owner of an automobile are unquestionably regulatory in origin at least in part because they affect me differently from how they affect others. A prohibition against speeding within the Ann Arbor city limits protects other drivers and pedestrians primarily (with a secondary safety benefit conferred on me). Banning me from using my car as a taxi in New York City without a medallion benefits current New York cabbies and confers no identifiable benefit on me. By contrast, the regulations that bar me from realizing profits by tearing down my home and putting up an apartment also benefit me because they prevent my neighbors from doing the same thing. Because land is immobile, these reciprocal relations are fixed, with each of us simultaneously forfeiting and benefiting in the same way. This reciprocity may mask, but hardly negates, the regulatory nature of the intervention of municipal land-use regulation.

ALTERNATIVES TO ZONING

The property-rights view of zoning is hardly universal. The most eloquent legal critic of the regime of municipal land-use regulation is Ellickson

(1973), who advocates a laissez-faire land-use regime based in nuisance law rather than proactive regulatory zoning. But despite the far-reaching nature of his market-oriented reforms, they seem surprisingly geared at replicating the low-density development pattern that has arisen under zoning, even as he argues against the regulatory regime underpinning the status quo. For example, Ellickson proposes doing away with conventional zoning for nearly all land-use conflicts, relying instead on a nuisance-based regime. Land uses that are in obvious conflict—such as heavy industry and residential neighborhoods—tend to segregate autonomously, according to Ellickson, and no proactive use zoning is called for. In contrast to his strictly reactive approach to these land-use conflicts, Ellickson's proposals single out "localized objectionable population concentrations" (771) for proactive regulatory exclusion. "Dense residential developments are likely to be considerably noisier and more offensive in appearance than *normal* neighboring land uses," Ellickson writes. "These unneighborly aspects of a development are proper targets for an internalization system. Localized costs such as noise can best be internalized through private nuisance actions. The unneighborly effects of an unusual population concentration, however, may also involve pervasive, but individually insubstantial, losses, such as overburdened street parking. These problems are likely to be best handled through systems of fines and *uniform mandatory public standards*" (771, emphasis added). If "uniform mandatory public standards" against dense residential development differ from conventional regulatory zoning, Ellickson does not explain how.

Why does market-driven dense residential settlement merit proactive exclusion in Ellickson's otherwise laissez-faire regime? Not because the harms are particularly onerous; where one land use tends to inflict tangible harm on another, market processes (aided by individuals' and firms' impulse to avoid nuisance litigation) will tend to separate potential conflicts, according to Ellickson. Rather, the justification for singling out dense residences for regulatory exclusion stems paradoxically from the amorphousness of the harm they impose on their neighbors, which he deems "pervasive but individually insubstantial." For concrete harms, laissez-faire will do; but when the harm is as unactionable as increases in parking along public streets, conventional zoning is called for.

Ellickson's singling out of dense multifamily housing for special exclusion harks back to the Supreme Court's decision in *Euclid*, the case that established zoning's constitutionality in the first place. Though the immediate question the case raised pertained to industrial use, the Court took pains to show that its validation of zoning extended to municipal segregation of single-family and multifamily uses as well. Like Ellickson's recommendations, the *Euclid* decision appears to single out apartment buildings for exclusion, notwithstanding the somewhat vague nature of the harm they inflict.

In general, Ellickson's views on development at higher-than-current densities can be understood through his definition of growth controls. Ellickson conceives of nuisance boards that will "publish regulations stating with considerable specificity which land use activities are considered unneighborly by that metropolitan population at that time" (763). Growth controls—defined as "governmental measures that restrict the prospective development of land parcels to a population density less than that generally prevailing in developed areas of the relevant metropolitan area" (768)—should generally not be exercised except where the restricted landowners are compensated. Thus by implication, nuisance boards' standards short of "growth controls" represent the ordinary and expected course of events. Proactive governmental exclusion of market-driven densification is par for the course, under Ellickson's nominally market-based scheme.

The benchmark from which a land-use intervention is assessed as "growth control" is not market-based densities but the status quo, which arose under a density-restricting zoning regime. Restricting development to two dwelling units per acre would not be growth control within the Ellickson framework if the rest of the comparison area is developed similarly—regardless of market pressures for denser development, and regardless of the role of zoning in shaping current development patterns in the first place. "Residents of a metropolitan area are overtly discriminating against outsiders," Ellickson writes, "when they apply prospective population density controls that prohibit new development that would be less dense than their existing neighborhoods" (768–69). By this standard, the community that excludes a transit-oriented development (or even conventional apartments) on the grounds that it would be denser than existing neighborhoods in the community is not engaging in discrimination against outsiders, and the nuisance boards that Ellickson advocates would be free to adopt standards designating these uses "unneighborly" (763).

Despite Ellickson's articulate critique of zoning, at times he seems to equate residential densities that developed under a zoning regime with those that would hold under market conditions. Arguing against planning agencies' capacity to "make intelligent decisions about the optimum gross spatial distribution of a population," he suggests that "optimal distribution is more likely to be achieved through private migration decisions" (769). Yet, given his definition of discrimination against outsiders, the primary threat he is concerned with appears to be density restrictions more severe than those of current zoning. Restrictions on market-driven densities are not problematic even though pressure for these densities is what arises when "[e]mployers and individuals faced with location decisions naturally weigh the overall advantages of their alternative environments" (769). Thus, despite their laissez-faire orientation, Ellickson's proposals remain, like conventional municipal zoning, largely geared at excluding market-driven densification of development. They are fully adequate to the task of zoning out many transportation and land-use innovations, which generally depend on denser settlement than their surroundings.

Critics of the current zoning regime have also proposed alternatives that employ deed restrictions, or covenants. Under a deed-restriction regime, the uses to which property owners may put their land are limited by contract, which is often put in place by the original developer. The famously unzoned City of Houston is the site of many such deed restrictions, which are significant there to the point that they constitute an alternative land-use approach—one that appears to rest on private action rather than governmental regulation. This section considers the extent to which the deed-restriction approach truly constitutes a nonregulatory form of land-use control. I argue that municipal enforcement is critical to the widespread adoption of such tools—and that this enforcement ends up recreating zoning under another name.

Having studied Houston extensively, Siegan (1997) notes that "[B]ecause enforcement of restrictive covenants can be costly for home-owners in lower-income subdivisions and small subdivisions, Houston adopted in an ordinance in 1965 enabling the city to enforce these covenants" (200). For Siegan this municipal enforcement is a benign alternative to private monitoring of these covenants, and one that presumably offers some economies of scale.

Ellickson, by constrast, sees a problem with municipal enforcement of private covenants, suggesting that "[t]o prevent the transfer of enforcement costs to government, a preferable solution in large subdivisions might be compulsory membership in a homeowners' association that polices the covenants and is financed by assessments on its members" (717). Ellickson's concern regarding municipal enforcement of private covenants appears restricted to costs, and then only to cases where the scale of the subdivision in question renders private enforcement feasible; covenants affecting smaller numbers of properties would apparently remain publicly enforced under Ellickson's recommendations.

The policy conundrums of municipal enforcement of private covenants extend far beyond the narrowly constrained cost-shifting problem. Without municipal enforcement—that is, under the ordinary operation of contract law—covenants negotiated between landowners or set in place by a developer would be enforced strictly through the courts. Landowners who violate the terms of the covenant would be subject to suit by other owners or representative homeowners' associations. No jurisdiction would have a proactive interest in the covenant's enforcement, just as administrative agencies have no interest in the enforcement of the contracts of private parties; the state gets involved only through the courts and only if a party brings action. Under this enforcement regime, covenants have some claim to being a private mode of land-use regulation, though the reliance on government to record the restriction on the deed in order to ensure that it binds successive owners suggests that completely private land-use controls remain elusive. In any case, under such a regime, any legal covenant (this excludes racially exclusive restrictions, for example) is properly enforceable by the courts.

When municipal enforcement enters, deed restriction systems can no longer be viewed as private land-use controls. Government is no longer neutral between parties but asserts a proactive interest in contract enforcement. Homeowners who, for example, add accessory apartments to their single-family houses in contravention of a restrictive covenant may expect municipal action against them, regardless of whether their neighbors are inclined to bring suit. Such municipal action begins to resemble conventional zoning strongly, in that the city enforces land-use restrictions administratively, independent of any finding of harm and independent of any litigation.

In this sense, municipally enforced restrictive covenants merely recreate zoning under another name. But unlike conventional land-use controls, which are enacted democratically by the elected representatives of city residents, municipally enforced land covenants effectively place power over municipal policy in the hands of private parties, with no democratic processes intervening. In the case of Houston, the State of Texas has authorized this in two ways: it allows municipalities both to issue commercial building permits according to private deed restrictions and to bring suit for violations of deed restrictions (Allen 1972). This contrasts markedly with the ordinary conduct of private contract law, under which administrative agencies are neutral regarding contract violations; if the aggrieved party seeks no judicial relief, administrative agencies have no independent interest in enforcement.

Growth in homeowners' and condominium associations (R. Nelson 1999) provides households with a potentially useful tool for managing their environments. But if enforcement costs are borne strictly internally, it is likely that their magnitude will limit the capacity of these private associations to replace, rather than merely augment municipal control of land use. In the meantime, most private associations exist as an added layer of control in communities that are otherwise zoned conventionally—or in the case of Houston, a city in which the zoning regulatory function has been recreated through municipal enforcement of deed restrictions.

Neither of the two major alternatives to municipal zoning discussed here—the nuisance-based approach associated with Ellickson or the deed restrictions analyzed by Siegan—would impede governmental exclusion of denser development, including transit-oriented development, New Urbanist neighborhoods, and other transportation and land-use innovations. Ellickson's nuisance-based recommendations specifically provide for the regulatory exclusion of "unneighborly" densities. And to the extent that a covenant-based land-use regime rests on municipal enforcement—as it does in Houston—it is likely to maintain local government's role as protector of low-density suburban areas from alternative development as a matter of policy. Yet both these proposals—as well as the "collective property rights" view of zoning—are advanced in the name of expanding the role of the market in the land-use regime of the United States. From a diverse range of theoretical approaches, observers seem to agree: public action to constrain development to lower-than-market densities is itself a market force.

PLANNING VERSUS "THE MARKET": AN IMAGINARY DICHOTOMY

Debates over U.S. metropolitan policy fall very quickly into the "planning versus markets" formulation, a problem definition that seems to suit both planning and market advocates just fine. But ultimately, the analysis of policies for land use and transportation cannot hinge on this construction because in the case of land-use controls, there is no agreement on what does and does not count as the "market." Where zoning is viewed normatively as a collective property right that is inherent to municipal government, its unfettered exercise is accepted as an integral part of the land-development market. Under this assumption, state- or regional-level limitations on municipal regulatory prerogative—whether judicial, legislative, or administrative—are viewed as counter to the workings of the market because they interfere with the ability of local families to act, within their municipal corporate structure, toward a common end.

But where municipal land-use regulation is viewed as governmental intervention into private economic transactions based on a delegation of the state's police power, actions to restrict municipal regulatory prerogative expand the role of the market—and enlarge market-driven choice—in metropolitan development. These can include judicial doctrines, such as that of the Pennsylvania Supreme Court, that limit municipalities' ability to zone out multifamily housing. They can also include requirements, like those of Oregon, mandating that in areas around transit stations, transit-oriented development must be allowed. This latter amounts to a legislative constraint on the ability of municipal governments to restrict the land-development market and is hence market-enabling—unless you subscribe to the view that zoning is an inherent right of municipalities and hence a market force, in which case the action constitutes a constraint on the free market. Apparently the call to "let markets plan" is never as simple as it appears on the surface.

Although the actions of judges since before *Euclid* reveal both views of local municipal power, the dominant stream in the United States—certainly the one pursued by the Supreme Court—has been to equate municipal zoning with an inherent right to protect private property. The judicial decisions reviewed here may reflect existing societal norms and perceptions of local government regulation, or they may play a significant role in shaping those norms. In either case, these views provide a method of understanding the implicit acceptance of the status quo in metropolitan land development as the default arrangement, a kind of state of nature from which deviations demand justification in science. This blurring of zoning's regulatory nature supports an equation of the status quo with the market, and thereby a miscasting of the debate over transportation and land use.

CHAPTER SIX

THE LIMITED POWER OF SMART-GROWTH REGULATION

The prospect of using land-use regulatory policies to promote compact development forms is simultaneously their proponents' hope and their detractors' fear. "We are in favor of compact development being subjected to a market test; we oppose attempts to impose these through command-and-control zoning and design regulations..." write Gordon and Richardson (1997, 97). The opposite use of such regulations—that is, zoning to limit compact developments in low-density suburbs—is by virtually all accounts the more common use of municipal regulatory power; as such it might be expected to attract more criticism for its "command-and-control" nature. But this chapter considers a somewhat more pragmatic question: Can land-use regulatory policy actually raise development densities and land-use mixing to levels that the market is not interested in providing?

Many smart-growth advocates hope so. Research and professional literature employs language like "encourage a better mix of uses" and "encourage developers to increase floor-to-area ratio" when discussing the goals of regulatory policy. But under most circumstances land-use regulations are incapable of raising development densities or land-use mix to levels above that which the market desires. Planning can allow and even facilitate higher-than-current development densities and land-use mix, but mandating development densities beyond those that the market deems feasible is generally impossible. This argument may appear sobering to those who would seek to plan proactively for smart growth but ought instead to be a source of encouragement. Commercially successful compact and mixed-used development that arises as a consequence of reforms in land-use policies constitutes *prima facie* evidence of the market's interest in these alternatives. Equally important, the impossibility of generating density by regulatory fiat renders chimerical any worries about the legitimacy of imposing it against the will of the market through regulation.

Bogart (1998) explains concisely why generating density through regulatory requirements is generally impossible. He considers two forms of land-use regulation: maximum and minimum capital-to-land limits. Maximum limits would take the form of restrictions on building density, height, or lot coverage, which Bogart identifies as the usual case. Minimum-density standards are far less common, and in any case, "the immobility of land ... makes that option unenforceable because capital is free to leave" (212). In other words, one can permit developers to build densely but cannot force this result by regulation because they always have other development opportunities from which to choose.

The physical development outcome on a particular site can be viewed as the product of the interaction of the site's economic conditions (which determine what can feasibly be built) with the allowed uses (which determine what can legally be built). Table 6-1 provides a schematic for this interaction. Consider first a parcel on which higher-density development would offer greater profits than lower-density development there or elsewhere. Under these circumstances, allowing such development would be expected to lead to the same results as requiring it; where the private market is interested in building densely in any event, the distinction between a permissive and mandatory stance in this case would not be reflected in the physical product. Although requirements for dense development can accommodate market forces that may be present, they cannot compel a product the market does not seek to provide. By contrast, regulations restricting development on the site to a low-density form could clearly result in an end product whose density is lower than that which its developers would have preferred.

Table 6-1. Interaction of Profit Potential and Local Regulation

Higher-density development offers...	Municipal land-use policy toward higher-density development	Development outcome
Greater profits than lower- density on-site and elsewhere	Prohibit	Lower density
	Allow	Higher density
	Require	Higher density
Lesser profits than lower- density development on-site and elsewhere	Prohibit	Lower density
	Allow	Lower density
	Require	Vacant

The lower half of the table considers the opposite condition, whereby higher-density development offers less profit than lower-density development there or elsewhere. A permissive municipal stance would be expected to lead to low-density development, since private developers would have little interest in compact development on such a site. Municipal prohibition of dense development would lead to an identical result. Requiring high-density development where only low-density is economically supportable would be expected to lead to no development at all, since investors would seek development opportunities elsewhere. If this situation were expected to persist into the future, it may be that the regulation "eliminates all reasonable return" (*Penn Central et al. v. City of New York et al.* 1977, 336) or may even constitute a "deprivation of all economically feasible use" (*Lucas v. South Carolina Coastal Council* 1992, 1016) and thus would invite a takings-based claim against the municipality. Thus in places where zoning for higher densities leads in fact to the prescribed development, evidence is provided that such development offers at least normal profits. Regulation imposing upper limits on density is certainly capable of altering the market outcomes fundamentally, but regulation imposing lower limits is not. Within this context, the following section considers individual land-use regulatory approaches and their potential to induce the production of higher-than-market levels of density.

SMART-GROWTH CODES

Smart-growth codes are zoning ordinances inspired by a New Urbanist or similar design approach. Such codes often specify smaller lots, narrow streets, alleyways, mixes of residential and commercial uses, and minimum development densities. "Design-oriented New Urbanist codes have been developed to *encourage* compact, mixed-use neighborhoods, usually in selected urban zones," write Duany and Talen (2002, *1452–53*). "For example, [the City of] Stuart's Urban Code *permits* high-density and mixed-use development in all sections of the city" (emphasis added). In other words, the tool such codes offer for "encouraging" this development is *permitting* it, in contrast to more standard suburban regulations that tend to zone it out.

Similarly, the Smart Growth Network (2003) reports on the Village of Winfield, Illinois, whose smart-growth-inspired Town Center District Plan "*allows* various uses and density types to exist in the same district without requiring variances from a typically homogeneous zoning district" (10, emphasis added). Such land-use policy reform is described similarly elsewhere: "Traditional zoning relies on the separation of uses as a means of managing development," explains the Smart Growth Network's report (2002, 5). "In combination with complementary building codes, this approach carefully dictates both the look and use of all buildings in a community. An alternative approach that *encourages* a better mix of uses is one that limits regulation to building type and that *allows* building owners to determine the uses" (emphasis added). In this instance as well, the task of "encouraging" innovation in land use amounts to refraining from banning it. Given the availability of alternative development opportunities, these codes ultimately cannot require such development unless a willing developer exists.

Reforms that stop preventing a particular form of development are frequently said to provide "incentives" for such development. Although these reforms cannot force an unwilling developer to build compactly on a site, such a proactive stance can nonetheless influence development outcomes. By conveying its interest in a particular form of development on a site, the municipality can signal developers that such proposals will be viewed favorably and treated expeditiously by the planning and permitting process. This can serve to elicit proposals that might otherwise not be forthcoming. And given developers' fundamental interest in building at a certain density level, the fact that the municipality holds the ultimate permitting power can be used as leverage to bargain for desired design elements.

An example of planning interventions to signal preferences to developers is offered by the Smart Growth Network (2002, 13): "The city of Boulder, Colorado, has encouraged new mixed-use and infill development by designing prototype projects to educate local developers about the preferences that the community had expressed. The planning office had architects create project prototype designs so developers could see exactly what the community was looking to have built. Local developers used these designs as guidelines to build many early mixed-use projects." But even though the city can signal its intent, the development package as a whole, including permitted development densities and required design elements, must offer at least normal profits to the developer to have any effect.

In special cases a minimum-density requirement could theoretically compel dense development regardless of market disinterest. O'Toole (1999) highlights this possibility: "Prescriptive zoning mandates higher densities whenever building or rebuilding occurs. If your house burns down, you may even be required to build an apartment in its place." This statement was based on a *Portland Oregonian* article (Peeples-Salah 1996) regarding the downtown transit zone in the Portland suburb of Gresham. The city does in fact view single-family homes in the zone as a nonconforming use and would require a homeowner to obtain special permission to reconstruct a residence that was at least 80 percent destroyed by causes outside her control. During the years in which the ordinance was in place, such permission has not been requested once (Vanderkooy 2004). Although the change in land-use regulation triggered some local controversy early on, this has been quelled by the significant appreciation that homeowners have enjoyed as a consequence of the upzoning, and in fact a number have realized substantial gains by selling their properties to developers of multifamily housing and for conversion to business. Single-family property within the zone sells at a premium of approximately 35 percent because of the potential for conversion to other uses, according to a real estate agent active in the zone (O'Halloran 2004). Even though the treatment of single-family houses as a nonconforming use in transit zones has spread to other municipalities, the possibility that this designation could exact the kind of sacrifice envisioned by O'Toole seems remote, and in any case its theoretical application bears no resemblance to the ubiquitous and very real restrictions of low-density zoning.

TRANSFER OF DEVELOPMENT RIGHTS

Transfer of development rights (TDR) is a land-use regulatory tool that allows developers or landowners who wish to develop in areas slated for growth to purchase the development rights from landowners in areas where growth is to be discouraged (Maiorana 1994). The land where growth is to be encouraged is referred to as the receiving zone; land where development is discouraged is the sending zone. Land in the sending zones remains the property of its original owner but becomes undevelopable, the rights to build having been sold. In contrast, the land in the receiving zone is permitted to be developed at greater density than would ordinarily be permitted by the zoning code.

This approach can clearly reduce development in the sending areas, since it creates a mechanism for rights to development in these zones to be sold permanently. But it is also frequently characterized as a tool for encouraging more intense development in the receiving zone. For example, Stevenson (1998, 1345–46) describes an urban program geared at historic preservation:

> In 1972 New York City, in its first area-wide TDR program, created a special South Street Seaport District to preserve several blocks of small, two-hundred-year-old buildings surrounding the Fulton Street Fish Market, located directly south of the Brooklyn Bridge... In order to accomplish both preservation and development goals, the City created a special district containing both a preservation area and a redevelopment area. Owners of historic properties in the preservation area were permitted to convey their development rights to a middleman or directly to a receiving lot in the redevelopment area... The use of TDRs and the TDR bank benefited the district by facilitating the preservation of the Seaport's Schermerhorn Row landmark buildings and simultaneously encouraging the development of valuable land in the adjacent South Street Seaport commercial area.

Can transfers of development rights in fact encourage development in a receiving zone? The program enables owners and developers in the receiving zones to purchase rights to such dense development. But the very fact that the rights carry a value such that a potential developer would be willing to purchase them implies their scarcity. The source of the scarcity is the municipality's regulatory stance against dense development to begin with. The fact that in some cases developers are willing to purchase the development rights provides *prima facie* evidence of private markets' interest in developing more densely than conventional planning regulations allow. Thus, whether TDRs can encourage development depends on the baseline against which their effect is judged. If that baseline is market-driven densities or intensities, TDRs are incapable of fostering additional development. If the baseline is the development permitted under restrictive municipal zoning to begin with, TDRs can indeed encourage development—by providing a rationale for the municipality to allow it, rather than by inducing developers to develop more densely than they might otherwise be inclined to.

INCENTIVE ZONING

Incentive zoning, also called density bonuses, is a regulatory approach that increases allowable density or floor-area ratio in exchange for some desired public contribution by the developer. For example, Seattle allows development at densities beyond the conventional zoning in exchange for amenities such as a daycare center, a shopping atrium, sidewalk widening, or urban plaza (reported in Garvin 1996).

Similar to transfer of development rights, incentive zoning is sometimes referred to as a technique for promoting dense development. For example, the Smart Growth Network (2002, 13) suggests using "density bonuses to encourage developers to increase floor-to-area ratio..." The report explains, "Density bonuses can promote many smart growth features in communities while also creating the land-use intensity that more efficiently supports public services. Density bonuses have been used to provide a variety of amenities including parks and plazas and structured parking. The basic premise is that a developer is granted the opportunity to increase the size of a building beyond that which is allowed by zoning, in exchange for providing a public amenity from which the community can benefit." Once again the "encouragement" of high floor-area ratios takes the form of allowing dense development that the municipality would otherwise zone out.

The Smart Growth Network (2003, 8) described a Washington, D.C., initiative "to encourage developers to build vertically rather than horizontally... Vertical development, which in many communities consists of at least six stories, can be achieved by...providing density bonuses for developments that include a mixture of uses on one site." The regulations amount to a method by which a District of Columbia developer can, through investment in public-serving amenities, overcome municipal limitations on building height. This is a far cry from a policy to "encourage developers to build vertically rather than horizontally"—it in effect merely allows developers to purchase rights to build densely. The reason it works is that rights to develop densely are limited and hence valuable; but the limitation in the first place is the product of zoning restrictions. Thus use of incentive zoning itself is additional evidence of the extent to which the private development market desires to develop more densely than conventional zoning allows.

INCLUSIONARY ZONING

Inclusionary-zoning policies are regulatory instruments either requiring or providing incentives for developers to construct affordable housing units or contribute to a fund dedicated for similar purposes. They can take the form of mandatory contributions or incentives under which the provision of a certain number of affordable units triggers a loosening of density or height limitations, allowing the developer to add units to a development.

The paradox is that in most cases, inclusionary-zoning policies are built on a foundation of exclusion to begin with (Fischel 1991). This is the case when inclusion of affordable units confers rights on the developer to increase the density of (market-rate) units in the project overall; without the capacity and willingness of the municipality to limit housing development, it would hold no leverage to spur creation of affordable units through inclusionary-zoning regulations. Furthermore, developers' acceptance of this deal is clear evidence of their desire to develop more densely than regulations would otherwise allow: if they would "pay" to have density restrictions relaxed, presumably they would seek to develop more market-rate units if those rights could be had without cost.

The desirability of inclusionary zoning depends on one's view of the affordable housing problem to begin with. If housing affordability is seen as an issue with relevance only for the poor, this could be a reasonable approach. By contrast, Fischel (1991) argues that the U.S. approach to zoning makes housing too expensive generally and leads U.S. suburbs to be too spread out. A deregulatory approach whereby municipal capacity to limit residential development densities was restricted could have a greater impact on housing affordability overall, since the potential of such policies to spur an increase in alternatives to large-lot, single-family development is significant and may dwarf that achievable under an inclusionary-zoning approach (Chapter 7).

The impact of an inclusionary-zoning ordinance that is drafted as a mandatory fee or requirement to develop affordable units is slightly less clear. Fischel argues that for the municipality to collect a charge from developers, "it is necessary that the developer not be able to develop as much market rate housing as he would like" (1991, 69). This is because develop-

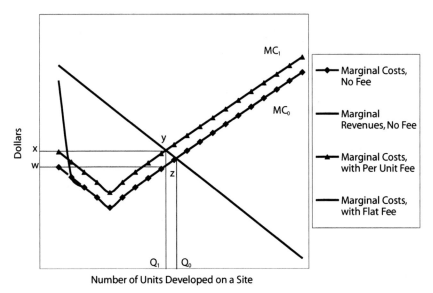

Figure 6-1. Impact of Inclusionary Zoning Policies

ers who are permitted to build at any economically feasible density by right would simply decline to pay the charge.

This section offers a different view on the special case of a mandatory (as opposed to incentive-based) inclusionary-zoning ordinance. Although the ability of a municipality to impose such a cost is clearly based on its capacity to deny a permit to the proposed development, such a fee does not necessarily depend on municipal willingness to limit development densities. A municipality could allow the development of market-level densities but condition the building permit on the payment of an affordable-housing fee, which would be viewed by the developer like other approval-related costs. As long as the development, net of all municipal approval costs, offered profits at least equal to the developers' alternative potential projects, the development would be expected to come to fruition.

The principle that mandatory inclusionary-zoning fees do not necessarily rest on municipal limitations of development density is illustrated in Figure 6-1. Developers able to select their desired density of development in the absence of land-use controls would be expected to equate marginal costs and marginal revenues of an additional unit on site, leading to the development of Q_0 units. An affordable-housing fee of xy assessed per unit shifts the marginal cost curve upward, to MC_1, leading to a reduction in market-rate densities to Q_1, a price of market-rate units of w, and collections to the affordable-housing fund equal to the rectangle wxyz. Although the per unit fee does reduce development densities of the market-rate housing, its imposition depends on the willingness of the municipality to withhold a development permit from nonpayers, not municipal willingness to restrict densities.

An alternative fee design could potentially mitigate the tendency of the fees to reduce development densities of market-rate housing. If the affordable-housing fee were assessed on per acre basis rather than per unit, it would not affect the marginal cost of developing an additional unit on a particular site. Thus MC_0 represents the marginal cost function under no fee and under a fixed fee per acre; the two are identical over all of their range except for the first unit developed, which triggers the fee. Under this scenario, although profits are reduced, development densities are not affected by the fee as long as the project, with its fees, offers profits at least equal to the developers' alternative investment opportunities. Should the fees reduce profits to lower-than-normal levels, the development would not be expected be built at all.

By considering strictly the number of units developed on a particular site, the foregoing analyses pertain to the density of developed acreage rather than the total number of units developed in a community or region. A fixed per-acre fee raises the marginal cost of developing additional land and thus could reduce the amount of land developed in a given year. Clapp (1981) developed a general model of the development impact of inclusionary-zoning requirements based on construction of a share of below-market units, and found their impact depends primarily whether consumers avoid the sector covered by the inclusionary regulations. Where such avoidance is feasible, housing production drops in the regulated sector. Where avoidance is more difficult, or where the municipality offers density bonuses sufficient to compensate the developer for the affordable-housing requirement, such regulations can increase supplies of affordable housing without reducing the development of market-rate housing. Although density restrictions are not a necessary precondition to inclusionary-zoning policies, their ubiquity creates opportunities for offering incentives for construction of affordable housing.

Viewed against a hypothetical situation under which municipal exclusion is eliminated, inclusionary regulations clearly fall short. Compared with the status quo of municipal regulatory exclusion, inclusionary regulations offer some opportunity for additional housing development. The ability of these tools to raise total densities to above-market levels would rest both on freedom from municipal density limitations and on the design of the fees themselves.

URBAN GROWTH BOUNDARIES

Unique among the land-use regulatory tools discussed in this chapter, a tightly drawn and rigorously enforced development boundary around the metropolitan region—not individual municipalities—can raise development densities inside the border. Such a line, termed an urban growth boundary (UGB) is designed to specify where urban and suburban development is and is not permitted; it aspires to contain metropolitan growth to specified areas. Where the other approaches discussed in this chapter represent a fundamental loosening of restrictive regulations, a UGB is an enforceable restriction on development. This growth-control tool properly—though hardly universally—goes hand-in-hand with reform of low-density regulations in areas within its territory. A region that seeks to contain growth with a UGB but maintains restrictive low-density development regulations within the boundary is effectively exporting growth to more remote locations.

When in fact a UGB designation is paired with easing of low-density regulations within the boundary, increases in the density of new development may result. Any observed increased in development densities may be due to the restrictions of the UGB, the liberalization of low-density development regulations, or some mix of the two; the relative effect of each of the two policies is not immediately apparent. To the extent that any densificiation is the product of the relaxation of low-density regulations, the UGB follows the pattern of the rest of the tools discussed in this chapter: it can allow more compact development but cannot force it. By contrast, if observed densification is attributable to the restrictions of the UGB, then densification compelled by regulation is plausible.

Portland, Oregon, an area whose growth is guided by a UGB, provides a useful case history. Metropolitan population increased 25 percent between 1980 and 1994, but the urbanized area increased by only 16 percent. Average new lot sizes in 1998 were 6,200 square feet, less than half the size of new lots in 1978 (Gibson and Abbott 2002, 430). Some of this effect would have undoubtedly occurred without Portland's distinctive planning approach, since other West Coast metropolises became denser over the period as well. To the extent that the change was associated with policy, it was presumably due to some combination of the growth boundary itself and the relaxation of low-density restrictions within it. (Mandated high densities within the urban growth boundary are insufficient as an explanation for processes of densification, since developers wishing to avoid the regulations could simply seek other development opportunities outside the UGB.)

Several elements suggest that the effect was due more to lowered restrictions inside the boundary than to the restrictiveness of the boundary itself. First, by state law, the boundary is required to incorporate a 20-year supply of developable land. Thus its ability to compel high-density development via tight constraints on metropolitan growth is limited by statute. Second, the Washington border, on the Columbia River, is just eight miles north of downtown Portland. A significant portion of the metropolitan region is outside the UGB in Washington. This implies the existence of a close substitute to location within the boundary. Homebuyers frustrated with small lots within the boundary have the option of residence on the more conventionally planned Washington side of the border; this significantly limits the ability of the UGB to compel above-market densities. In this way, the portion of the Portland region that is outside the UGB constitutes a kind of safety valve that limits the extent to which the boundary can raise development densities by regulatory fiat.

Finally, metropolitan regions do not exist in isolation; they compete with one another for residents and firms. This fact would similarly limit the ability of Portland's UGB to raise development densities to above-market levels, since individual or business locators chafing against the regulation could move to any of Portland's competitor regions, such as Seattle, San Francisco, or Denver. For these reasons, densification in Portland may have been more a function of the loosening of low-density restrictions within the boundary than a result of any development pressure created by the boundary itself.

Alone among the land-use regulatory tools discussed in this chapter, urban growth boundaries hold the theoretical potential of increasing development densities to above-market levels. But this potential is limited by competition between metropolitan areas for residents and jobs, suggesting that greater permissiveness—in the form of restrictions on low-density zoning—rather than the greater restrictions are responsible for densifying effects within the boundaries.

CAN SMART GROWTH BE COMPELLED?

"In a free society," writes Bernard Siegan, "government should not have power to tell people who want to live in a single-family home in a suburb that they must instead live in a multiple-family building in a city" (2001, 696). In his view, smart-growth advocates "urge elimination of conventional zoning regulations and opt instead for regulations permitting, or even requiring, traditional neighborhood developments..." (698). Surely advocates concerned about government's power to tell people how to live ought to find no fault with regulations *permitting* compact development; without that liberalization, zoning would raise precisely the specter they ostensibly fear. And this chapter has shown that given the mobility of capital, even regulations requiring traditional neighborhood development can yield such physical forms only if developers perceive their designs to offer at least normal profits.[1] Even urban growth boundaries, a hallmark of metropolitan Portland's planning approach criticized by Siegan, cannot compel developers to build densely within them in the presence of alternative development opportunities in the metropolitan region or elsewhere. Hence the compact development observed provides evidence of market interest.

On the surface, this may appear disheartening to advocates of smart growth or transportation and land-use integration. Many explain their policies as a search for land-use regulatory devices to spur development markets to produce alternatives that the ostensibly unconstrained market fails to produce. But upon examination, nearly all the policies that are designed to "encourage" certain forms of development amount simply to refraining from excluding those development forms. Rather than being a source of discouragement, this finding establishes a fundamental congruence between the development of smart-growth alternatives and the desires of individuals and households as expressed through markets. Where supportive land-use regulations lead to the successful development, construction, and sale or rental of such alternatives, development markets provide evidence that these options meet the needs and preferences of some market segments. By contrast, there is no real market check on conventional low-density regulations: where these are ubiquitous, we have no information regarding the market potential of the more compact alternatives. The difference stems from the mobility of capital versus the immobility of land; landowners wishing to escape maximum-density limitations cannot take their territory elsewhere and are thus left no choice but to develop at low densities. By contrast, developers wishing to escape minimum-density limitations most certainly can seek other investment venues.

Policies facilitating or preventing compact development ultimately represent choices among alternative rules governing the generation of physical form. "People choose from the menu of choices that are available to them," writes Gerald Frug (2001, 5). "But the background legal rules and institutions shape the world in which people are making their choices. Background legal rules frame choices; different rules frame different choices." The reform of current exclusionary land-use policies, and even the adoption of rules facilitating alternative development, hardly represent the initiation of planning intervention into free markets—they are just a shift from one set of rules to another. In many ways, the smart-growth agenda for regulatory reform in fact gives greater play to markets than does the status quo. In this policy dispute, neither set of rules can legitimately lay claim to the status of a neutral default that ought inherently to be chosen should evidence of its competitors' benefits turn out to be uncertain. The relevant policy framework is not the tired and fallacious dichotomy of "planning versus the market" but the competing legal and institutional arrangements within which transportation and land-use choices develop. None of these arrangements can reliably produce alternative development options where markets for these are wanting.

CHAPTER SEVEN

DEVELOPERS, PLANNERS, AND NEIGHBORHOOD SUPPLY

"Smart growth is an orphan when it comes to having a constituency," says Fairfax County, Virginia, Board Chairman Gerald E. Connolly. "It's something many people can support until it comes to their neighborhood" (*Washington Post*, February 8, 2005). The missing constituency is not that of the potential home buyer or renter, but rather the local body politic willing to allow compact development in its own back yard. The dual constituency required for smart growth—buyers and renters on the one hand, and local governments that allow it on the other—suggests new directions for empirical research. Transportation and land-use research has focused on the travel behavior impacts of alternative neighborhood forms but has largely ignored the more fundamental issue: how such neighborhoods are supplied and why there are relatively few of them. These questions call for research on the processes by which transportation and land-use alternatives are generated in the first place, the forces that constrain or facilitate particular choices, and how the choices generated meet the transportation and land-use preferences of various populations. This chapter presents findings of empirical studies that focus on the interaction of private development and the planning function in the provision of neighborhood choices. These include a national survey of developers, a natural experiment in which the New Jersey and Pennsylvania suburbs of Philadelphia were subjected to different planning regimes (the work of Mitchell 2004), and case studies of development in California and Michigan.

Research on these phenomena faces several distinct challenges. Land-use regulations in municipalities across a metropolitan area are exceedingly difficult to quantify consistently because they can be rigid or malleable (Shlay and Rossi 1981); moreover, municipal land-use regimes do not consist exclusively of written regulations but operate in large measure on the basis of invisible negotiated agreements between planners and private developers (Field 1997). Perhaps more importantly, there is a great deal of consistency between the planning regimes guiding new development across U.S. metropolitan areas, a phenomenon that deprives research of potential sources of variance. Research in this realm has sought to overcome these challenges by making use of differences that nonetheless hold between states and metropolitan regions, stated preference techniques, and perceptually based survey research.

Myers and Gearin (2001) argue that a "tyranny of the minority" exists in housing development markets: developers are oriented to the preferences of new-home buyers or renters, but in any given year, perhaps only 1 percent of the population occupies newly constructed housing. Since today's new construction becomes tomorrow's previously occupied home, the choices available in the housing market in any given period are formed by the accretion from thin sets of preferences in previous years.

This framework is particularly useful when viewed together with the impacts of land-use regulation: the neighborhood environments of a given period result from the interaction of new-home buyers and renters of previous periods and the land-use regimes that guided development then and since. Remote or fringe areas that develop at low densities during one era may be ripe for infill or redevelopment after economic conditions change or the metropolitan region expands. But the low-density preferences of the first-comers are translated into municipal land-use regulations. If these are not adjusted, alteration of the physical characteristics of the area will be significantly hampered, and developers seeking to provide more compact environments will be constrained. Evidence for this proposition, from a variety of research perspectives, is presented in this chapter.

DEVELOPERS' PERCEPTIONS OF ALTERNATIVE DEVELOPMENT

Land developers represent major actors in the production of neighborhoods and, ultimately, metropolitan form. They work within—and frequently seek to alter—the framework of land-use regulations guiding development in a particular community. Research into the price impacts of these regulations (Chapter 3) suggests that in many areas these interventions represent binding constraints that restrict supply and lower development densities. This insight can be corroborated and augmented through a direct study of developers' perceptions of the impact of land-use regulations on their product. If municipal zoning were so malleable—or pressures for denser development forms so low—that regulations did not constrain development outcomes, developers would be expected to view the relaxation of those regulations as inconsequential to their products. Similarly, if developers viewed the status quo in metropolitan development as adequate to serve current markets for smart growth, they would be unlikely to perceive systematic undersupplies of compact neighborhood forms. Studying developers directly facilitates comparisons of their interactions with the land-use regulatory function in a variety of settings, including urban, inner suburban, outer suburban, and rural.

To assess developers' perceptions of markets for alternative development forms, a national survey was conducted in 2001 (Levine and Inam 2004). The survey sample was randomly drawn from the database of the Urban Land Institute in Washington, D.C., the premiere national organization of land developers. The survey was distributed by mail to 2,000 developers nationwide; 36.5 percent of the sample ultimately completed and returned usable survey forms (Table 7-1). Principal themes of the survey included the following:

- *Perceptions regarding the market for alternative development.* Is it currently sufficient or insufficient to expand the provision of alternative development forms? Is the supply of such development currently adequate to satisfy its demand? If not, what are obstacles to its expansion?
- *Developers' experience with proposing and developing these alternatives.* How are such proposals handled, modified, accepted or rejected by the planning system?
- *Strategic behavior in response to planning interventions.* In what ways do developers modify their behavior in anticipation of the intervention of the planning function?

Table 7-1. Response to Survey Questionnaire

Questionnaires mailed	*2,000*
Returned for bad addresses	47
Returned incomplete with indication that the survey respondent was not a developer	19
Returned completed	706
Response rate	36.5%
Qualifying respondents (i.e., residential, commercial, or mixed-use developers)	693

Table 7-2. Comparison of Survey Respondents' Location with Urban Land Institute Developer Population

Region of office location	Percentage of respondents (n = 693)	Percentage of respondents in institute database (n = 4,183)
Northeast (CT, MA, ME, NH, NJ, NY, RI, VT)	10.3%	11.8%
Mid-Atlantic (DC, DE, MD, PA, VA, WV)	10.5%	9.5%
Southeast and Caribbean (AL, FL, GA, KY, MS, NC, PR, SC, TN)	19.2%	18.8%
Midwest (IL, IN, MI, MN, OH, WI)	13.5%	13.1%
South-Central (AR, LA, NM, OK, TX)	8.0%	10.0%
Great Plains and Rocky Mountains (CO, IA, KS, MO, MT, NE, ND, SD, UT, WY)	9.9%	7.1%
Pacific and Northwest (AZ, CA, HI, ID, NV, OR, WA)	28.6%	29.7%

- *Impact of regulations on the densities and land-use mixing of development.* How do developers believe that their products would change if land-use and transportation regulations were liberalized?

To analyze the survey data, multistate regions were defined based on the regions of the Department of Housing and Urban Development (HUD). In some cases, two HUD regions were combined to ensure reasonable sample sizes within each geographic unit. As a check on sample bias, locations (the only variable comprehensively available) were compared for respondents and the developer population as a whole; the two distributions matched closely (Table 7-2).

The survey defined *alternative development* broadly in the following fashion: "This survey is concerned with alternatives to conventional, low-density, automobile-oriented, suburban development. These alternatives can include higher than usual densities, a mix of land uses, a variety of housing types close together, pedestrian-oriented design, availability of a range of transportation modes, and easy accessibility. The alternatives can include New Urbanist designs, transit villages, clustered developments, ecological designs, attached housing, and others." Questions focused on respondents' experiences with alternative development, their perceptions of the adequacy of current supplies, perceptions of any obstacles to meeting current demand for alternative development, and the impact of municipal land-use regulation on their own products. Respondents' views of what constituted alternative development undoubtedly varied: "alternative" for one respondent may be quite conventional for another, and the data regarding a developer's individual experience with alternative development must be assessed in this light. Data regarding developers' desired density of construction and land-use mixing would not be subject to this limitation. Nevertheless, the entire survey was designed to measure developers' perceptions as evidence—within the context of the growing literature on the topic—of the impact of land-use and transportation regulations on the capacity for the current U.S. planning regime to provide for alternative development forms. The survey is thus best viewed as studying developers' perceptions of the market for whatever they conceived of as alternative development.

The Market for Alternative Development

Developers perceive considerable market interest in these alternatives. Three-quarters of the nationwide sample estimated that at least 10 percent of the local market is interested in alternative development, and more than one-third of the developers perceived a market of at least 25 percent (Table 7-3). On a nationwide basis, these findings are consistent with residential preference surveys that find similar shares of households interested in these environments (Myers and Gearin 2001). Developers in regions of intense urbanization—the Northeast and Mid-Atlantic—tended to perceive the highest levels of market interest, while those in the center of the country perceived the least. But even in these regions, most of the developers surveyed believed that at least 10 percent of the market was interested in alternative development. It seems that in developers' minds, the market for alternative development is considerably greater than "niche."

Respondents were asked to assess the adequacy of current supplies of alternative development, given their perceptions of market interest. Majorities of developer-respondents in every region of the country believed that current supplies of alternative development were inadequate relative to market interest. These ranged from just over half the developers from the South-Central region to nearly 9 developers out of 10 in the Northeast

Table 7-3. Percentage of Developers Perceiving at Least 25% of Market Interested in Alternative Development

Mid-Atlantic	50.0%
Multiregion	44.0%
Pacific and Northwest	39.6%
Midwest	39.5%
Northeast	36.2%
Great Plains and Rocky Mountains	35.5%
Southeast and Caribbean	28.8%
South-Central	21.5%
Total sample	36.6%

Table 7-4. Developer Perceptions of Adequacy of Current Supply of Alternative Development

| | Is there adequate supply of alternative development in existing housing and new construction? | | |
	Enough and in right locations	Enough but not in right locations	Not enough	n
Northeast	1.7%	12.1%	86.2%	58
Multiregion	12.8%	10.6%	76.6%	47
Pacific and Northwest	13.6%	14.8%	71.6%	176
Great Plains and Rocky Mountains	13.5%	15.4%	71.2%	52
Mid-Atlantic	19.3%	12.3%	68.4%	57
Midwest	15.2%	22.8%	62.0%	79
Southeast and Caribbean	18.9%	25.8%	55.3%	132
South-Central	18.2%	30.9%	50.9%	55
Total sample	14.6%	18.6%	66.8%	656

(Table 7-4). In addition, nearly 1 developer in 5 believed that although current supplies of alternative development are sufficient, these developments are undersupplied in the areas where they are most in demand. In total, fewer than 15 percent of developers assess current supply of alternative development to be both adequate and in the right places.

The previous two tables suggest that developers perceive a systematic mismatch between demand for and supply of alternative development. Their views on the barriers to the further expansion of developments of this kind are reported in Table 7-5. Respondents were asked to indicate all significant obstacles to the expansion to the supply of alternative developments. With the exception of developers in the South-Central region, few respondents saw lack of market interest as an obstacle, but an overwhelming majority of respondents viewed local regulations as a significant obstacle. The second most broadly recognized obstacle was opposition on the part of neighborhood residents. It should be pointed out that in practice,

Table 7-5. Perceived Barriers to Expansion of Alternative Development

Region	Regulation	Neighborhood opposition	Financing	Insufficient market interest	Cost of development	Land availability and assembly	n
			Which are significant barriers to the expansion of alternative developments?				
Northeast	87.3%	65.1%	34.9%	14.3%	4.8%	14.3%	63
Mid-Atlantic	86.5%	65.5%	32.2%	22.0%	0.0%	5.1%	59
Southeast and Caribbean	71.8%	57.3%	37.7%	30.5%	8.2%	6.0%	134
Midwest	75.6%	59.3%	27.2%	22.2%	1.2%	9.6%	83
South-Central	69.1%	46.3%	40.0%	41.8%	5.4%	5.4%	56
Great Plains and Rocky Mountains	81.5%	53.7%	40.7%	27.8%	3.6%	1.8%	55
Pacific and Northwest	77.8%	65.7%	32.8%	26.1%	4.9%	7.7%	182
Multiregion	86.0%	59.2%	44.9%	24.0%	10.0%	2.0%	50
Total sample	78.2%	60.2%	35.3%	26.3%	5.0%	6.9%	682

"neighborhood opposition" and "regulation" are identical obstacles to the development of alternatives. Neighbors opposed to development are unable legally to halt such development through direct action; rather, their mobilization is channeled through the municipal land-use authority, such as the city or the county. The authority in turn can choose to use the regulatory power delegated to it from the state to exclude, modify, or permit the development in question.

The other significant difficulty reported is securing financing. Developers often portray lenders as conservative and unwilling to finance alternatives to conventional development. In the current survey, roughly one-third of respondents voiced this claim.

Respondents were then asked to identify the single most significant obstacle to the expansion of alternative development forms. Consistent with the results above, only a small minority of developers (15 percent) believed that a lack of market interest was the primary factor blocking such expansion. Difficulties in financing such development were mentioned by less than 10 percent of respondents. By contrast, 43 percent of respondents considered local development regulations the most significant obstacle; another 17 percent identified neighborhood opposition as the most significant obstacle. If "neighborhood opposition" and "regulation" are fundamentally the same obstacle, more than 60 percent of the developer-respondents implicated local regulation as the most significant obstacle to alternative development.[1]

Table 7-6. Firms' Experience with Proposing Alternative Developments

	What share of your firm's proposals for alternative developments has been rejected by local governments? (n = 663)	What share of your firm's proposals has been significantly altered by the planning and approval process? (n = 654)
No proposals made	35.3%	35.9%
None	35.9%	19.9%
1% to <10%	9.8%	8.3%
10% to <25%	6.8%	8.7%
25% to <50%	5.4%	9.9%
50% or more	6.8%	17.3%

Respondents were asked about their firms' own experiences with proposing alternative development. More than one-third of the firms reported no such proposals (Table 7-6). Of those who had proposed such developments, nearly half said their proposals were rejected. A larger number had proposals for alternative development significantly altered by the planning process; more than two-thirds of firms that presented such proposals had at least some aspect significantly altered. Modifications commonly imposed by the planning process included reduction in densities (81.7 percent of respondents), reductions in mixed-use character (47.2 percent), and a change in the share of mixed-use or attached development (33.2 percent).

Developers' anticipation of the modifications that the planning process imposes tends to lead to strategic behavior on their part. For example, some developers avoided proposing alternative development in areas where it might be commercially successful because they presumed the proposals would be rejected (36.8 percent of respondents reported that they sometimes employed this strategy). Similarly, some proposed lower-density developments than they would have preferred in order to make the developments more acceptable to the planning authorities (39.5 percent of respondents). Conversely, some proposed higher-density developments than they actually intended in order to have something to negotiate during the planning process (49.8 percent of respondents). That nearly half the developers reported proposing densities higher than they intended to develop suggests that in their minds, the planning process was likely to compel a reduction in development densities—a finding consistent with economic studies concluding that land-use regulation in fact induces the development of metropolitan areas that are physically larger than they would otherwise be (Chapter 3).

Finally, respondents were asked how land-use regulation affected their own products with the following question: "What difference would relax-

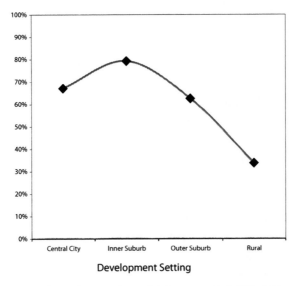

Figure 7-1. Share of Developers Reporting Intent to Build More Densely with Relaxed Land-Use Regulations

ation of density, floor-area ratio, setback or lot size regulations make to your firm's developments in central city; inner suburbs; outer suburbs; and rural areas?" Respondents were asked to choose between the following answers: "we'd develop less densely; no change; we'd develop more densely; and we don't develop in that market." Figure 7-1 illustrates results as the percentage of respondents indicating that their development densities would increase.

Overall, significant majorities of developers perceived that relaxed land-use regulations would be met with increased development densities—a plausible result, since land-use regulations tend to be designed as caps on development rather than as specification of minima. The sole exception was in the context of rural areas, where few developers indicated interest in developing more densely than current regulations allow. By contrast, in close-in suburban regions, nearly 80 percent of developers indicated that relaxed land-use regulations would lead to higher development densities. This figure was higher than that for central city development (where reasonably high densities are allowed in any case) and outer suburban development (where pressures for dense development are less than in the close-in suburbs).

The nationwide pattern was replicated in nearly every region of the country, with developers indicating the largest impact for the relaxation of land-use regulation in close-in suburban areas. These results suggest a manner in which land-use regulations affect development patterns. It may be that in areas beyond the metropolitan fringe, municipal regulations have little effect, and the observed low density of development matches market conditions well. But as the metropolis grows and yesterday's fringe areas become today's close-in suburbs, the pressure for denser development begins to exceed that permitted by the land-use regulations established by residents already in the community. At that point, the gap between developers' preferred densities and those actually permitted becomes the greatest, as evidenced by the consistent peak in Figure 7-1.

Results of this study thus suggest that developers perceive both considerable market interest in and an undersupply of alternative development. They dominantly view municipal land-use regulation as the impediment barring a significant expansion of such development. If developers are in fact keen on denser development in accessible suburban areas, the search for proven travel behavior (or other) benefits to justify such development is a misspecification of the relevant policy task.

The data presented here are strictly based on developers' perceptions; confirmation of these views would come in on-the-ground responses to a change in land-use regime. Such a response is observed in the suburbs of Philadelphia. In the 1970s, the supreme courts of Pennsylvania and New Jersey embarked on different approaches to the problem of exclusionary municipal zoning. James Mitchell (2004) studied the impact of the bistate divergence in policy on housing mix; his research is summarized in the following section.

THE PENNSYLVANIA–NEW JERSEY EXPERIMENT

New Jersey's approach to exclusionary zoning is perhaps the nation's best known. In the Mount Laurel decisions (Kirp et al. 1995), the New Jersey Supreme Court developed an approach under which municipal zoning ordinances were required to provide for low- and moderate-income housing. The primary mechanisms for accomplishing this goal were a developer charge that would be used to bring the municipality into compliance with its fair share of affordable housing, and legal tools that would enable developers to overcome municipal exclusion if their projects included sufficient shares of affordable units. For example, permission for greater density (a "density bonus") could be awarded to developers who dedicated a portion of their development to affordable housing (Rubin et al. 1990).

The approach of the Pennsylvania Supreme Court, beginning with the *Girsh Appeal* in 1969, differed significantly. Pennsylvania municipalities were required to provide zones for all reasonable types of housing to accommodate population growth of all income groups—but no subsidies were mandated, and no specific fair-share targets were established. Municipalities that failed in this duty were vulnerable to the "builder's remedy," under which excluded developers were granted injunctive relief in the form of specific court-mandated authorization to build on a particular site, not merely an invalidation of the exclusionary zoning regulation. The Pennsylvania Supreme Court based its argument on property rights rather than on the principle of "fair-share" affordable housing. That is, developers could not be unreasonably denied the opportunity to construct multifamily housing in areas where there was sufficient market; any beneficial impact on affordable housing production was ancillary to this establishment of the right to develop multifamily housing. Municipalities' claims that multi-family housing needed to be excluded because of service or infrastructure cost considerations were explicitly disallowed. Although the "builder's remedy" was irregularly available in New Jersey as well, the New Jersey remedy "was focused not on housing type but on low- and moderate-income families by facilitating cross-subsidization from market-rate units to affordable units through the intermediary of the developer" (Mitchell 2004, 124).

The tortuous history of the Mount Laurel doctrine through New Jersey courts, administrative agencies, and municipalities has been well documented (e.g., Kirp et al. 1995; Calavita et al. 1997). Many observers have concluded that its impact on affordable housing development in New Jersey has been modest. An early assessment held that "[i]f all the wood fiber in all the books and papers written about the original Mount Laurel decision were converted into construction materials, it would conceivably amount to more low-income housing that was built as a result of the decision" (Fischel 1985, 320). In the 1980s, administrative and judicial whittling away at the decision led to a situation under which "a determined developer, confronting a particularly recalcitrant township, might have been able to...compel the rezoning of a parcel for a planned inclusionary development, [but] the circumstances under which that was legally feasible...were becoming more and more rare" (Calavita et al. 1997).

Given ambiguities about the affordable housing regime in New Jersey, a comparison of Pennsylvania and New Jersey housing development is not an entirely clean natural experiment. Although New Jersey is not a typical state regarding treatment of exclusionary zoning, neither does it represent a

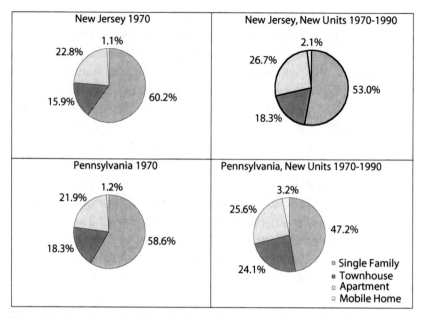

Figure 7-2. Housing Units, New Jersey and Pennsylvania Suburbs of Philadelphia

Note: X^2 test shows Pennsylvania-New Jersey differences significant with >90% confidence.
Sources for data: Mitchell (2004) and personal communication with author.

consistent and rigorous application of inclusionary zoning policies. In the context of the current study, data on New Jersey housing development are best interpreted in one of two ways. Given the erosion of fair-share housing doctrine in the state, New Jersey may be seen as similar to other states whose home-rule traditions are not fundamentally challenged by fair-share housing requirements. Alternatively, it may exemplify the most likely outcome of a fair-share housing regime. In either case, a comparison with neighboring Pennsylvania can shed light on the impact of state-level action restricting municipal prerogative.

The Mitchell (2004) study investigated housing supply change from 1970 to 1990 in suburban Philadelphia—238 municipalities in Pennsylvania and 114 in New Jersey. Housing and sociodemographic characteristics were roughly comparable between the New Jersey and Pennsylvania municipalities in 1970; incomes and housing valuations were somewhat higher in the Pennsylvania municipalities but grew more rapidly over the study period on the New Jersey side. Similarly, the Pennsylvania side in 1970 was home to municipalities with lower minority populations, higher shares of white-collar employment, and higher education levels, but interstate differences were small in all cases. Although the Pennsylvania suburbs

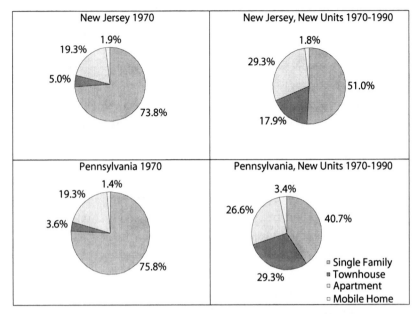

Figure 7-3. Housing Units, High-Growth New Jersey and Pennsylvania Suburbs of Philadelphia

Note: X^2 test shows Pennsylvania-New Jersey differences significant with >90% confidence.
Sources for data: Mitchell (2004) and personal communication with author.

were marginally denser than their New Jersey counterparts in 1970, distribution of housing by type was nearly identical (Figure 7-2 and Figure 7-3).

Although preexisting differences were small, most of them would be expected to lead to greater proportions of single-family development on the Pennsylvania side. Thus the environment in 1970 constitutes a good test for the impact of the zoning reforms begun by the Pennsylvania Supreme Court in 1969. Figure 7-2 depicts the distribution of the housing stock by type (single family, townhouse, apartment, and mobile home) in 1970, and the distribution of the housing units added between 1970 and 1990. Although the initial breakdown of units was similar, the housing stock in other-than-single-family units added between 1970 and 1990 was nearly 6 percentage points greater in the Pennsylvania municipalities than in the New Jersey communities.

Figure 7-2 includes both high- and low-growth municipalities. In municipalities with few growth pressures, one would not expect markets to tend toward higher-density development. It is useful for this reason to separate out a high-growth subsample for further analysis; this consisted of communities that added at least 3,000 units over the period. High-growth communities accounted for just over half of all housing-unit growth. This high-growth subsample (Figure 7-3) reveals an even greater difference than the population of municipalities as a whole: alternatives to single-family development represented less than half of the New Jersey units but nearly 60 percent of the units built in Pennsylvania.

The foregoing description is strictly bivariate, accounting for state regime differences only. The Mitchell (2004) research also estimated a multinomial logit model, with the four housing types as the outcome variables. Demand-side controls (aggregated at the municipal level) included variables for age distribution of the population, mean family income, number of families with children, white-collar employment share, share of college graduates, and number of black and Hispanic residents. Supply-side controls in the multinomial logit model included indicators of sewer availability, undeveloped land, housing distribution by type in 1970, and municipal population size.

Using the estimated discrete choice model, Mitchell simulated a change in the distribution of housing units by type by state, holding all other variables constant. At the mean values of the independent variables, a Pennsylvania (compared with New Jersey) location led to a predicted increase of 20 percent in the share of townhouses constructed between 1970 and 1990, an increase of 13 percent in apartments, and an increase of 1 percent in mobile homes. Holding all independent variables constant, a Pennsylvania location is associated with a corresponding drop in the single-family units' share of all housing growth of 35 percentage points. The multivariate analysis thus amplifies the results described above: the Pennsylvania regime was associated with a richer mix of alternatives to single-family housing development than its New Jersey counterpart.

If the New Jersey regime was guided by at least a nominal commitment to fair-share accommodation of affordable housing, it stands to reason that comparisons with states lacking even this legal commitment would reveal starker differences. But could Pennsylvania's reliance on the "builder's remedy" have accounted for the differences observed? Clearly, there were not nearly enough lawsuits to account for the increased share of multifamily housing in the Pennsylvania suburbs. Observed housing-development differences would be attributable to the legal regime set in motion by the Pennsylvania Supreme Court only if municipalities zoned proactively for multifamily housing to stay out of court. A statement from an adviser to a Pennsylvania municipality that had been accused of exclusionary zoning (provided by Mitchell 2004, 131) suggests that this is exactly what is going on: "Failure to act [to provide reasonable zoning for apartments where a demand existed] would only increase the risk that builders could obtain court approval for apartment in the area of *their* selection. It was therefore important that the township act responsibly to provide a reasonable area for apartment use consistent with the orderly development of the township and the furnishing of necessary township services." Thus inadequate provision for multifamily housing in the Pennsylvania system threatened loss of cherished local control; in that environment it behooved the municipalities to zone proactively for housing alternatives, lest a disgruntled developer seek the "builder's remedy."

CASE STUDIES OF DEVELOPER-PLANNER INTERACTION

The natural experiment in suburban Philadelphia suggests a set of relationships between private developers and the planning function. Greater local regulatory prerogative appeared to lead to more restrictions on multifamily development, and limitations on local power led to more acceptance of market-driven development of denser housing forms. Yet compact, mixed-use, and transit-oriented neighborhoods are in fact developed in a number of locales, even though local government would have little trouble excluding them by regulation. Why are some such development proposals successful, but others are either excluded by municipal authorities or extensively modified?

That issue was studied at a micro scale by Inam, Levine, and Werbel (2002) in four case studies of alternative development proposals; this section draws from that study. Two of the proposals—in San Diego, California, and in Dearborn, Michigan—were approved and developed. The other two—in the Silicon Valley area of Northern California and in suburban Detroit—were severely modified by the planning function in a fashion that lowered development densities and changed the "alternative" nature of development. The case studies sought, in a detailed fashion, to assess any regulatory obstacles to alternative development forms and to investigate how these can be successfully overcome.

Pembrooke Park, West Bloomfield Township, Michigan

One case that clearly demonstrated regulatory obstacles to compact development was the Pembrooke Park proposal in West Bloomfield Township,

Michigan. The site is at the growing edge of the Detroit region, 24 miles from downtown Detroit and 9 or 10 miles from the suburban centers of Southfield and Troy. West Bloomfield Township had identified the site for development as part of its master-plan review process and called for consolidation of preexisting lots and minimization of curb cuts to promote free-flowing traffic. The original zoning on the 20-acre site, R-15, was the largest lot zoning in the township and would have allowed for only 30 single-family homes on 15,000 square-foot, 100-foot-wide lots.

Given the high visibility and accessibility of the site, the developer sought to respond to a perceived market of childless young professionals and seniors for development considerably denser than that allowed by existing regulations. The initial proposal entailed 122 units of attached condominiums for the site. The developer proposed a rezoning to RM-6, the only zoning that would have allowed condominium development on this site. Such a rezoning would have permitted 6 dwellings to the acre, which would have come close to enabling the 122 proposed units on the 20-acre site. Thus, although the site was slated for development, the developer proposed something considerably denser than what the township had in mind.

The proposed development certainly would have qualified neither as a transit-oriented development nor as a mixed-use, pedestrian-oriented neighborhood. But as a neighborhood considerably denser than its surroundings in a relatively high-accessibility location, the development would have offered a number of attributes to its target market that were otherwise unavailable. The density and shared-wall construction lowered development costs and would have yielded a more affordable and energy-efficient product. Although the location offered no high-quality transit, it was closer to high-employment areas of suburban Detroit than many of its alternatives and could have offered its occupants a shorter and less expensive commute.

Interaction with the township's planning commission led to significant modification of the project; from the initial proposal, the concept was reduced to 110, then 100 attached units, then finally to 61 detached units, or 3.2 units to the acre. Concerns focused on traffic impacts of a large number of units at an already busy intersection. Yet even the modified proposal generated significant public opposition and a close vote when it was considered by the township's board of trustees. About 100 vocal opponents from neighborhoods up to three miles away from the site attended the hearing. Concerns centered predictably on traffic, noise, property values, and the existing single-family character of the neighborhood. The reduced project was ultimately approved by a 4-3 vote of the trustees.

There is little doubt that the modification imposed by the planning process reduced the development's affordability, together with its compactness: "If you are going to reduce that density then you need to really change the product dramatically in order to reach a higher price point to compensate for value of land," indicated the township's planning director (Inam et al. 2002, 53). The process led to a doubling of zoned densities but only half the units that the developer sought,

Although some argue that increasing market pressures for compact development ultimately would lead to revised land-use regulations, the project's developer sees things differently. "A lot of communities [such as West Bloomfield] don't have the tools set up to react to, respond, review and approve the kind of development that is now being proposed," he explains. "As the market changes, as the demand for certain product types change, residential development demand changes. Unfortunately, many of the communities that have established planning and zoning have very traditional tools" (Inam et al. 2002, 531). The developer's perception that land-use regulations failed to accommodate growing demands for this type of housing seems correct, but the fault may not lie with the "traditional tools." In fact, a zoning designation existed in the township that would have allowed his development to go forward. The tools to facilitate the compact development were present, but the willingness to employ them in this particular circumstance appeared lacking; in the process both housing affordability and the potential for relatively close-in living for 61 households in metropolitan Detroit were reduced.

Whisman Station, Mountain View, California

Housing affordability is an even greater issue in California's Silicon Valley, where local regulatory processes halved the proposed density of a development immediately adjacent to Santa Clara County's light-rail system. Whisman Station is a 517-unit residential development built on a 40-acre site in the City of Mountain View, near the high-technology industrial heart of Silicon Valley. A lively market for denser development exists in the area, driven by the proximity of Silicon Valley employment, a young and mobile workforce, a steady influx of technology-related professionals, and a widespread desire to reduce exposure to the area's legendary traffic jams. Even well-paid professionals are frequently unable to afford single-family living

Figure 7-4. Whisman Station Streetscape

Photo by Aseem Inam

in the closer-in communities of Silicon Valley, leading to considerable markets for attached housing forms.

The land in question, a former industrial site, became available for residential development after the owner failed to attract new industrial development. The City of Mountain View was at the time searching for new housing sites. A report by a consultant hired by the city concluded that densities of around 21 units per acre were supportable on the site, and that a significant market existed for rental housing. The city's plan for the area called for high-density development; given housing shortages in that region, units in such a development would almost certainly have been readily accepted by the market. In fact, the Draft Whisman Precise Plan proposed allowing up to 25 or 30 dwelling units per acre. The president of the Whisman-Middlefield Neighborhood Association, who worked to change the original proposal, nonetheless acknowledged that demand in the area was so high that "even if it was built up at twice the density I think people would have bought it" (Inam et al. 2002, 43).

The developer apparently agreed; after a consultation with Mountain View's planners, who encouraged dense development because of the proximity to light rail, he proposed 1,000 units, or 25 units per acre. One might have expected this market-driven impulse toward densification to be welcomed. But critics of the proposed development argued that Mountain

View already had its "fair share" of dense housing development—in fact the city does have higher shares of multifamily housing than its neighbors—and that other communities should now accept additional such development before Mountain View. Neighbors protested the high density of the proposal, citing the "small-town feel" of the community. This claim was oddly dissonant with the alternative charge—that Mountain View, much more than its other Silicon Valley neighbors, already had more than its fair share of multifamily housing. Proponents of the project included the regional transit agency, which was interested in developing markets for its light-rail service; local employers keen on increasing housing supplies for workers; and environmental groups, which sought alternatives to auto-intensive, sprawling development. Not evident in the process were potential occupants of the site, who in any event would not largely have been current Mountain View residents and voters.

Presented with the reality of the development, the planning commission and city council backed off their commitment to high-density living, even on this accessible, transit-oriented site in a growing high-technology region. Ultimately, the planning process halved the development density and number of units. Notwithstanding the use of regulation to reduce development densities significantly relative to those proposed by the developer, the neighborhood's 12.5-unit-per-acre density is compact for a suburban setting, and the development retains an orientation toward its namesake light-rail station. Though planning intervention halved proposed densities, the city's website touts the neighborhood and its planning process, noting that "[t]he City used its Precise Plan process to lay out the objectives and specify zoning and design standards for Whisman Station. Key goals were to create a new residential neighborhood that embraces the rail station as the focal point, to ensure an interesting mix of unit types, to bind together the residential areas on either side of the rail lines and to strengthen community identity through a sense of openness and public parks."[2]

West Village, Dearborn, Michigan

In contrast to those cases, in which the planning process severely curtailed compact development, in West Village in Dearborn and Rio Vista West in San Diego, private-sector interest in dense development was facilitated through public action. Dearborn is an industrial suburb 10 miles west of Detroit, and home to Ford's world headquarters. Though most of the town is laid out according to a low-density, auto-oriented template, there was the sense both among city officials and some developers that a market existed for a more compact and walkable neighborhood near Dearborn's downtown. Perceived elements of this market included large nearby employers, such as Ford Motor Company, the University of Michigan–Dearborn, Henry Ford Community College, and Oakland Hospital. With Dearborn's per capita income slightly below the state average, there was also the feeling that younger residents needed a more affordable alternative to the traditional single-family homes that dominated the community.

Around 1986 Mayor Michael Guido became interested in an alternative development form on a 4.1-acre site near downtown. The city had acquired the site, which had previously been characterized by marginal retail uses and low occupancy rates. The city requested proposals for a compact, mixed-use development, and three developers responded. One proposal was rejected for its strictly residential nature; the other came from a developer judged to have insufficient experience. The third developer was selected and ultimately saw the project through to completion.

Some regulatory changes were required for the development. Fifty-one separate variances were needed to allow the setbacks, building heights, and densities the developer proposed. Although the existing zoning did allow a combination of apartments and condominiums with businesses, it would ordinarily have required 100 more parking spots than the 83 that were actually constructed. "There was some selling or educating to the planner and the Public Works Department in terms of curves and parallel parking," explained the developer, "but with help [from the mayor and the economic and community development director] we worked through those...without a lot of trouble" (Inam et al. 2002, 40–41). Construction codes needed to be adapted as well, since the city's building department was unfamiliar with the kind of attached housing construction that was proposed.

In contrast to the two developments discussed above, neighborhood opposition to this proposal was minimal, largely because the previous zoning had been commercial. The site was ultimately developed with 76 housing units, neighborhood-scale retail, and a plaza. It has been very favorably accepted by the market; an initial list of interested potential residents grew to 2000, and units have increased in price considerably since the first sold.

To make West Village a success, the City of Dearborn did not simply agree to a developer's proposal; rather, the city actively sought out developers to build the kind of neighborhood it wanted. According to virtually all parties, the personal leadership of the mayor was the key. But without developers willing to invest in that particular vision, no political leadership would have been able to produce the neighborhood that was ultimately developed. The planning function here was used to signal the market that a denser development proposal would be welcomed, rather than dragged through interminable battles.

The West Village story offers a telling postscript as well. The project offered spinoff benefits to subsequent development in terms of regulatory liberalization. The 51 variances required by the development spurred promulgation of a new set of rules for stacked condominium developments. As a result, a subsequent townhouse development on the east side of Dearborn required only two variances.

Rio Vista West, San Diego, California

Rio Vista West in San Diego was similarly a product of municipal initiative and private capital. The project, located on the Mission Valley extension of the Blue Line trolley, was initiated in 1992 when Cal-Mat, the real estate subsidiary of a sand- and gravel-mining company, sought to develop a 95-acre parcel the company owned in San Diego. The site was thus already in the developer's ownership prior to any development plans; this distinguishes the San Diego case from the others, where the developers acquired the site with development plans in mind. When the company approached the City of San Diego, it was informed that the parcel was to be developed as a transit-oriented development (TOD), according to rezonings and TOD regulations that had been enacted in the previous two years. This designation was a product of the Mission Valley Planned District Ordinance, which prescribes transit-oriented development guidelines at transit stations and encourages mixing of land uses. The ordinance was inspired largely by the city's finding that although only 17 percent of city households included two adults with children living at home, a much greater share of recent development appeared to be geared toward this demographic segment. In addition, the local tourist industry generated large numbers of moderate-income jobs and thus significant demand for denser and more affordable housing forms. The developer was also aware of a cultural preference by some younger households and empty nesters for urban living and alternatives to a single-family, auto-oriented lifestyle. Unfamiliar with the concept of transit-oriented development, the company sought the advice of Peter Calthorpe, a leading New Urbanist planner, who was ultimately commissioned to assist with the master plan for the site.

The vicinity of the site was primarily commercial, a factor that tended to mute any neighborhood opposition. Enabling the development required significant modification of existing regulations and policies, including amendments to the general plan, community plan, and specific plan; adoption of design guidelines; a plan development permit; a tentative map; and rezoning. To streamline the permitting process, the planning staff bundled these modifications in its proposals for action by the planning commission and city council. The planning function thus interacted closely with private sector investment to produce this transit-oriented development: the initial designation of the area for TOD led the developer to rethink plans for the area flexibly. The second important element was regulatory streamlining, without which the development would have been considerably more costly.

The development was ultimately built at 11 dwelling units to the acre, with both retail and residential development on site. The residential development offers easy access to the transit station, though the retail development lost some of the desired transit-oriented flavor through its orientation to the major arterials rather than to the station. And not all elements envisioned by the TOD polices were present; notably, a retail focus on the station area was lost in favor of a more auto-oriented, big-box retail development. Even these commercial areas, however, were designed with considerably more attention to pedestrian amenities than similar retail developments elsewhere.

Lessons from the Four Developments

The four developments described above—two in California and two in Michigan—were selected as examples of alternative development proposals that met different fates: two were successfully developed, and two were substantially modified by the planning process in a way that reduced their "alternative" character. Although this small group of projects is not a statistical representation of the universe of development proposals, it does suggest certain lessons regarding alternative development.

Most notably, in none of the four cases was the planning function neutral; that is, in no case did municipal planners adopt a laissez-faire approach to development densities. In Whisman Station and Pembrooke Park, planning regulations were employed to reduce development densities below those desired by the developers. West Village in Dearborn was based on municipal specification of development type; nonetheless, there was little problem attracting developers willing to build at the desired densities.

Thus, even though the city took a proactive stance toward compact development, this policy could only facilitate market forces—it could not compel such development in the absence of a willing developer.

A slightly different circumstance held in Rio Vista West, where a subsidiary of the previous landowner also served as developer. The city presumably carried some leverage to compel compact development even in the face of developer resistance, since the land was owned by the developer's parent company. And in fact, the subsidiary company was initially unfamiliar with the TOD concept called for by city policy on the site and needed to adapt its plans accordingly. Yet the result hardly seems to be the product of any regulatory forcing: the developer believes that the project met market demand quickly and is happy with the outcome (Inam et al. 2002, 35). Moreover, the several smaller developers that handled individual components of the project could certainly have declined the work if they had thought the TOD regulations would lead to subnormal profits. Finally, it is worth noting that where the developer had doubts about economic feasibility of the TOD formula—local retail clustered around the train station—the outcome was modified, and a more conventional auto-oriented, big-box center was developed. Thus the image of heavy-handed planning regulation compelling the private sector to develop in ways inappropriate to the preferences of purchasers and renters appears illusory.

In fact, in the cases described above, a proactive municipal stance toward dense development appeared to be a virtual prerequisite. Where developers initiated proposals for denser-than-planned construction (in Pembrooke Park and Whisman Station), their proposals were halved in density by the planning process. The role of the municipality was underscored by the developer of West Village in Dearborn, who said that without the involvement of city officials, he would not have offered the proposal he did. The municipal leadership was thus able to signal to the private developer that a compact development proposal would be facilitated rather than resisted.

The fate of the development proposals appeared to hinge on the legal and geographical situation of the site as much as market acceptance of the development process. Existing zoning facilitated compact development in the Dearborn case but frustrated it in Pembrooke Park in West Bloomfield. Where zoning needed to be changed, a previous industrial designation (as opposed to lower-density residential) may have eased the shift as in Rio Vista West, yet such designation was insufficient to guarantee adoption of developers' proposals in Whisman Station. Physical distance from existing neighborhoods appeared to facilitate acceptance in Rio Vista West, and proximity spurred opposition in Mountain View and Dearborn. In no case was a developed single-family residential zone proposed for denser development, and given the history of these cases, it is difficult to imagine such a proposal succeeding.

The presence of rail transit in the San Diego and Mountain View cases appeared to provide the planning rationale for accommodating relatively high development densities (even if the Mountain View process cut proposed densities in half). Yet given housing shortages in San Diego and particularly Mountain View (and the findings of the survey reported above), it is likely that developers there would welcome the opportunity for dense housing regardless of distance from a transit station. Impacts of the two developments on transit use are not known in detail, but the best available estimates in Santa Clara County are that 15 percent of employed residents living within a five-minute walk of a light-rail station commute via transit at least three days per week (Santa Clara VTA 2002), as do 20 percent of those both living and working near light-rail stations (Santa Clara VTA 1998–1999). Similar results were found for San Diego, where 15.8 percent of residents living near Mission Valley–San Diego trolley stations used transit for commuting at least three times per week (Lund et al. 2004, 46). On one hand, this compares very favorably with the 3 percent of residents countywide commuting regularly by transit. On the other hand, it does not represent overwhelming reliance on transit, especially since transit-mode shares for nonwork trips for residents living near transit were considerably lower.

Thus the extent to which these developments encourage transit use is fairly debatable. But given high housing costs in these areas, and the potential for these developments to provide an alternative to long-distance commuting, the rationale based exclusively in transit mode-share impacts is incomplete. Facilitating these housing developments in close-in areas was a worthwhile goal independent of the transit impacts they may offer: the developments enabled hundreds of households to live in highly accessible locales. Although hoped-for increases in transit use may have provided the rationale for accommodating these developments, the greatest benefit may have been the increase of housing where dwelling units were acutely needed. The two neighborhoods also offer an alternative to long-distance commuting and a choice in transportation and land use. Each household living in these two neighborhoods opted for more compact homes and neighborhoods than they could have afforded at more remote locations.

Zoning out these developments would have denied these households the opportunity to make the particular tradeoff between space and accessibility that they did. By contrast, accommodating these developments facilitated the link between household preference and neighborhood choice.

THE CONSEQUENCES OF MUNICIPAL LAND-USE CONTROL

This chapter presented evidence from three studies pertaining to the impact of land-use regimes on the production of metropolitan form. The national survey of developers suggested significant interest in building in a more compact form, if municipal regulations were to allow such development. These findings received considerable support in the natural experiment that has been occurring since 1970 in the suburbs of Philadelphia. Those suburbs on the Pennsylvania side were subject to the state supreme court's restrictions on the ability to zone out multifamily housing; the New Jersey suburbs were subject to a judicially mandated fair-share housing policy. The Pennsylvania policy supported a markedly larger share of multifamily housing growth, despite the similarity of municipalities on the two sides at the start of the study.

On a micro scale, the four case studies of alternative development proposals in California and Michigan explored the interaction of private developers and the planning function in producing alternatives. In none of the four cases can the development outcome be described as the product of an uncontrolled market; rather, municipal regulations shaped development intimately in all cases. In the West Bloomfield and Mountain View developments, the planning function lowered development densities considerably below those desired by their developers. By contrast, Dearborn and San Diego wanted compact development. In Dearborn, the city sought developers interested in such development for a city-owned site; its proactive engagement signaled that such proposals would be welcomed rather than undermined by the planning process. In San Diego, the transit-oriented designation of the area signaled a particular form of development to the existing landowner. The development company was satisfied with the compact housing aspect of the TOD designation but successfully sought to modify the provision for local-serving retail. The San Diego case suggests a crucial but market-limited role for planning in alternative development. In some circumstances, planning can prod private developers to produce neighborhoods that they would otherwise not be inclined to develop. But the need for private profits imposes limits; when the developer became convinced that a retail center at the transit station would not have made economic sense, he persuaded the city to relax its guidelines.

In all cases, municipal planning powers are highly consequential to metropolitan development outcomes and in many cases are deployed in a fashion that constrains alternatives to low-density, auto-oriented development. The studies presented here also suggest research questions currently understudied by transportation and land-use scholars. This research tradition has long been engaged in the question of the travel behavior implications of alternative urban forms. Although this question fits the social science mold, it relates poorly to the actual policy dilemmas raised at the intersection of transportation planning and municipal land-use planning. By contrast, the alternative supply-based perspective presented here implies a rich family of policy-relevant research in the production of transportation and land-use choices.

Through investigations into the interaction between private development and the planning function, this chapter has argued that municipal regulations frequently constrain the supply of alternatives to low-density, auto-oriented development. If this is the case, then another effect should be evident on the demand side: a systematic gap between the transportation and land-use preferences of some households on the one hand, and their actual neighborhood choices on the other. Households who prefer pedestrian- and transit-oriented environments should be less likely to get what they want in transportation and land-use terms than those who prefer low-density, auto-oriented neighborhoods. Metropolitan regions that provide for a richer mix of neighborhood types ought to support a closer fit between household preferences and actual neighborhood choices; areas where a single neighborhood model is dominant should demonstrate a looser connection between preferences and choices. This question is explored in the following chapter through an analysis of household preferences and neighborhood choices in Atlanta and Boston.

CHAPTER EIGHT

THE DEMAND FOR TRANSPORTATION AND LAND-USE INNOVATION

I f land-use regulations present a constraint on the supply of the alternatives to sprawl, three effects ought to be evident. First, the quantity of compact development ought to be reduced by the regulations (Chapter 3). Second, neighborhoods that have attributes of compactness, walkability, and transit accessibility which are made artificially rare by regulation ought to command a price premium (Eppli and Tu 1999; Tu and Eppli 2001; Song and Knaap 2003). Finally, households faced with constrained choices would be expected to be less satisfied with their choices than households to whom a fuller range of neighborhood types were available; supply constraints would lower the utility that households derive from their housing choices and would leave latent demand for alternative development.

This chapter investigates this third dimension through an analysis of household preference and neighborhood choice in two similarly sized U.S. metropolitan areas, Atlanta and Boston (and is based on Levine et al. 2005). Boston was selected as a metropolitan area that offers a range of neighborhood types, from auto-oriented to transit- and pedestrian-friendly.

This is not so much a product of superior planning practice as an artifact of the historical era within which the Boston region developed. By contrast, the housing stock of metropolitan Atlanta is much more dominantly in zones developed for automobile access under a modern suburban zoning regime in the post–World War II era. If municipal regulations constitute a binding constraint, limiting compact, walkable, and transit-friendly development, an effect ought to be observed in the preferences and choices of residents of these two areas. Specifically, residents of Boston—as an area with a wide variety of neighborhood types—should exhibit a closer fit between their transportation and land-use preferences and their actual neighborhood choices than will residents of Atlanta, which is a more uniformly automobile-dependent metropolitan region.

This notion is hardly self-evident. If nearly all households preferred low-density, auto-oriented neighborhoods even at the cost of high auto use—"the American dream"—an environment that uniformly matches this description would support a tight fit between preferences and choices. The mismatch that is measured here is a product of a divergence between the distribution of housing units across neighborhood types on the one hand and the distribution of transportation-land use preferences among the population on the other.

This mismatch is gauged through a comparison between people's stated preference for transportation and land-use characteristics and the attributes of the neighborhood in which they actually reside. The design is intended to overcome respective weaknesses of both revealed-preference and stated-preference research in isolation. Revealed-preference research seeks to learn about people's desires from their actual choices of items like consumer products, transportation modes, or neighborhoods. This approach excels in its realism, since it depends on actual choices for which people had to invest time and money, rather than easy-to-answer survey instruments. But revealed-preference research helps little when the problem is investigating people's preferences for options that are absent or undersupplied. By contrast, stated-preference research can readily investigate preferences for these undersupplied options, but its results are subject to considerable uncertainty, since research subjects may provide the answer they think the researcher wants or may answer strategically or fancifully. To overcome these weaknesses, the study related stated-preference measures with households' actual neighborhood choices to assess the capacity of different metropolitan environments to satisfy households' transportation and land-use preferences. Although the stated-preference measures in isolation remain subject to the concerns mentioned above, they are not the primary subject of this analysis. Instead, the closeness of fit between the stated- and revealed-preference measures is used to gauge the capacity of each region to satisfy its residents' preferences for a transportation and land-use environment.

People's ability to satisfy their transportation and land-use preferences is limited by the characteristics of the neighborhoods from which they must choose, which are in turn constrained by municipal land-use policy. The study finds that in the relatively uniformly auto-oriented Atlanta region, people with preferences for walkable or transit-oriented communities were poorly able to act on those desires. By contrast, the greater variation of neighborhood types in metropolitan Boston supported a closer match between transportation and land-use preferences and actual household choices.

The match was assessed in three principal steps. First, the territory of metropolitan Atlanta and Boston was divided into five classes each, based on transportation and land-use characteristics. Second, original survey data of 800 households in each area were analyzed to classify residents' transportation and land-use preferences along a continuum from pedestrian- and transit-oriented neighborhoods to auto-oriented neighborhoods. Finally, a discrete-choice model was estimated to test the sensitivity of respondents' choice of neighborhood type to their transportation and land-use preferences. Because of the broader range of neighborhood offerings in Boston, neighborhood choices were much more sensitive to transportation and land-use preferences than in Atlanta; simply put, the Bostonians who had strong preferences for transit and pedestrian-oriented communities were much more able to translate these preferences into actual neighborhood choices than their Atlanta counterparts.

THE ATLANTA-BOSTON STUDY

The regions studied here include the 10-county area of the Atlanta Regional Commission and the 101-town region of Metropolitan Boston, the area of the Boston Metropolitan Planning Organization. The two areas were roughly comparable in population, with 1.1 million households in metropolitan Atlanta, and 930,000 in the Boston region, though the land area of the much more densely built Boston is considerably less: 1,400 square miles as opposed to 3,000 for metropolitan Atlanta. The geographical unit of analysis is the traffic analysis zone (TAZ). TAZs are geographical units developed for transportation modeling purposes; they are sized to contain roughly 2,000 residents and/or employees and to serve as a logical neighborhood unit for purposes of transportation analysis. The Atlanta study area was divided into 928 TAZs; the Boston region contained 613 such zones.

Clustering Methodology and Results

The hundreds of zones in each region represent neighborhoods or neighborhood agglomerations. For the purposes of this study, these geographic units needed to be combined into larger neighborhood types based on their transportation and land-use characteristics. This grouping of neighborhoods into broad classes serves two purposes. First, it defined comparable areas between Boston and Atlanta, such that neighborhoods classified into a single category would demonstrate similar land-use and transportation characteristics. Second, the grouping of hundreds of zones into a limited set of neighborhood types from which households choose facilitated the tractability and interpretability of the choice model described below.

Neighborhood transportation and land-use characteristics as generally measured at the metropolitan scale include attributes of density, road network characteristics, and regional and local accessibility. Since neighborhoods vary across multiple dimensions, a statistical technique was required for their grouping. Cluster analysis is a multivariate technique that groups cases based on their similarity across multiple measured attributes. A K-Mean cluster analysis (Aldenderfer and Blashfield 1984) was performed on TAZs of the two regions, using the 13 variables listed in Appendix A. To render the meaning of the clusters as consistent as possible between the two areas, clustering was done for Atlanta and Boston in the same analysis; that is, the TAZs of the two regions were combined in a single dataset, and clusters were created without regard to the region in which they were located. In this fashion, the statistical meaning—if not the perceived land-use and transportation implications—of a given cluster is the same between the two regions.

To divide the two regions into neighborhood types based on the multidimensional data above, a set of five clusters was specified *a priori*: central business district (Cluster A), other central city (Cluster B), inner suburban (Cluster C), middle suburban (Cluster D), and outer suburban and exurban (Cluster E). For both Boston and Atlanta, the clusters fall into a distinct concentric pattern, with generally increasing accessibility and transit and pedestrian orientation toward the center of the metropolitan area. Most of the ter-

Table 8-1. Households by Cluster, Atlanta and Boston, 1995

Cluster	Atlanta households	Boston households
A	0.5%	2.6%
B	2.9%	17.3%
C	8.4%	34.6%
D	27.9%	33.2%
E	60.3%	12.4%

Source: Estimates by Atlanta and Boston metropolitan planning organizations.

ritory of Atlanta is occupied by neighborhoods in Cluster E, the outermost and least pedestrian- and transit-friendly cluster. Boston, in contrast, presents observably more territory in Clusters B and C, which rank much higher in the many dimensions that constitute accessibility and transit and pedestrian friendliness.

Differences in the area of the various zones tend to understate the contrast between the two regions in terms of availability of housing in different neighborhood types. For example, although less than 3 percent of Atlanta households were located in Cluster B neighborhoods, more than 17 percent of Boston households lived in this zone, a difference greater than that of the relative areas of the zones (Table 8-1).

Notwithstanding the identical procedure for designating neighborhood types in the two regions, the nature of the development within a given cluster differed considerably between Boston and Atlanta. Examples of Cluster A neighborhoods in Boston included five-story lot-line apartment buildings and a public housing complex adjacent to a downtown of similar density (Levine et al. 2002). The parallel zone in Atlanta included some centrally located gated residential developments as well as apartments incorporated in large built-up blocks downtown (Figures 8-1 and 8-2). Cluster B in both Boston and Atlanta included neighborhoods of mixed single-family homes and small apartments, generally with nearby retail (Figures 8-3 and 8-4). Examples of Cluster C in Boston included a mix of apartment buildings along major routes, with single-family neighborhoods adjacent; Cluster C neighborhoods in Atlanta included small, 1940s bungalows with neighborhood commercial zones (Figures 8-5 and 8-6). Cluster D in Atlanta included single-family development of the 1950s–1960s on midsized lots (Figures 8-7 and 8-9). Examples in Boston included older villages incorporated into the Boston metropolitan area and their surrounding development. Cluster E in both Boston and Atlanta included newly constructed single-family homes of 3,000 square feet or more and three- and four-car garages. In Boston, large, new single-family homes were combined with some of the more remote older villages of the region; in Atlanta, some large-lot suburban development of the 1960s and 1970s was included in this outer zone (Figures 8-9 and 8-10).

Survey Methodology

A survey was developed and pretested for administration by telephone. The survey focused on respondents' transportation and land-use preferences, regardless of the neighborhood in which the respondents actually resided. Many of the questions were phrased in tradeoff format, since people may hold internally contradictory preferences; for example, they may want walkability on one hand, but only low-density, land-use-separated development forms on the other. The tradeoff questions forced them to choose between potentially contradictory elements of their preferences and reveal which was a higher priority.

Examples of pairs of statements follow, in Table 8-2. Respondents were asked to select between a and b and then indicate the intensity they felt for their chosen statement.

The survey sample was developed through a random selection of individuals in a consumer database drawing on multiple sources, including credit reporting data. Overall, 1,607 individuals completed the survey, for a response rate of 38.9 percent. Weights were applied to the sample to ensure that the distribution of households in the sample matched the distribution of households across the neighborhood types.

The questions were designed to elicit respondents' preferences along a number of dimensions pertaining to transit or automobile orientation and pedestrian environments. Preferences tended to move together; for example, an individual indicating strong preferences for transit tended to indicate similarly strong preferences for pedestrian environments. Under conditions such as these it is possible to use principal components analysis to create a limited number of indices, or factors, that capture the underlying similarity between individuals' responses to questions that are related in the fashion described above. By creating a small set of factors that represent a significantly larger number of variables, this technique can facilitate further modeling without using the full set of variables. In this analysis, a single factor, interpreted as an indicator of neighborhood transportation/land-use preferences, was extracted. For each respondent a factor score was calculated along a continuum from –2.2, indicating preference for transit- and pedestrian-oriented neighborhoods, to +2.3, indicating preference for

Figure 8-1. Cluster A, Atlanta
Photo by Aseem Inam

Figure 8-2. Cluster A, Boston
Photo by Aseem Inam

Figure 8-3. Cluster B, Atlanta
Photo by Aseem Inam

Figure 8-4. Cluster B, Boston
Photo by Aseem Inam

Figure 8-5. Cluster C, Atlanta
Photo by Aseem Inam

Figure 8-6. Cluster C, Boston
Photo by Aseem Inam

Figure 8-7. Cluster D, Atlanta
Photo by Aseem Inam

Figure 8-8. Cluster D, Boston
Photo by Aseem Inam

Figure 8-9. Cluster E, Atlanta
Photo by Aseem Inam

Figure 8-10. Cluster E, Boston
Photo by Aseem Inam

Table 8-2. Examples of Trade-Off Questions Designed to Elicit Neighborhood Preference

1a. I like living in a neighborhood where people can walk to places like stores, libraries, or restaurants, even if this means that the houses and commercial areas are within a block or two of each other.	1b. I like living in a neighborhood where the commercial areas are kept far from the houses, even if this means that people can't walk to places like stores, libraries, or restaurants.
2a. I like living in a neighborhood with single-family houses on larger lots, even if this means that public transit is not available.	2b. I like living in a neighborhood with a good bus and train system, even if this means a neighborhood with a mix of single-family houses and multifamily buildings that are close together.

auto-oriented neighborhoods. The distribution of this factor among the samples is displayed in Table 8-3 and indicates the significantly different preference structures of the Atlanta and Boston samples, with the latter being considerably more inclined toward transit- and pedestrian-oriented neighborhoods. Nonetheless, it is worth noting that more than 29 percent of the Atlanta respondents (and 40 percent of the Boston respondents) expressed at least some degree of preference for transit- and pedestrian-oriented neighborhoods.

Given the combination of the divergent preferences of residents of the two areas and the significantly different metropolitan form of each area, it may be that differences in the characteristics of people's neighborhood environments are explained by differences in their preferences. For example, on the whole, Atlantans live in more car-oriented environments than Bostonians. Is the difference in their preferences sufficient to explain the differences in the neighborhood environments in which they find themselves?

Data presented in Figure 8-11 suggest that this is not the case. The figure graphs the probability of residence in Cluster A, B, or C, the three most transit- and pedestrian-friendly zones in Atlanta, by people's transportation/

Table 8-3. Distribution of Neighborhood Preference Factor, Boston and Atlanta

Neighborhood preference	Very strong pedestrian neighborhood preference	Pedestrian neighborhood preference	Mean preference	Auto neighborhood preference	Very strong auto neighborhood preference
Factor score standard deviations from mean	−1.5 to −2.2	>−1.5 to −0.5	−0.5 to <0.5	0.5 to <1.5	1.5 to 2.3
Boston	4.5%	35.5%	31.2%	24.3%	4.5%
Atlanta	6.4%	23.0%	29.7%	34.2%	6.7%

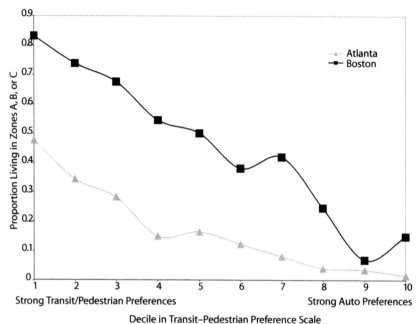

Figure 8-11. Relationship of Transit/Pedestrian Preference to Residence in Transit- and Pedestrian-Friendly Zones

land-use preferences. For example, people with the strongest (i.e., top-decile) preferences for pedestrian neighborhoods in metropolitan Boston had an 83 percent probability of living in those zones; their Atlanta counterparts with identical preferences had only a 48 percent chance of living in Cluster A, B, or C. This gap suggests that there is demand in Atlanta for residence in transit- and pedestrian-friendly zones that is not satisfied.

The graph appears to validate the transportation and land-use preference scale used in these analyses, since the likelihood of living in a transit- and pedestrian-oriented area declines regularly as people's preferences move in a more automobile-oriented direction. But more importantly, it illustrates that the variation in residence in pedestrian neighborhoods is only partly explained by the difference in households' preferences between the two regions; households expressing identical preferences are likely to live in very different environments. For example, Atlanta households in the second decile (i.e., with transit and pedestrian-neighborhood preferences stronger than 80 percent of the sample) had less than a 30 percent chance of living in a transit- and pedestrian-friendly zone. Such a low probability of living in these zones is not observed in Boston until nearly the eighth decile (i.e., people with auto-neighborhood preferences stronger than 80 percent of the sample).

Differences between Boston and Atlanta residents can also shed some light on the role of neighborhood self-selection in the relationship between urban form and travel behavior. Given the gap depicted in Figure 8-1, it seems unlikely that new transit-oriented housing in Atlanta would fill up with average Atlantans; rather, such housing would tend to be occupied by people who previously could not satisfy their residential preferences in Atlanta. Self-selection in this case would be a real effect, but it would hardly negate the impact of urban form on travel behavior. Absent a full range of choices, those households would be unlikely to reside in a pedestrian neighborhood and would have to adopt auto-oriented travel patterns. Where pedestrian neighborhoods are undersupplied because of regulation or other constraints, the self-selection effect associated with expansion of these neighborhoods can be a very real result—perhaps even the most significant impact—of the urban form, rather than a source of statistical bias to be isolated and discarded. For this reason, studies linking travel behavior to urban form are uninterpretable in the absence of an underlying theory of neighborhood production.

Discrete-Choice Modeling of Choice of Neighborhood Clusters

Thus far, the Atlanta-Boston study is strictly bivariate and thus we cannot yet analyze the relationship of preference and choice for particular zones or particular groups. Such an analysis would depend on a modeling framework in which individual households choose from among the identified neighborhood types. Since neighborhood types here are conceived of discretely—they are real places whose character shifts over time and space in a discontinuous fashion—the tools of discrete choice are employed. In particular, the choice from among the five neighborhood types identified is modeled as a multinomial logit (Ben Akiva and Lerman 1985). Six models were estimated for each metropolitan area: a model for the population as a whole, and models for whites, nonwhites, and households of low, medium, and high income. Each model has two sets of independent variables: neighborhood-specific constants, and the neighborhood-preference score described above (interacting with neighborhood choices). In all cases, neighborhood type E is the omitted category, and Clusters A and B have been combined because of low sample sizes in Cluster A.

The models are constructed to assess the closeness of the "fit" between people's transportation and land-use preferences and their choice of actual neighborhood, and the sensitivity of people's choices to their preferences. That is, how readily can people act upon their transportation and land-use preferences when selecting a residential location?

The models are presented in Table 8-4. All coefficients are significant with at least 95 percent confidence, with the exception of the models for nonwhites and the Boston model for low income. All coefficients of the preference score variable carry the expected negative sign; lower preference scores mean greater preferences for pedestrian neighborhoods. In all cases (save the model for nonwhites in Boston) the coefficients become progressively more negative as the choices approach the central A and B zones, indicating the impact of stronger pedestrian-neighborhood preferences on the utility of residence in one of those zones.

All of the Atlanta models have significantly greater explanatory power than their corresponding Boston model. This can be gauged with the pseudo-R^2 statistic, the multinomial logit analog to regression's R^2—a measure of the model's overall explanatory power. The statistics range around 0.3 to 0.4 for Atlanta, and around 0.1 to 0.2 for Boston. This is an artifact of the lopsided distribution of households in Atlanta, where 60 percent of households reside in zone E; Boston's more even distribution of households among zones tends to lead to less explanatory power in the models. Two approaches are used to control for this distribution effect. First, models with neighborhood alternative-specific constants—but no transportation–land-use preference data—were estimated. These models were then compared with models that also incorporated information about the respondent's transportation and land-use preferences. In five of six models estimated, the incorporation of preference data boosted the models' explanatory power more for Boston than for Atlanta. In other words, knowing what a respondent prefers in transportation and land use gives us greater information about what kind of neighborhood she actually gets if that person is a Bostonian rather than an Atlantan. That preferences predict choices in Boston better than in Atlanta suggests a disconnection between what people want and what they get in the more sprawling region.

The effect of transportation and land-use preferences on neighborhood choices is seen even more distinctly through the marginal effects of neighborhood preference scores on neighborhood choice.[1] Marginal effects are interpreted as the change in probability of selection of a neighborhood

Table 8-4. Multinomial Logit Models of Choice of Neighborhood Type

	All		Whites		Nonwhites		<$35,000 income		$35,000–$74,999 income		$75,000+ income	
	Boston	Atlanta	Boston	Atlanta	Boston	Atlanta	Boston	Atlanta	Boston	Atlanta	Boston	Atlanta
Coefficients of alternative specific constants												
Zone A or B	-0.28	-3.26	-0.40	-3.58	1.14	-2.59	-0.07	-3.22	-0.57	-3.15	-0.54	—
(t-statistic)	(-1.5)	(-10.6)	(-2.0)	(-8.5)	(1.4)	(-5.6)	(-0.2)	(-4.8)	(-1.6)	(-5.8)	(-1.5)	—
Zone C	0.85	-1.74	0.75	-1.70	2.39	-1.89	0.92	-1.44	0.81	-1.99	0.55	-1.89
(t-statistic)	(6.5)	(-12.2)	(5.6)	(-10.7)	(3.3)	(-5.6)	(3.8)	(-5.3)	(3.6)	(-6.7)	(2.2)	(-7.2)
Zone D	1.05	-0.48	1.01	-0.58	1.91	-0.13	1.17	-0.31	0.97	-0.79	0.96	-0.76
(t-statistic)	(8.5)	(-5.3)	(8.0)	(-5.5)	(2.6)	(-0.73)	(5.2)	(-1.6)	(4.6)	(-4.3)	(4.2)	(-4.4)
Coefficients of neighborhood preference scores (interacting with neighborhood choices)												
Zone A or B	-1.97	-1.73	-2.05	-2.02	-1.05	-0.91	-1.51	-2.35	-2.16	-1.62	-2.45	—
(t-statistic)	(-10.4)	(-6.0)	(-10.4)	(-5.6)	(1.0)	(-1.7)	(-4.6)	(-4.3)	(-6.1)	(-2.9)	(-6.8)	—
Zone C	-1.22	-1.25	-1.2	-1.31	-1.41	-0.88	-1.04	-1.39	-1.14	-1.25	-1.44	-1.26
(t-statistic)	(-8.4)	(-8.1)	(-8.2)	(-7.8)	(-1.4)	(-2.3)	(-4.0)	(-4.8)	(-4.5)	(-3.9)	(-5.4)	(-4.7)
Zone D	-0.55	-0.48	-0.55	-0.81	-0.30	-0.13	-0.30	-0.90	0.97	-0.65	-0.75	-0.80
(t-statistic)	(-4.0)	(-5.3)	(-4.1)	(-7.3)	(0.3)	(-0.7)	(-1.3)	(-4.5)	(4.6)	(-3.4)	(-3.2)	(-4.5)
Marginal effects of neighborhood preference scores on neighborhood choice												
Zones A or B	-0.25	-0.03	-0.26	-0.03	-0.13	-0.03	-0.19	-0.061	-0.26	-0.04	-0.29	—
Zone C	-0.26	-0.08	-0.25	-0.09	-0.31	-0.06	-0.22	-0.11	-0.025	-0.07	-0.27	-0.07
Zone D	-0.12	-0.14	-0.12	-0.14	-0.06	-0.10	-0.07	-0.17	-0.12	-0.11	-0.17	-0.12
Overall model statistics												
n	798	800	748	653	50	147	241	191	262	215	245	284
Adjusted pseudo-R^2	0.13	0.38	0.13	0.41	0.23	0.27	0.12	0.33	0.12	0.40	0.15	0.36
Adjusted pseudo-R^2, model with alternative specific constants only	0.05	0.31	0.05	0.33	0.19	0.25	0.07	0.21	0.05	0.34	0.02	0.30
	Δ=+0.08	Δ=+0.07	Δ=+0.08	Δ=+0.07	Δ=+0.04	Δ=+0.02	Δ=+0.05	Δ=+0.12	Δ=+0.07	Δ=+0.06	Δ=+0.13	Δ=+0.06
Average neighborhood preference scores*	-0.38	0.40	-0.39	0.46	-0.24	0.16	-0.46	-0.04	-0.42	0.39	-0.34	0.59

*Note: Boston–Atlanta differences significant with >0.99 confidence. Differences within Atlanta groups (ethnicity, income) significant with >0.99 confidence. Differences within Boston groups not statistically significant.

type that is associated with a one-point move in the transportation and land-use preference score. For example, a one-point move in a person's preference score towards auto-oriented neighborhoods is associated with a 25-percentage-point reduction in the chance of living in Cluster A or B in Boston but only a 3-percentage-point reduction in Atlanta. The converse is true as well: a one-point move toward pedestrian neighborhood preference boosts the probability of living in Cluster A or B by 25 percentage points in Boston but only 3 percentage points in Atlanta. Thus, the marginal effects are interpreted as an indicator of the sensitivity of a household's neighborhood choice to its transportation and land-use preferences.

The difference between Boston and Atlanta is dramatic. Relative lack of choice in Atlanta rendered one's neighborhood selections much less sensitive to one's preferences than in Boston. In general, marginal effects for Clusters A, B, and C were much greater in Boston than in Atlanta; by contrast, marginal effects for Cluster D were somewhat greater in Atlanta. Given the greater supply of suburban housing in Atlanta, people with preferences for this type of housing were slightly more able to satisfy those preferences than their Boston counterparts. However, Boston's relative disadvantage in this neighborhood type is considerably less than its relative advantage for the more pedestrian neighborhoods; this is further supported by the fact that the marginal effect on explanatory power of the addition of transportation and land-use preference as an independent variable is consistently greater for Boston than for Atlanta.

Similar analyses are displayed for population subgroups. For example, marginal effects for nonwhites in both Boston and Atlanta were significantly less than for whites, suggesting a more constrained ability on the part of the nonwhites to act on transportation and land-use preferences. Analysis of marginal effects at different income levels is revealing. In the case of the Boston sample, the marginal effects increase markedly with income. This is as is expected: the higher one's income, the greater the effect one's neighborhood preferences would have on one's neighborhood choices. Results for low-income people in Atlanta are anomalous in this regard in that both the marginal effects and the additional explanatory power of neighborhood preferences appear to be highest in the low-income group.

The multinomial logit model described in Table 8-4 can be employed to estimate probabilities of residence in the various zones for households of different socioeconomic characteristics and transportation and land-use preferences (Table 8-5). These results can help illustrate the difficulty of satisfying preferences for pedestrian neighborhoods in an area with con-

Table 8-5. Estimated Probabilities of Residence in Neighborhood Types, by Transportation–Land-Use Preference and Socioeconomic Group

	Estimated probability of residence in zone											
	All		Whites		Nonwhites		<$35,000 income		$35,000–$74,999 income		$75,000+ income	
	Boston	Atlanta	Boston	Atlanta	Boston	Atlanta	Boston	Atlanta	Boston	Atlanta	Boston	Atlanta
Respondent with pedestrian neighborhood preference greater than 75% of sample												
A or B	25%	7%	26%	6%	14%	7%	23%	8%	31%	7%	29%	N/A
C	41%	20%	39%	20%	68%	13%	42%	21%	51%	17%	36%	19%
D	28%	36%	29%	40%	16%	40%	28%	43%	10%	34%	30%	39%
E	6%	38%	7%	35%	2%	40%	7%	27%	8%	42%	6%	42%
Respondent with median pedestrian neighborhood preferences												
A or B	11%	2%	10%	2%	14%	4%	12%	2%	9%	3%	10%	N/A
C	33%	9%	32%	10%	50%	7%	33%	12%	34%	8%	29%	9%
D	41%	34%	42%	31%	31%	42%	42%	36%	42%	28%	44%	29%
E	15%	55%	15%	57%	5%	48%	13%	50%	16%	61%	17%	62%
Respondent with pedestrian neighborhood preferences greater than 25% of sample												
A or B	4%	1%	3%	0%	12%	2%	5%	0%	1%	1%	2%	N/A
C	22%	4%	21%	4%	30%	4%	22%	5%	11%	4%	17%	4%
D	48%	28%	48%	21%	48%	42%	52%	24%	76%	20%	47%	18%
E	27%	68%	28%	74%	9%	53%	21%	70%	13%	76%	34%	78%

strained supply of these neighborhoods, like Atlanta. For example, a person with transit and pedestrian preferences stronger than 75% of the sample would have a 25% probability of living in Cluster A or B in Boston but only a 7% probability in Atlanta. If the household were nonwhite, the relevant probability in Boston would drop to 14% but remain unchanged in Atlanta. A white household with median transportation and land-use preferences would have a 15% probability of living in the outer zone, Cluster E, in Boston but a 57% probability in Atlanta. Thus even when preferences are held constant, the results suggest that the physical form of Atlanta tends to result in choices of residential environments that are less accessible than in metropolitan Boston.

None of the foregoing analysis is meant to suggest that preferences for the physical characteristics and accessibility of neighborhoods dominate, or should dominate, other aspects of the residential-choice decision. Clearly, school quality and neighborhood safety tend to be more important to the locational decisions of many if not most households. But this analysis does not rest on any assumption of primacy of transportation and accessibility factors. Instead, where greater choices are available, more households will be able to satisfy their preferences even for nonprimary characteristics in their neighborhood wish list. For example, consider a household whose first priority is a neighborhood with good schools, and whose second priority is a neighborhood that facilitates walking and offers transit and a short commute. If all the affordable neighborhoods that have good schools are located in auto-oriented suburbs with poor accessibility characteristics, this household would likely choose such a locale, and its preferences for accessible living, transit, and pedestrianism would never be revealed. On the other hand, if because of greater diversity of choice, the desired mix of neighborhood characteristics could be found in affordable communities with good schools, this household could satisfy its preferences—both primary and secondary.

THE PREFERENCE-CHOICE DIVIDE

Whereas the previous chapter focused on questions pertaining to private developers and the production of neighborhood choices—that is, the supply side—the Boston-Atlanta study focused on the extent to which available choices satisfy household demand for more accessible, pedestrian- and transit-friendly metropolitan form. Clearly, there is much greater interest in transit- and pedestrian-friendly neighborhoods in Boston than in

Atlanta. It might be the case, then, that the relative paucity of such neighborhoods in the Atlanta region is not a problem but a simple reflection of consumer preferences in the region.

Results presented here suggest that this is not the case. Atlantan households with strong preferences for transit- and pedestrian-friendly neighborhoods are much less likely to reside in such zones than their Bostonian counterparts. In a discrete-choice model of neighborhood choice between the two regions, knowing a household's transportation and land-use preferences contributes considerably more in explanatory power in Boston than in Atlanta. This is not surprising, given the differences in physical form between the two regions. An Atlanta household may have strong preferences for transit- and pedestrian-friendly neighborhoods but is unlikely to be able to act on those preferences in an environment of constrained supply. By contrast, a Boston household with such preferences has considerably greater opportunity to make a neighborhood choice in line with its transportation and land-use preference.

Although this study was centrally concerned with regulatory constraints on compact, mixed-use development, the evidence it developed—the mismatch between preferences and choices in a constrained environment—was indirect. Yet this evidence, in conjunction with other studies on supply and price impacts of municipal regulatory constraints, suggests that the current land-use regime indeed zones out transportation and land-use choices that could satisfy a significant minority of households in U.S. metropolitan areas.

APPENDIX A:
VARIABLES USED TO CHARACTERIZE NEIGHBORHOODS

Density variables

Population density. Total population divided by total residential land area. Residential land extracted from land- use Geographic Information Systems (GIS) coverage. This variable used in natural log form for cluster analysis.

Employment density. Jobs divided by total land area. Used in natural log form.

Road network characteristics

Percentage T intersections. The number of T intersections (as opposed to 4-way or more intersections) divided by total intersections. Indicator of connectedness of a street network.

Intersection density. Intersections per square mile of total land area. Used in natural log form.

Street length density. Total roadway length divided by total land area.

Average speed. Average congested speeds of major streets in and surrounding the TAZ. "Average speed" used created polygons bordered by links of the transportation modeling network; these polygons were overlain onto TAZs and values calculated by weighted average of land area.

Average number of lanes. Average number of lanes in major streets in and surrounding the TAZ. Calculated in a similar fashion to average speed.

Regional and local accessibility

Automobile accessibility. Accessibility to employment via the automobile network. For zone i, one of j total zones, $access_i =$

$$\sum_{j=1}^{n} f(c_{ij}) \times employment_j$$

This is the denominator of the production constrained gravity model:

$$T_{ij} = P_i \times \frac{A_j \times f(c_{ij})}{\sum\limits_{z=1} A_z \times f(c_{iz})}$$

Where

T_{ij} = Trips between zones i and j

P = Trip productions

A = Trip attractions

$f(c_{ij})$ = The friction factor associated with travel time c between zones i and j.

z = all zones

For consistency of interpretation, friction factors estimated for Boston by the Central Transportation Planning Staff were used for both areas. The choice of Boston factors has little impact on results, as Pearson correlation (r) between the Boston and Atlanta friction factors = 0.98. Friction factors:

$$f(c_{ij}) = e^{-b(cij)}$$

Where

e = the base of natural logarithms

b = a parameter empirically and iteratively estimated to maximize the fit between predictions of the gravity model (left) and observed distribution of trip lengths, times, or costs.

Transit-auto ratio. Ratio of employment accessibility by transit to employment accessibility by auto. Transit accessibility calculated as automobile accessibility above. Some TAZs offer no transit access; value become zero for these zones.

Land-use intensity: quarter-mile. A measure of land-use mixing: The number of surrounding quarter-mile grid cells with a different land use from the center cell, averaged over a TAZ.

Land-use variety: quarter-mile. A measure of land-use mixing: The number of land uses in surrounding quarter-mile grid cells different from the land use of the center cell, averaged over a TAZ.

Land-use intensity: two-mile. As above, but a two-mile radius used.

Land-use variety: two-mile. As above, but a two-mile radius used.

CHAPTER NINE

A NEW FOUNDATION
FOR POLICY REFORM

The city of Salonika, Greece, incorporates many elements that planners in the United States would refer to as smart growth. The country's second-largest city, this Aegean port town is compact,[1] with residential settlement characterized by apartment buildings of five to eight stories. Mixed land uses are the norm. The ground floors of apartment buildings on streets of any significance tend to be devoted to restaurants, retail, and other businesses. Pedestrians flood the streets and plazas virtually around the clock. While enjoying these benefits, the city also struggles with the disadvantages of density, including roadway congestion, scarcity of open space, noise, and a heat-island effect.

Like most of the world's cities, Salonika did not begin the 20th century in its current form (Yerolympos 1995). Much of the city's current territory was developed in the 1920s in small detached bungalows built hastily to accommodate a rapid influx of refugees. As these structures aged and the city grew, they were generally replaced with multifamily structures of increasing heights. As part of this process, the maximum allowable building heights were increased in a stepwise fashion. Here and there one can

Figure 9-1. Redevelopment at increasing densities with eased height limitations, Salonika, Greece
Photo by Theodoros Natsinas

still see the small older structures remaining, evidence of the evolutionary process that led to the current city form (Figure 9-1).

The era of lower-density settlement in early 20th-century-Salonika coincided with the advent of modern zoning in the United States. This fact led me to hypothetical speculation: what if the town's bungalow neighborhoods had been protected by an American-style single-family-detached zone? Without relaxation of these standards, older deteriorating units might have been replaced by larger homes, but the transformation into today's compact city would have been precluded. Salonika would have assumed a much more sprawling profile, since most growth could have been accommodated only at the periphery. The city's lively street life, short travel distances, and pedestrian and transit orientation—bus, walking, and cycling accounted for at least half of all trips in 1999 (Thessaloniki Master-Plan Organization 1999)—would not have been supportable. To be sure, the costs of dense development would have been avoided as well. But the compact development form hardly emerged from tough regulatory requirements for dense development. Quite the opposite: in practice, it was the easing of density limitations as the city grew that enabled it to respond to

Figure 9-2. Municipal regulations preclude redevelopment at higher densities, Sunnyvale, California
Photo by Hillel Levine

changed economic conditions with significant densification, as well as with outward growth.

That evolution stands in sharp contrast to the manner in which urban form in the United States adapts to economic change. Few areas in the United States have transformed as markedly in recent decades as California's Silicon Valley, the high-technology region at the southern end of San Francisco Bay. Much of the territory surrounding the valley's current industrial heartland was developed in suburban single-family neighborhoods in the 1960s. At the time, the region was growing as the fringe of the San Francisco Bay Area. The term Silicon Valley was coined in 1970, and over the next few decades, the formerly agricultural territory was converted into the world's premiere center of high-technology industry. Yet throughout this transformation, the residential settlement pattern that took root under earlier economic conditions remained largely intact. In contrast to Salonika, the neighborhoods of California ranch houses and split-levels, developed in the pre-Silicon Valley economic environment, were protected against transformation that would have made them any denser. The value of the land on which homes in this region sit has grown to the point that a well-located but modest suburban unit can easily command $800,000 or more.

The presence of basic structures on expensive land might be seen as a harbinger of redevelopment at higher densities, but the single-family settlement form inherited from the 1960s remains enshrined by the zoning enacted during the territory's initial development. Although significant densification has occurred through multifamily development in other zones, growth is largely accommodated through the spread of residential neighborhoods into agricultural territory scores of miles away, with the predictable legendary commutes (Purvis 2003).

This is not to suggest that without this manner of municipal regulation, the region would have—or should have—adopted the dense urban form of a Salonika. The urban form that might have emerged under a different land-use regulatory regime is unknown, and it would almost certainly differ from those of traditional cities. The physical form of the region is still evolving, but its direction is constrained by planning interventions in the form of low-density zoning and other land-use regulations. Given current municipal powers and the nature of local land-use politics, it is difficult to envision significant transformation of low-density, single-family zones laid out in the 1960s and 1970s even several decades into the future. Despite the evident harm that this regulatory process imposes on households excluded from neighborhoods near the region's main employment concentrations, transportation and land-use debates persist in constructing the municipally regulated status quo as a more or less free market. In this view, deviation from the norm requires scientific proof of travel behavior modification.

The debate hinges more properly on the design of institutions and legal rules that guide development—each of which entails "planning" and "market" in varying combinations. None of these arrangements are neutral, since each shapes metropolitan development in different ways. Will these rules permit transformation in already-developed areas as economic conditions change, or will they lock in the low-density, land-use-separated settlement patterns that arose under a previous era? When municipalities are empowered to pursue the latter goal, they simultaneously impede innovation locally, force increased shares of development to the fringes at the regional scale, and systematically reduce the supplies of accessible, walkable, and transit-friendly neighborhood options to households that might otherwise have chosen them.

Salonika and Silicon Valley represent dramatic urban transformations, but the ordinary evolution of metropolitan areas also presents a choice between alternative development paths. With rapid metropolitan growth, the expanding urban fringe of one era becomes centrally located territory, generating pressures for development of passed-over sites and for redevelopment at higher densities than those of the original settlement pattern. But if land-use regulations, notably single-family zoning, preclude much of this transformation, growth is channeled outward while inward and upward development is constrained. Thus the issue at stake in transportation and land-use debates is the manner in which metropolitan areas are able to evolve.

THE DISCONNECTEDNESS OF TRAVEL BEHAVIOR DEBATES

Municipal intervention into land-use markets is ubiquitous, and is broadly acknowledged that such intervention frequently excludes denser development proposals. Nevertheless, transportation and land-use policy debates proceed by implicitly treating the status quo as a neutral default choice from which deviations require justifications in travel behavior science. Suppose that a consensus emerged that alternative development offered no beneficial travel behavior impact, at least in the short term. The policy prescription emerging from this finding would depend on one's theory of metropolitan growth. If a more or less free market controls metropolitan change, failure of the travel behavior evidence could undermine the rationale for policy intervention. By contrast, if regulations preclude the development of walkable and transit-friendly alternatives desired by some share of the market, lack of scientific evidence would not justify the perpetuation of these exclusionary governmental interventions. Thus a belief that policy reform should hinge on the results of travel behavior studies implies acceptance of the former model—that a more or less free market guides metropolitan growth. This equation of the free market with the status quo is a surprising premise, given the current massive interventions of municipal government in the land-use realm.

One reason for the apparent tenability of this premise may be the very ubiquity of the land-use interventions. In U.S. metropolitan areas, municipal zoning is so much the norm that it tends, in some debates, to disappear as a factor determining metropolitan form. This renders possible analyses that presume that it is the "invisible hand" of free markets that "guides the conversion of land to urban use" (Brueckner 2000, 163). This explanation for the treatment of the current development regime as a neutral default seems insufficient, however. In realms such as exclusionary zoning or the siting of regional facilities, awareness of the impact of municipal regulation (often fueled by "not-in-my-backyard" sentiment) in public and academic debates is quite keen.

Local Zoning as a Market Force

A view equating an intensely controlled land-use regime with the market is a product of more than the regulations' ubiquity. The decentralized application of land-use controls is also a factor; they are exercised by municipalities so numerous that zoning regulations seem to be an autonomous force akin to market exchange. This view is clearly reflected whenever local governments are grouped together with individuals and firms in a class of decentralized marketlike entities (e.g., Schultze 1977), rather than as a governmental level like their state and federal counterparts.

Local government actions are likened to marketplace buying and selling for reasons beyond the numerousness of municipal entities, however. Instead, this equation is embodied in a legal tradition that goes back centuries and is reflected in a much newer economic approach that dovetails perfectly with its legal counterpart. Municipal governments have historically been viewed with ambivalence in both the United States and England; are they agents of governance and hence legitimately subjected to checks and balances lest they become oppressive? Or alternatively, are local governments the expression of the free association of their constituent households, and hence to be granted maximum latitude of action? Are they to be allowed to perform only those actions that have been specifically delegated to them, or are all actions permitted that are not expressly forbidden? When acting in the public realm of governance, municipalities have been subjected to a more constrained view of their rights and powers. But where U.S. local governments take privatelike actions—and zoning to protect private property falls squarely within this realm—the latter, more expansive view has predominated. When acting in this capacity, municipalities are seen less as a level of government and more as a voluntary association of their members, akin to a modern homeowners' association. When judges see municipal governments in this way, they tend to defer to local prerogative as if it emanated from an inherent right of local families to protect their property.

The historical concept of local government action as a private market force received formal economic justification with Tiebout's (1956) model of consumer-voters' "shopping" among competing communities. But the

Tiebout model alone does not explain why municipal capacity to zone out denser development forms ought to be viewed in this marketlike fashion. The rationale for viewing municipal zoning within this framework was not fully explicated until Hamilton (1975) argued the need for exclusionary zoning to prevent unstable "musical suburbs" games whereby poorer households constantly attempt to locate in wealthier communities to reap fiscal advantage, with wealthier households in perpetual flight. Under one interpretation of the Tiebout model, a "household's ability to select a place of residence from among a host of fully autonomous jurisdictions offering different amounts of public spending" is tantamount to "freedom of choice in the public sector" (Brueckner 2000, *169*). Yet this vision of freedom of choice necessarily—and paradoxically—rests on the capacity of those jurisdictions to exercise police-power regulation over land-development market.

Moreover, it is not self-evident that a municipal exclusionary zoning capacity is either necessary or sufficient to prevent the musical-suburbs games that worried Hamilton (1975). Quite the opposite: such games seem already to be in full swing in many U.S. metropolitan areas. Many suburbs are experiencing processes of decline reminiscent of the problems of the cities a generation ago (Orfield 2002). The exclusionary prerogative that municipal governments cherish was clearly insufficient to stem a flight of wealth from these communities. It may be that the search for municipalities that provide even more thorough exclusion than one's current town motivates part of this exodus. If this is the case, then local exclusionary prerogative may actually trigger as many musical-suburbs moves as it forestalls. If households become convinced that relocating will not afford them any greater protection by exclusionary zoning than their current community offers, some incentive to move may be eliminated.

If the model of voting with one's feet is undergirded by police-power, market-constraining regulation, choosing among competing communities cannot be seen as marketlike unless municipal zoning itself is reinterpreted as a market force. This was accomplished with Fischel's (1985) exposition on zoning as a collective property right. Rejecting views of zoning as governmental regulation—whether benign and omniscient, or arbitrary and unwarranted—Fischel articulated a view that zoning represents a particular assignment of property rights. Rather than being vested entirely with the landowner, development rights are partially granted to the community, with the municipal government being the agent empowered to act on these rights. Under this view, the regulatory nature of zoning is fundamentally altered. As with market-based ordering in general, government's role is the establishment and enforcement of property rights—with the difference being that in the case of land-use controls, some of those rights are assigned collectively. This view of zoning as an assignment of property rights, including the right to exclude at the municipal level, is shared by Webster and Lai (2003, *123*) who write that "[o]nly a political philosophy that denies the legitimacy of *any* private property can ignore the issue of optimal exclusion. If we accept the market as an allocating mechanism then we accept exclusion since, as we have noted, markets cannot function without exclusive property rights."

The zoning-as-collective-property-rights framework is presented as a positive analysis from which normative policy recommendations may be derived. Yet inherent to this view is the normative position that municipalities ought, as a matter of legal right, to be able to employ the zoning function in this way. An alternative view might hold, for example, that zoning may be used only in a fashion consistent with state-level public purposes. The distinction is important. Municipalities may well view the ability to zone out apartments or exclude transit-oriented development from the vicinity of rapid transit stations as a collective property right. But their capacity to use the land-use regulatory function in this fashion depends on the latitude granted them by legislatures and courts.

The normative nature of this position is underscored through parallels with alternative legal positions on the nature of municipal zoning. In contrast to the view that municipal zoning is strictly a delegation of the states' police power to municipalities, judges frequently rule as if the right to zone stems inherently from the property rights of local families. This normative legal position implies that municipal land-use regulations are grounded in a source other than the state's police power. Implicit judicial adherence to this view—even as judges nominally reiterate that municipal zoning is in fact a delegation of such power—tends both to loosen requirements that municipal regulations serve a proper state-level public purpose and to legitimate parochial uses of the power. In this way, the view that municipal zoning is rooted in the property rights of local families is a perfect legal parallel to the economic view of zoning as a collective property right, and it similarly assists in explaining the treatment of current patterns of metropolitan development as a marketlike neutral default option. When municipal land-use controls are seen as something other than governmental regulation of economic processes, the status quo can be taken as the market's solution.

Under this semantic redefinition, alterations of municipal powers are tantamount to interventions in the market that are justified only by conclusive scientific proof of benefit.

Analyzing zoning as a collective property right rather than governmental regulation of economic activity may be defended on pragmatic grounds. As long as municipalities are unlikely voluntarily to cede any of their prerogative in land-use control, they are likely to behave as if zoning is in fact their property right; they will enact whatever legal zoning policies please local homeowner-voters, regardless of the impact these may have on excluded households. It may be argued that accepting this is simply an adaptation to political reality, and the best one can hope for is to reduce support for exclusionary policies by compensating, insuring, or providing other incentives for suburban homeowners to relax their not-in-my-backyard opposition to development that does not fit their preferred mold. This position is unobjectionable as a pragmatic judgment of what is and is not politically feasible in the U.S. metropolitan context. But defining zoning as collective property right rather than as governmental regulation and calling political support for zoning a marketlike demand (Fischel 2001) beg the question: should U.S. municipalities wield the extensive prerogative that they do over land uses within their jurisdiction? Different states have pursued varying policies in this regard. Current municipal land-use prerogative is hardly an inevitable state of nature—it is but one choice of institutional arrangements from many possible alternatives. Redefining local zoning as a kind of market force obscures its regulatory nature and thereby short-circuits public debate over its appropriate scope.

By way of illustration, consider the growing call for applying cost-benefit analysis to governmental regulations to sift out the efficient and legitimate from the misguided (Sunstein 2002). Identifying local zoning as a governmental regulatory exercise could conceivably subject it to the legitimacy test of cost-benefit analysis—and most observers would agree that many municipal regulations would fail the test. By contrast, when local zoning is seen as a collective property right, the notion of subjecting it to an economic efficiency test becomes as nonsensical as requiring individuals to file cost-benefit analyses before buying or selling their property. In standard economic analysis, consumption decisions are not evaluated for their efficiency but rather taken axiomatically as evidence of individuals' preferences. By extension, if a municipality uses its collective property rights to (for example) limit the number of unrelated individuals who can live together in a single-family zone, the "collective property rights" view implies that the legitimacy of this legal action stems simply from the fact that the community prefers the (legally permissible) outcome. No higher regulatory justification is required.

The collective-property-rights view thus alters the regulatory nature of zoning by rendering it a kind of market force. Yet there is no *a priori* reason why regulations enacted at other geographic scales—regional, state, or even federal—could not similarly be defined as an exercise of the collective property rights of the individuals who compose the relevant political juris-diction. If anything, regulations imposed by the larger governmental units could have a stronger claim to the mantle of collective property rights, since higher proportions of the benefits and the costs of the regulations would be internal to the enacting jurisdictions. By contrast, regulations by smaller jurisdictional units are characterized by geographic spillover effects because of their size and interconnection with other municipalities (Fischel 1985, *100*). In any case, redefining municipal governmental intervention as the workings of private markets in property-rights terms does not alter the reg-ulatory nature of local zoning.

LET MARKETS PLAN?

Urban planning researchers and practitioners frequently ground their pol-icy problem definitions in the "planning versus the market" dichotomy, often arguing for greater planning interventions into market ordering. Voices skeptical of planning practice often frame their analyses within the same dichotomy but argue for a greater role for market-based solutions. The power and apparent clarity of this problem definition carry over to the transportation and land-use realm, with recommendations for "more plan-ning" competing with calls to "let markets plan."

Notwithstanding the apparent neatness and appealing symmetry of this particular problem definition, these formulations are almost entirely devoid of meaning as long as there is no agreement over what counts as market ordering in the land-use realm. Whether local zoning is regulation or the market is very much in dispute. Even proposals for land-use control options based on private-law techniques, such as deed restrictions or common-law nuisance structures—ostensibly the epitome of market-based controls—rarely get local government out of the land-use regulation business, but rather set it up as the public enforcement arm for private agreements. If local government regulation of land uses is a market force, then regional or state limitations on it represent market intervention. Under that definition of municipal regulation, state requirements—that local zoning allow apartment buildings, say, or that transit-oriented development not be excluded from the vicinity of transit stations—would represent interferences into the market that demand justification. By contrast, if municipal zoning is viewed as police-power governmental regulation into market processes, then the state-level actions can actually expand the role of the market by restricting the prerogative of municipalities to enact market-constraining regulations. Rather than the meaningless planning-versus-the-market formulation of the problem, the controversy would be far better characterized as a debate over alternative legal and institutional arrangements regarding metropolitan development, each of which mixes regulation and markets in different ways.

The call to let markets plan hardly asks to eliminate regulatory land-use controls. Rather, it is a demand for noninterference in municipal regulatory prerogative, which is transformed into a market force through semantic redefinition. With this definition of the market, a search for market failures as a rationale for governmental intervention appears to make sense. If markets guide development and travel behavior can be modified by urban forms, then interventions on behalf of compact development are worth considering as a remedy for market failure. But ambiguous travel-behavior findings could undermine the logic of policy reform because intervention would require reasonable scientific certainty regarding the land-use and transportation connection.

This book has argued for an alternative position. To reiterate: when municipal land-use controls are recognized as a form of governmental intervention into market processes, the market-failure formulation of the transportation and land-use policy problem is fundamentally altered. If urban sprawl and the paucity of alternative development forms are not primarily the result of market failure but of governmental regulation, then the issue of scientific proof of benefit is flipped on its head. Uncertainty regarding the travel behavior impacts of urban form ceases to be a basis for maintaining land-use regulations that exclude compact, pedestrian- or transit-oriented development from areas where markets could support these alternatives. And in areas where insufficient demand for such development exists, even supportive regulations would not generate walkable or transit-friendly neighborhoods.

THE PRESTIGE OF SCIENCE

Rein and Winship (1999) warn of the dangers of a mode of policy thinking they refer to as strong causal reasoning. Policy analysis has become steeped in the social sciences, and governmental actions are assessed on their capacity to demonstrate desired policy outcomes, often in realms removed from the intervention. For example, antipoverty efforts may be justified on the basis of their ability to induce improved school performance by children from low-income families. The problem is that causation in social science is often weak, with explanatory power low and estimated impacts of independent variables on policy outcomes modest. In an environment in which policy is justified by science, advocates of such policies feel pressed to assert significant and strong relationships—that is, to engage in strong causal reasoning—to supply an objective basis for their desired policies. This is a risky game, argue Rein and Winship. When such reasoning is not warranted by the evidence, advocates ought not to shy away from morally based normative arguments and hide behind the ostensible objectivity—but ultimate vulnerability—of social science evidence. Thus, for example, antipoverty efforts may be advocated on moral grounds quite independently of their ability to raise school scores.

The case of transportation and land use offers another alternative to strong causal reasoning. Invoking science in the name of policy reform automatically sets up a policy default should scientific evidence regarding the desired impacts come up short. Yet that very default status may at times be unwarranted. Examination of the implicit default can provide a way out of the bind of strong causal reasoning: where the default is itself the product of unjustified policies, the burden of demonstrating strong causal effects of the policy reform must logically be shifted.

Such a shift is challenging, given the respect commanded by science in general and the scientific formulation of policy problems in particular. The question of how urban form affects travel behavior is an example of a classically formulated question in social science: the impact of a policy-relevant independent variable on an outcome of interest is modeled using multivariate statistical techniques. The promise of objectively assessing the truth regarding the urban-form–land-use relationship lends considerable impetus to this particular problem formulation. In addition, as a reasonably complex question not given to clean and conclusive experimentation, this problem formulation supports a research industry of ever-increasing capacity and quality. Since 1970, social scientific methodologies applied to the travel behavior question have become progressively more sophisticated, with increasing controls for extraneous sources of variance, correction for neighborhood self-selection, and specification of behaviorally-based demand models. Rapid growth since the 1980s in the availability of georeferenced data, together with geographic information systems for their analysis, has led to increasingly fine-grained representations of neighborhood physical attributes. The diffusion of discrete-choice statistical models over the same period has facilitated detailed disaggregate investigations into travel-behavior questions. This application of technical virtuosity to the scientific question supports a lively methodological debate and spurs funders who are oriented toward scientifically based definitions of policy issues.

It is not a denigration of the legitimacy of this scientific enterprise to state that its results map poorly onto the transportation–land-use policy question. Although scientific findings linking alternative land-use practices with improved travel behavior may legitimately be a consideration for relaxation of restrictive low-density land-use regulations, any failure to establish that link would hardly justify the perpetuation of these interventions. But a more robust foundation for policy reform may be found in expansion of transportation and land-use choice. Rather than pursuing the elusive promise of certainty regarding the link between urban form and travel behavior, advocates for alternative development forms would do well to articulate why policy reform is desirable even in an environment of pervasive uncertainty.

SELF-SELECTION

Nowhere is the attraction of a scientific definition—or its mismatch with actual policy questions in transportation and land use—clearer than in the debate over the interpretation of neighborhood self-selection. This book has argued that, given alternative understandings of the self-selection phenomenon, travel behavior studies themselves cannot be interpreted without a theory of production of metropolitan form. Conversely, one's interpretation of the phenomenon implicitly reveals one's view of the processes that produced neighborhood choices. A view that neighborhood self-selection is inherently a source of bias to be eliminated in search of the pure urban design effect assumes that there is little latent demand for pedestrian neighborhoods—a situation that could arise if a more or less free market controlled metropolitan development. By contrast, if the supply of walkable and transit-oriented neighborhoods is constrained by municipal regulation, as this book argues, there would be a backlog of households seeking the opportunity to select these environments. In other words, the neighborhood self-selection processes that produced current travel behavior outcomes would still be alive and well. Thus a theory of undersupply of transit- and pedestrian-friendly neighborhoods would lead to a view that policy reform can affect travel behavior both through the pure urban design effect and through the neighborhood self-selection effect. By extension, travel behavior studies that treat the neighborhood self-selection effect as a source of bias by definition implicitly adopt the theory that metropolitan development is guided by a more or less free market that leaves little latent demand for transit- and pedestrian-oriented neighborhoods. But given the pervasive interventions of local regulation, such a free market can best be imagined if zoning itself is construed as a market force.

A CONSTRAINED VIEW OF BENEFITS

The ability of markets to satisfy preferences is not contingent on the scientific validity of those preferences. Using science to predefine which benefits do and do not count regularly leads to fallacious policy-making. For example, *The New York Times* (McNeil 2004) reported the case of Creekstone Farms, a premium beef producer that had lost its overseas markets—notably Japan—because of discovery the previous year of a case of bovine spongiform encephalopathy, or "mad-cow disease," in the U.S. meat supply. Creekstone responded by individually testing its own cattle, a move that promised to reopen the lucrative Japanese market to the producer. The U.S. Department of Agriculture (USDA) forbade Creekstone to test its cattle, arguing that "there was 'no scientific justification' for testing young steers like those Creekstone sells." The absence of scientifically proven benefits was seen as ample basis to curtail Creekstone's profit-motivated activities, given that other nontesting producers feared negative consequences. The reasoning is clearly deficient, even assuming that the assessment of lack of scientifically demonstrable benefits is correct, because benefits accrue well beyond the statistical prevention of disease. With optional private testing, Japanese consumers—who apparently demand an individually certified supply of beef—get their preferences satisfied; Creekstone Farms makes profits supplying that market demand.

The analogy with transportation and land-use planning is apparent. When travel-behavior research asserts that the lack of proven transportation benefits of alternative land-use forms undermines the logic of policy reform, it is adopting the stance of USDA: notwithstanding that current policy constrains market choice for alternative development forms, an absence of scientifically proven benefits justifies the continued constraint. Such a position construes benefits far too narrowly. The answer to the question "Are there transportation benefits to the alternative land-use approaches?" depends on the definition of a transportation benefit. These benefits are frequently narrowly construed to include reduction in congestion or vehicle miles traveled (VMT). But this book has argued that the U.S. municipal regulatory regime has systematically constrained choices to the point that people who prefer pedestrian- and transit-friendly environments are poorly able to satisfy those preferences.

Yet even researchers and policymakers who have acknowledged the choice-constraining characteristics of the current land-use regime have largely persisted in seeking benefits in congestion relief and VMT reduction as a prerequisite to policy change. In contrast, this book has argued that accepting a problem definition based in planning failure rather than market failure implies a broadened view of the benefits of policy reform, since increased availability of more walkable alternatives represents a transportation benefit as surely as reduced congestion or VMT.

Benefits of policy reform are frequently evaluated in a highly compartmentalized fashion that likely underestimates the impact of cross-cutting urban strategies. For example, research focusing on narrowly construed transportation benefits of alternative development forms frequently concludes that even though congestion benefits remain unproven, there may be other good reasons to pursue these alternatives, including housing affordability, community cohesion, or public health. The implied next step is an isolated analysis of each of these benefits; presumably policy reform rests on adequate scientific proof of at least one of the claims. Under this logic, if each claim is considered on its own and found lacking, there is then no reason to alter the status quo.

That approach reflects an unwarranted insistence on the specific treatment of individual urban ills and would reject a policy reform that has plausible but uncertain benefits in multiple realms—even when that reform amounts to liberalizing regulatory obstacles to innovation. This is poor logic because a policy bearing uncertain benefits in multiple realms can have a larger expected payoff than narrow tactics that offer virtually certain benefits in a single realm. Much current policy research is built on this compartmentalized thinking and represents an axiomatic rejection of the more holistic view. Government structures are arranged similarly; transportation departments may consider transit- and pedestrian-oriented forms for their potential to reduce VMT but generally exclude housing affordability or public health considerations from the analysis.

One form of this compartmentalization is particularly relevant to integrated transportation and land-use planning. Suburban low-density single-family zoning is thought to reduce housing affordability by retarding market-driven innovation in smaller lots and attached housing forms. There is broad acknowledgment of the relevance of municipal zoning practices to housing affordability, and exclusionary zoning is seen as an equity issue relevant to the housing choices available to the poor. Yet housing affordability and location are intimately linked; the former problem is not primarily an absolute shortage of housing but a shortage of affordable housing near one's work and nonwork destinations. Under these conditions, households frequently need to bear either the heavy cost of long-distance travel or the more onerous costs of inaccessibility. In both the housing and transportation cases, land-use regulatory practices hinder some households from meeting their combined housing, transportation, and neighborhood needs and preferences. This regulatory regime, rather than being strictly relevant to affordability and equity, is similarly central to the ability of metropolitan areas to provide alternatives to low-density, auto-oriented development.

PERMISSIVE VERSUS RESTRICTIVE LAND-USE CONTROLS

Chapter 6 considered how land-use controls alter market outcomes, arguing that maxima for heights, density, or intensity encourages more sprawling development than the market would otherwise produce. By contrast, minimum standards in this regard cannot generate markets for denser development where there are none. Zoning an area for compact development cannot generate such an environment unless private developers—who always have numerous alternative opportunities—choose to invest in the locale. Conversely, when developers respond to high-density zoning with high-density proposals, they are providing *prima facie* evidence that they anticipate profits from this form of development that are at least equal to the best alternative use of their capital.

This does not imply that planning requirements for transit-oriented developments, New Urbanist neighborhoods, or smart growth do not shape development. Given developers' interest in building at a particular density, planning requirements can condition permissions on design elements, sidewalks, connections to transit, and so forth. But these can be successfully mandated only if the developer is interested in building at a certain density. Given the mobility of development capital, minimum density requirements are fundamentally permissive rather than restrictive, since developers uninterested in building at a higher density will simply seek alternative venues.

By contrast, interventions such as urban-growth boundaries are unambiguously regulatory interventions into market processes. Proponents of integrated transportation and land-use planning would do well to articulate and clearly distinguish the two fundamental elements of their agenda: liberalized land-use regulations in areas slated for development, combined with tightened controls in areas designated for protection (or development at a later stage). More clearly distinguishing the permissive elements of the smart-growth agenda can serve to channel debate toward the restrictive elements. Smart-growth proponents are currently called upon illogically to justify both the permissive and the restrictive components of their policy proposals with scientific proof of benefit.

BURDEN OF PROOF

This book has argued that a proper assignment of burdens of proof for policy reforms is a prerequisite to productive debate in the transportation and land-use arena. To the extent that an alternative-development or transportation–land-use integration agenda rests on the relaxation of restrictive municipal regulations, it is not logically conditioned on the scientific establishment of benefit. This is because policy analysis in a market economy presumes that it is the regulatory restriction, not its relaxation, that demands some manner of justification.

Proper assignment of burdens of proof does not imply any hostility toward zoning per se or the public regulation of land use in general. The current regime of land-use controls was set in place a century ago by urban reformers to cope with unhealthful urban conditions, a consideration that remains valid today and has even been broadened to include elements like physical activity. But a debate that presupposes that restrictive municipal land-use regulations are the default state of affairs distorts the policy issues, leading to such absurdities as when arguments for reform of low-density zoning practices are met with stern lectures about the virtues of the market.

The notion that the current land-use regime has opened a gap between the transportation and land-use preferences and actual neighborhood choices of households is not axiomatically true, but rather is subject to empirical investigation. It may be, for example, that the current land-use regime simply replicates what would be produced by an unconstrained market, thereby leaving no such gap between preferences and choices. This possibility appears not to withstand the test of empirical investigation, however. By all accounts, neighborhood resistance to proposed denser-than-average development is fierce, often leading to the exclusion of the development. At a minimum, these objections, when operationalized through police-power zoning, move high-density uses to more remote locations. But the economics-based research referred to in Chapter 3 suggests that the current municipal land-use regime constitutes a binding constraint that lowers development densities in aggregate and creates more exclusive communities than would otherwise arise. If this is the case, the current regime does more than shift land uses around. Evidence of a price premium of up to 25 percent associated with New Urbanist developments (Eppli and Tu 1999) suggests a scarcity of these developments relative to their demand in the marketplace.

Although this evidence does not identify the source of the scarcity, it is consistent with the supply limitations that would result from municipal zoning practices that exclude these alternatives. Meanwhile, information presented in Chapter 8 regarding the gap between households' preferences and choices suggests that these effects are significant. This evidence is corroborated through findings regarding the divergence between the current products of land developers and those that they indicate they would prefer to develop under a less restrictive municipal regulatory regime.

A shift in the way transportation and land-use options are debated—as advocated here—would open up the enterprise of empirical research to a range of scientifically interesting questions that would more closely align academic inquiry with the relevant policy questions.

BEYOND TRANSPORTATION BENEFITS

This book has focused on the transportation–land-use sides of the metropolitan development issue, but its argument is applicable to other realms in which advocates of alternative land-use practices seek to justify reforms through measurable scientific benefits. For example, a growing line of research explores the connections between land use, physical activity, and health. In particular, researchers are testing the contention that urban sprawl, by rendering the automobile both necessary and easy for most trips, reduces walking and cycling and contributes to obesity. Tests for that kind of causality are squarely within an epidemiological or public health research tradition. Yet by evaluating the health impacts of alternative urban forms without considering the legal and institutional processes by which those forms arise, the research misconstrues the policy questions in a fashion similar to that of travel behavior research. To see this, assume—for the sake of discussion only—that any negative health impacts of low-density development are ambiguous or negligible. This finding would certainly be inadequate to justify regulations excluding compact, walkable development. Scientific research would hardly relish making the following policy recommendation: "Since the obesity effects of sprawl are ambiguous, there is no health-based reason to alter low-density municipal zoning. People who, for health reasons, might want to choose residence in neighborhoods where they can walk to destinations should be informed that these places will continue to be zoned out because there is no valid scientific reason for allowing them."

On the particular issue of health, the analysis of alternatives to sprawl differs markedly from treatment of health-based claims in the marketplace that are not land-use related. For example, Peter Van Doren (2003, 32) of the libertarian Cato Institute celebrates the ability of markets to satisfy preferences independently of scientific merit:

> In fact, the market's delivery of private goods is not related at all to the scientific validity of people's preferences. Markets can and do supply organic lettuce regardless of whether it really is "better" for your health. The market's ability to deliver Miller Lite is not at all contingent on the resolution of the "Great-Taste, Less-Filling" debate. European consumers do not want genetically modified food regardless of scientists' arguments that consumer concerns about such food are without merit. And people pay good money for light trucks because they feel "safer" in the vehicles even though scientific evidence challenges that sentiment.

By contrast, Gordon and Richardson (2001, 147) dismiss the argument linking sprawl to obesity as "silly," even as they acknowledge that "[t]here are many examples of broader community objections to high-density projects" (140) that lead to their exclusion by municipal zoning. In juxtaposition, these two positions of Gordon and Richardson imply that scientific judgment ought to trump the consumer preferences of the households who might otherwise buy or rent housing in these high-density projects. A more consistent market-oriented philosophy would, like Van Doren's, seek to remove regulatory obstacles to market satisfaction of preferences for such alternatives, even those that some scientists might judge baseless.

THREE LEVELS OF POLICY REFORM

Metropolitan development is a complex system involving numerous actors, including developers, builders, bankers, citizens, and public officials at municipal, county, regional, state, and federal levels. Each set of actors faces its own incentives and constraints, and each interacts with the institutional structures that frame the entire development process. Comprehensive planning for enhanced land-use–transportation integration would consider all classes of actors and all institutions with which they interact as a prelude to designing policy reform.

This book has instead focused on two interrelated aspects of the current system: the tendency of unchecked municipal regulation to exclude compact, walkable, and transit-friendly development, and the related inclination of American scholarship and public debate to identify these regulatory actions with the market. This phenomenon is surely not the only factor behind metropolitan sprawl and the paucity of its alternatives. Desires of a majority of Americans for low-density living, developers' inclination to stick to tried-and-true formulas, and bankers' conservatism all play at least as big a part in generating the form of the U.S. metropolis today. There is a difference between these forces and the forces of governmental regulation, however. Regulation and policy are supposed to correct the excesses of the marketplace, not exacerbate them. Where a governmental institution like local land-use regulation accelerates market processes that cause concern, that institution is logically the first target of reform, since it is a lever of policy control already in public hands. Moreover, seeking to alter consumers' preferences or developers' behavior—whether possible or not—while regulatory obstacles to compact development remain in place seems both futile and hypocritical. For this reason, local land-use policy reform is a necessary and logical first step toward increased availability of alternatives to sprawl.

Many of those reforms are geared toward open-space preservation in the name of sprawl containment. Such policies can succeed in preserving open space. But if they are not paired with policies to accommodate urban densification, they are incapable of increasing the supply of alternatives to sprawl and, as a consequence, incapable of containing sprawl itself. Thus land-use regulatory reform must focus on overcoming barriers to compact, mixed-use development in close-in, high-accessibility areas.

There are three categories of such reform. First are approaches that leave municipal regulatory prerogatives untouched but encourage compact development. The second family of approaches uses incentives from higher-level bodies to spur municipalities to land-use regulations more amenable to alternative development. The third group distributes land-use regulatory power between municipal governments and higher-level governments both to facilitate land-use coordination and to overcome local resistance to denser development forms in areas where there is sufficient market interest.

Regulatory Reform Generated Internally

Notwithstanding the pervasiveness of the regulatory obstacles discussed in this book, a number of municipalities around the country have begun to permit and facilitate compact development forms in their boundaries. The settings vary significantly. Dearborn, Michigan, an industrial suburb of Detroit, actively sought developers to build a compact, mixed-use, walkable neighborhood near its downtown. San Diego worked with a landowner to promote a transit village surrounding a station of its light-rail line (Chapter 7). Westminster, a suburb of Denver, revised zoning to permit a developer to build a compact community (Chapter 1). The Congress for the New Urbanism (www.cnu.org) lists hundreds of developments in a partial database of projects. Not every one would satisfy every smart-growth advocate, but most represent alternatives to low-density, auto-dependent neighborhoods. Increasing visibility can trigger a snowball effect: growing numbers of people are encountering new neighborhoods that are compact, mixed-use, and oriented toward pedestrianism or transit and seeing that they can be pleasant, amenable places. This can help overcome the equation in many people's minds of denser development with environmental, social, and quality-of-life problems. Over the years, this exposure ought to lessen people's political resistance when denser development forms are proposed for their community.

The urban planning profession can play an important role in this shift. Frequently, compact developments are rejected by planning commissions or city councils despite positive recommendations from planning staff. Many planners in municipal practice are keenly interested in development alternatives, notwithstanding political opposition in their communities. The planning profession can adopt the role of an educator in these circumstances, explaining to local citizens and decisionmakers the importance of accommodating a broader range of housing and neighborhood types than in the past—not because of any proven benefits of the compact development forms but because they provide amenable environments for a broad range of household types, foster walkable neighborhoods, and promote vibrant downtowns.

Assisting local planners in this regard is a move toward zoning reform called form-based coding. Whereas traditional zoning codes focus on the uses to which a building is put—largely with an eye to strict segregation of different land uses—form-based codes focus on building design. The guiding notion is that while buildings change uses over their lifetimes, their form largely remains the same. An ancillary benefit is the implicit permitting of mixed land uses, since what goes on inside a building is less important, under a form-based code, than the characteristics of the building itself. By focusing on these attributes, the code can aid in the creation of streetscapes and public spaces that are the fundamental building blocks of urban physical development (Walters and Brown 2004).

A different approach to regulatory reform stems from thinking based in economics. Economists who are concerned about local governments' exclusion of denser development will seek structures that, without challenging municipal regulatory prerogative, can lessen its tendency for overuse. Thus Fischel (1985) argues for open trade, barter, and even the sale of zoning rights between developers and municipalities. Under the current regime, entrepreneurs who propose a compact development for which a large market exists lack the legal means for translating that strong demand into local government approval. If local governments perceive greater costs of dense development (in fiscal burdens, roadway congestion, school overcrowding, and others) than benefits to current residents, they are likely to disallow the proposal regardless of its overall societal benefit. To the extent that the societal benefit is embodied in potential developer profits, these profits can be used to buy permissions that might otherwise not be forthcoming. Gyourko (1991) argues that development impact fees represent a mechanism to inject greater flexibility into local land-use decisionmaking, a flexibility that may overcome part of the local tendency to exclusionary zoning. Mechanisms like transfer of development rights or incentive zoning (Chapter 6) may similarly overcome local exclusion by striking a bargain that makes an explicit *quid pro quo* for accepting the development in question.

Regulatory Reform Spurred by External Incentives

Approaches that leave in place the incentives that municipalities face and the prerogatives that they retain can take the policy reform agenda only so far. Demonstrated successes in the form of high-quality, livable, amenable neighborhoods developed for walkability and transit-friendliness will surely help convince some recalcitrant municipalities that compact development need not evoke the urban ills they are trying so hard to avoid. Reforms that rely on municipalities' internal motivations will still leave considerable regulatory exclusion in place, however, for a number of reasons, including a strong endowment effect: rights tend to "stick" where they are initially assigned (Chapter 3). In the case of municipal land-use regulation, the implication is that when local governments are granted the rights to exclude development, they will tend to use them rather than give them up for fair exchange. This is exacerbated by "fiscal zoning," land-use regulation to maximize net municipal revenues from development.

In that environment, even the apparent successes of compact and transit-oriented development may obscure regulatory exclusion. For example, Whisman Station, the transit-oriented development built on formerly industrial land in Mountain View, California (Chapter 7), could have been built at twice its actual density, based on the developer's proposals and stated desires. Increasing housing supplies in the heart of the Silicon Valley, a location known for its housing shortages—and on a rail transit line no less—would have been a desirable outcome to most observers. Yet the municipal planning process led to the halving of the project; the costs and benefits to the local constituency were the deciding factor.

Incentive-based policies can help move municipalities toward reduced regulatory exclusion. Regional governments in the United States tend to lack land-use powers, being organized instead around special services like sanitation, water, parks, highways, airports, and public transit (Transportation Research Board 2001). This does not mean that they are powerless to influence local land use. Some cases, such as the Georgia Regional Transportation Authority, have been granted specific powers to withhold funds from noncooperative local governments (Nelson 2000). Regional organizations tend to shy away from employing such disincentives in all but the most extreme cases, however. The American political system is much more adept at distributing incentives than disincentives, even when the latter may be considerably more effective (Altshuler 1979).

Sometimes those incentives can take the form of transit itself. In regions where transit extensions are desired by local communities, the metropolitan transit organization can condition such extensions on appropriate land-use planning on the part of municipal governments, as the Bay Area Rapid Transit (BART) District (1999) has begun to do. Communities choosing low-density zoning are finding their priority for BART extensions reduced under this policy; those that commit to transit-oriented development in station areas become better candidates. Given the organizational disconnection between transportation planning and land-use planning in the United States, this would seem to be a broadly applicable approach.

Incentives can also take the form of payments to communities. For example, the Metropolitan Transportation Commission in the San Francisco Bay Area offers payments to "local governments that build housing near transit stops" under the Housing Incentive Program of the Transportation for Livable Communities initiative (Metropolitan Transportation Commission 2005). Since local governments do not generally build housing but either allow or exclude it, this program is a subsidy not to the housing itself but to the regulator who permits it. As such, it clearly stems from an understanding that municipal allowance of the desired developments is a scarce commodity.

Regulatory Reform Based on Shared Land-Use Authority

Incentive-based systems can convey regional interest in local land-use policy to municipal governments, but they will remain limited by budget constraints. Moreover, the communities that engage in the severest forms of exclusion may be wealthy enough that incentives would have little likelihood of spurring regulatory reform. By contrast, systems in which land-use authority is shared between local governments and higher-level bodies are in place worldwide and are frequently geared—at least in part—to overcoming local resistance to compact development.

U.S. examples of higher-level authorities seeking to ensure that local government accepts development are rare, however. The U.S. norm is little state involvement in local land use in any case (Transportation Research Board 2001, 93). State growth-management programs currently exist in California, Florida, Georgia, Hawaii, Maine, Maryland, New Jersey, Rhode Island, Vermont, and Washington but have little power to compel local government to accept development (A. Nelson 1999). The Twin Cities Metropolitan Council in Minneapolis–St. Paul has been granted authority to "review the metropolitan significance of major public and private projects" (Rothblatt 1994, 501), meaning that it is able to deny certain projects but cannot require others to be allowed. Similar powers were granted to the Georgia Regional Transportation Authority to require that "developments of regional impact" conform to regional air-quality and transportation goals. These again represent indirect powers to disallow projects but, as in nearly all U.S. cases, no ability to require municipalities to accept development (Nelson 2000).

As described in Chapter 7, Pennsylvania has charted a judicially-driven (as opposed to planning-driven) policy to limit local governments' capacity to exclude a range of housing forms, including multifamily housing. The result has been an increase in multifamily housing as municipalities zone to forestall planning by judicial fiat that would undermine their prerogatives (Mitchell 2004). For this reason, the approach, which is based in developers' property rights, has much to recommend it. But Pennsylvania's judicially-based approach fails to embed its mandates on local governments within the regional coordinating function that a planning-based system can offer. While Pennsylvania municipalities have apparently responded to the regime by allowing more multifamily housing, there is little in the Pennsylvania Supreme Court rulings to encourage compact development along transit lines specifically, foster intermunicipal coordination, or promote contiguous compact development to create walkable urban zones. There are clear metropolitan-level interests in these outcomes, and although augmenting developers' property rights is a necessary step, it is probably not sufficient.

Oregon stands out as the sole U.S. state with significant powers to require its communities to allow compact development (A. Nelson 1999). Portland's "Metro," unique among U.S. metropolitan planning organizations, can require that municipal land-use plans are consistent with the regional plan (Transportation Research Board 2001). An important component of this is that it can require the municipalities to accept development they might otherwise be inclined to exclude. The result has been significant increases in density in new development (Gibson and Abbot 2002) and a quadrupling of land zoned for multifamily housing, to more than 25 percent of buildable acreage (Bollens 1992). Nelson (2002, 37) aptly characterized the changes in property-rights arrangements associated with Oregon's planning approach and its urban-growth boundaries (UGB) not as a massive increase in planning restrictions at the expense of private property rights, but as a reallocation of property rights on both sides of the boundary. "Outside UGBs," Nelson writes, "property owners have only the right to use their land for open space purposes, such as farming, forestry and natural resources; urban scale development is not allowed." By contrast, the policy increases property rights within UGBs:

> Inside the UGBs, property owners not only gained the explicit right to develop land for urban uses, but they were given substantially more development rights than perhaps they have ever enjoyed. Those rights included higher-density and intensity development of land, infrastructure commitments, and expedited review of development proposals...Since I am familiar with both metropolitan Portland and Atlanta, it is my personal observation that rezoning proposals to build higher-density housing and mixed use development in metropolitan Portland take a few months but rarely much more than a year (even with court appeals), while the same sorts of proposals in metropolitan Atlanta take a year and often more, and up to a decade if the courts are involved.

Thus Portland and other Oregon cities take an approach that cannot inherently be characterized as either more or less market-based than other metropolitan areas: property restrictions outside the boundary are coupled with enhanced property rights within. In fact, Nelson identifies this pairing as an essential element of urban-containment policies, criticizing other policies that lack an increased property-rights component because they are "patently exclusionary, are fraught with permitting delay, do not consciously accommodate the regional demand for development, and are not done from a regional or metropolitan perspective" (37–38). The problem with Florida's urban-growth boundaries, for example, is that they "are not accompanied by such strong property rights policies inside UGBs as are found in metropolitan Portland, and development processing there can take years for even the simplest development proposal" (38). Similarly, many municipalities in the San Francisco Bay Area have adopted piecemeal UGBs that "arguably save open space" but, because they are deficient in property-rights enhancements, push "new low-density subdivisions into the San Joaquin Valley, the nation's fruit and vegetable basket" (38).

Given the two-part shift in development rights in Portland—restrictions outside the UGB paired with enhanced property rights within—Lewis (1996) rejects any equation of regional powers with reductions in market forces, arguing that "[d]espite the Portland region's relative centralization of goals, guidelines, and procedures for development, it may be viewed as a more *free*—or at least, more *neutral*—political-economic land market than Denver, where progrowth elites and antigrowth interests seek out or even create institutions that will accommodate their specific visions" (207). The insight that smart growth properly entails a pairing of increased property rights together with its open-space protections is regularly glossed over. Ostensibly market-oriented observers criticize smart-growth policies for limiting the land available for urban growth, but rarely credit them with actually increasing property rights in areas slated for compact development. This stems in large measure from ambivalence over the legitimacy of preempting municipal prerogative to begin with, even when the municipalities are inhibiting the development of more compact and accessible metropolitan forms. Is metropolitan or state limitation of municipal regulatory prerogative market expanding or market limiting? The answer depends on the regulatory or market nature of municipal land-use controls in the first place.

Few other planning systems view local governments in the way the United States does. Local government regulation in countries around the world is not equated with the market but understood as public action. As such, it is accountable to higher governmental levels, which frequently weigh in on the side of the right to develop. For example, the Australian national government has been pursuing policies to enable urban densification primarily by promulgating and promoting codes for adoption by the states that limit local power to regulate development. The Australian Model Code for Residential Development, for instance, has reduced development regulations and standards as a means for enabling more compact development (Stilwell and Troy 2000). Far from market forcing, these regulations are geared at enabling property-development markets to operate in communities that had previously zoned out market-driven densification. Japan has pursued a similar approach: spurred by large property-development companies, the national government has promulgated rules that weakened local regulations to promote urban regeneration and increase housing supplies (Sorenson 2003).

The national governments of Germany, the Netherlands, and Great Britain are similarly involved in the land-use planning process and require local regulations to conform to national guidelines (Transportation Research Board 2001). To many Americans these powers sound draconian, but they are frequently deployed to keep local officials from overregulating the market. For example, in Great Britain people whose development applications have been rejected by local authorities may appeal to the Secretary of State (Rao 2002).

Canada presents a particularly interesting case for the United States because of cultural and geographic similarities. The important higher-level governmental actor there is generally the province, and municipal land-use plans must conform to those of provincial boards (Transportation Research

Board 2001). Although the powers of the provinces vary, they can be very influential actors in Canadian planning processes. In British Columbia, a municipality's official community plan is required to identify its relationship with the regional growth strategy, though this formulation does not directly impinge on the locals' right to limit densities in their jurisdictions (Meligrana 2000).

By contrast, the Ontario Municipal Board wields significant power over local planning processes; like the cases discussed above, it can intervene on behalf of development proposals that local authorities might otherwise exclude by regulation. The workings of the board are prosaic but powerful. Consider the following case, reported in the *Toronto Star* about Oakville, a lakeside town 25 miles southwest of Toronto (Swainson 2005):

> The Ontario Municipal Board has approved a controversial luxury 12-storey condo development on a strategic section of Oakville's waterfront. In a written decision handed down this week, adjudicator Susan Rogers gave the go-ahead to build no higher than the proposed condo's 12-storey neighbour. The developer, The Daniels Group, had sought to build a 14-storey project. Oakville officials wanted it to conform to the town's four-storey limit downtown....The town and four major residents' groups had opposed the project, arguing it was located in the Central Business District, where there is a four-storey height limit. Oakville Mayor Ann Mulvale said yesterday the decision is "disappointing for our community"...Oakville's lawyer told the hearing that the town was prepared to accept a building no higher than six storeys, terraced to appear like four. But anything taller would be out of step with the downtown's no-high-rise policy, which was adopted 30 years ago.

Regardless of one's feelings about the Ontario Municipal Board's decision in this case, it is clear that any equation of local planning with markets, or land-use planning at higher governmental levels with greater market constraints, is specious. Instead, nonlocal land-use powers are the globally proven technique for overcoming the tendency of municipal governments to exclude compact development. In contrast to economics-based approaches that may seek to reduce the *demand* for local-government exclusion through incentives, planning structured in this hierarchical fashion can directly challenge the *right* to exclude.

Needless to say, these higher-level planning authorities also constrain markets, reserve open space, and set minimum standards for development; they are hardly the dream of those who would seek to minimize governmental involvement in the land-development process. But regional interests frequently demand that local governments permit market-driven compact development, especially along transit lines and in high-accessibility areas;

planning structured in a strictly local fashion, as in the United States, is often unable to respond to these needs.

The fact that U.S. metropolitan areas and states generally lack these powers does not imply that domestic land-use regulatory institutions are immutable. The presence of regional powers in Oregon and (albeit failed) 1960s experiments in New York and Massachusetts (Cullingworth 1993) provide evidence that these options are not forever barred from the American land-use planning system. The "quiet revolution" that ushered in state involvement in land-use planning (Weitz 1999) may evolve into greater degrees of shared land-use authority between municipalities and higher governmental levels; this would hold the promise of reducing the ability of local governments to exclude compact development.

It is significant that in some cases, environmental and development interests are lined up on the same side of this issue, since both seek to allow denser development in close-in areas. This alliance may prove a potent coalition, particularly given state growth-management laws that require some form of municipal consistency with state planning goals (Orfield 2002). For instance, in 2003, a group of private developers seeking to build a 2.9-unit-per-acre, mixed-used development on a 150-acre parcel brought suit against Scarborough, Maine, a town of 17,000 lying eight miles southeast of Portland. The parcel in question had been designated in the town's comprehensive plan as a "village district" and slated for compact growth. Maine law requires that municipal comprehensive plans designate "growth areas" and that a town's zoning ordinance be consistent with its comprehensive plan. Scarborough passed a comprehensive plan—endorsed at the time by the Maine Office of Community Development as "masterful"—that designated the plaintiff's property as just such an area slated for focused development, referring to it as a "designated village compact" (Conservation Law Foundation 2004). The town council had approved the proposed development but was overturned by referendum and the area's zoning remained at 2 acres per dwelling unit. The developers brought suit, contending that the low-density zoning was invalid because it conflicted with the town's comprehensive plan. The developer-plaintiffs were supported in an *amicus curiae* brief by both the Maine Real Estate and Development Association and two smart-growth groups: the Conservation Law Foundation and GrowSmart Maine. The superior court's judge ruled the zoning to be inconsistent with the comprehensive plan (Kim 2005), and gave the town three months to reach a compromise with the developer. The city council ultimately enacted a zoning change that would enable a somewhat reduced version of the original proposal to be developed (*Portland Press Herald* 2005).

The case illustrates several points. The primary obstacle to relatively compact development in this area was not lack of market interest or a willing and able developer. Rather, it was the deployment of local regulatory power in a fashion that demanded very low-density growth. It also illustrates the inherent compatibility, in many circumstances, of development and smart-growth interests. Both share an interest in overcoming regulatory obstacles to compact development in close-in and high-accessibility locations.

Although that shared interest can form the basis of coalitions to overcome parochial use of the local zoning power, the success of such partnerships requires access to legal levers that trigger action. Market pressures for development alone would be unlikely to alter low-density zoning in a town like Scarborough as long as its citizens perceive greater cost than benefit to accepting the development. But creative use of statewide growth-management mandates holds some potential for overcoming local governments' regulatory obstacles to compact growth. The triggering mechanism is based in planning rather than in property rights alone; the zoning ordinance is required to conform to the comprehensive plan, which owes some fealty to statewide planning goals. As such, cases like this hold the potential for lending teeth to statewide growth management, which has largely deferred to local prerogative on the issue of accepting compact growth.

PLANNING OVER THE SHORT AND LONG RUN

This book has argued against conditioning land-use policy reform on scientifically established benefits in travel behavior. Nevertheless, the book is motivated by the hope that a different approach to transportation and land-use policy—and the different metropolitan patterns that could arise under a reformed regime—could hold significant payoffs in travel patterns, environmental protection, social equity, and quality of life in metropolitan areas. Yet these benefits are phenomena that can materialize in a meaningful way only over the long run. Travel behavior effects of an isolated pedestrian- or transit-oriented neighborhood are likely to be modest if its regional context is strictly auto-oriented. By contrast, as significant parts of a metropolitan region grow in patterns friendlier to transportation alternatives, their agglomeration may generate beneficial effects beyond those of each part in isolation.

Yet planning in hopes of long-run uncertain benefits is a risky business. If there were no short-run payoffs to reform of land-use policy, it would be difficult to justify. Some smart-growth proponents respond to this challenge by redoubling their efforts to demonstrate short-term benefits in travel-behavior modification or other scientifically verifiable outcomes. And it may be a symptom of American impatience that many governmental priorities, from air-quality requirements to congestion-mitigation planning, seem to push toward demonstrating (or at least modeling) benefits from one year to the next. Given this pressure, it is hardly surprising that smart-growth advocates have sought to provide the evidence demanded. Arguments presented here can offer an alternative. The benefits of allowing households to bring their neighborhood choices more in line with their transportation and land-use preferences are visible and immediate: they do not depend on scientific evidence of travel-behavior modification.

The hope for effects that materialize over the long run—while generating other benefits in the shorter term—can inform the planning approach to compact, walkable, and transit-friendly development forms. For example, designating land around a transit station for transit-oriented development can ensure that if there is a market for such development, it will not be preempted by low-density development that does not relate to the station. Such preemption can occur for a number of reasons, including the style of a particular developer or vagaries of the business cycle (since higher-density development may be less attractive in recessionary times). Similarly, planners can encourage and facilitate the market by seeking accessible, transit- and pedestrian-friendly proposals for development. This action can represent an important signal for developers that proposals for denser-than-usual projects will be welcomed rather than shot down in costly and protracted disputes. But while planning can designate territory, facilitate development, and encourage its productive agglomeration, it is ultimately the market that will decide what does and does not get built. Parcels designated "transit-oriented development" or "New Urbanist" for which no developer perceives a market will remain vacant, and pressures will mount for its rezoning to allow lower-density development forms.

The worry that the planning function can compel dense development against the wishes of the market is misplaced. Yet awareness of this role of the market does not imply a hands-off or laissez-faire approach to physical development. Rather, it suggests liberalization of land-use regulations that unduly lower development densities, separate land uses, and specify wide roads and huge parking lots. But relaxation of the regulatory template for urban sprawl is only a necessary condition for the development of alternatives. Such development will occur where it is not prevented by regulation, where sufficient market interest exists, and where the planning function is used in the coordinating fashion described above.

The current U.S. approach to land-use regulation was developed in an era when the dominant evil to be combated was the overcrowded, unhealthy city. The planning approach of U.S. municipalities accordingly sought to improve urban conditions through measures that reduced development densities per se. But the state of knowledge in urban planning and infrastructure has developed significantly since *Euclid v. Ambler*. Improved sanitation, transportation infrastructure, and legal and institutional arrangements provide new tools for rendering a full range of metropolitan densities livable. Even zoning itself can be "just like an effective sewer system, which allows for larger cities by making high densities healthier and more amenable" (Fischel 1999b, 420). Rather than fighting density per se, reformed planning institutions can focus on those infrastructure, connectivity, design and open-space elements that support a high quality of life at all market-supported densities.

The challenges entailed in these transportation and land-use policy reforms can hardly be overstated. But a more immediate shift—a change in the terms of the transportation and land-use policy debate—must precede longer-term reform. When the status quo in metropolitan development is constructed as the market, debates over the adequacy of travel behavior evidence to legitimate intervention appear to draw straight from the compelling logic of objective science. By contrast, when we acknowledge the role that pervasive governmental intervention has played in molding U.S. metropolitan areas to a sprawling development template, we must alter our assessment of both what counts as a transportation-policy benefit and the role of scientific evidence in legitimating reform.

NOTES

CHAPTER TWO

1. I am grateful to Daniel Rodriguez of the University of North Carolina for this point.

2. Similarly, if cars per person are endogenous—i.e., in part a function of one's neighborhood environment—modeling the impact of urban form while controlling for auto ownership would bias estimates of the impact of urban form downwards. This problem attends a great number of studies modeling the impact of urban form on travel behavior.

CHAPTER THREE

1. For example, in 1994, 2 percent of developable land in Fairfax County, Virginia, was zoned for townhouses or apartments (Choppin 1994, 2049), despite planning language that reads, "[opportunity] should be available to all who live or work in Fairfax County to purchase or rent safe, decent, affordable housing within their means" and that this goal should be "encouraged through more flexible zoning wherever possible" (Choppin 1994, 2065). An early study of

exclusionary zoning found that 99.2 percent of the land zoned as residential in metropolitan New York was zoned for exclusive single-family development (Mitchell 2004, 120, referring to the 1968 Douglas Commission Report, *Building the American City*).

2. A review by Quigley and Rosenthal (2004) concludes that "a number of credible papers seem to bear out the theoretical expectations" that "excessive land restrictions limit the buildable supply, tilting construction toward lower densities and larger, more expensive homes." At the same time, they lament the state of research in this area "because variations in both observed regulation and methodological precision frustrate sweeping generalizations."

3. Tiebout (1956) employed the term "public goods" and defined them in a way consistent with current economic usage: public goods are ones that "should be produced, but for which there is no feasible method of charging the consumers" (417). Yet many of the goods that Tiebout listed as candidates for efficient provision in a decentralized regime do not have that attribute at all: schools, municipal golf courses, beaches, and parking facilities (418) are all examples of goods that are frequently provided by the public sector but do in fact readily allow for charging of consumers. Two publicly provided goods that influence residential location choice particularly strongly are schools and public safety. The former is certainly not a public good; exclusion of nonpayers is technically feasible, as the existence of private schools demonstrates. Public safety is more of a true public good, yet building a theory on the notion that households have varying tastes for freedom from crime would have strained plausibility. As Frug (1999, 171) writes, "it seems odd to suggest that the division of America's metropolitan areas into areas with good schools and safe neighborhoods and areas with deteriorating schools and high crime rates is explicable in terms of people's differing 'tastes.'" Perhaps this tension underlies the rhetorical sleight-of-hand entailed in the use of the term "public goods" to describe private goods provided by the public sector. This chapter prefers the term "publicly provided" goods for this reason.

CHAPTER FOUR

1. For example, in the City of Cupertino, although 45 to 50 percent of the territory zoned R-1 in 1962 is currently in other zones, this was primarily undeveloped territory. Territory that was developed as R-1 remains predominantly unchanged (Gary Chao, Community Development Department, City of Cupertino, CA, October 10, 2003). The single-family neighborhoods of the 1960s in Los Altos remain single-family today (Curtis Banks, Community Development Department, City of Los Altos, CA, October 10, 2003). There have been rezonings of a few single-family properties along arterials in Santa Clara, but for the most part these did not allow for the development of multifamily housing because of minimum lot-size requirements. Apart from these, virtually all properties zoned and developed as single-family in the 1960s remain in a similar status today (Gloria Sciara, Community Development Department, City of Santa Clara, CA, October 10, 2003).

2. For example, 66 percent of the developed acreage of the seven-county Detroit metropolitan area was in the single-family land use in 1995 (www.semcog.org/ Data/CommunityProfiles/index.htm).

CHAPTER SIX

1. This chapter considers the potential of land-use regulatory policy to generate above-market development densities. Not considered here are policies based in subsidy. Two kinds of subsidy are relevant in this regard: payments to the municipality and payments to the developer. But since neither cities nor counties generally build housing directly, the former type of payment constitutes an incentive for communities to allow or facilitate such housing, and as such is consistent with the view that municipal regulation—not market disinterest—is a central obstacle to overcome in the development of such neighborhoods.

   By contrast, public subsidies to developers can render feasible projects that would not have been economically viable without the subsidy, and as such can potentially generate higher levels of transit-oriented housing than might otherwise arise. Tools include standard elements of the economic development planner's kit, including tax abatement programs and tax increment financing (whereby increased property taxes collected on the development site are recycled back to retire the developer's investment debt). Critics will view such public subsidy as an unwarranted interference in the market for transit-oriented development; moreover, these may in some cases represent inefficient expenditures of public funds for developments that could have arisen even without the subsidy. Both criticisms contain more than a kernel of truth. But these subsidies are hardly unique to planning efforts on behalf of transit-oriented development and need to be viewed within the context of the spectrum of municipal financial incentives to attract development.

CHAPTER SEVEN

1. Another 15.6 percent of developers indicated a miscellaneous set of obstacles to alternative development.

2. http://www.ci.mtnview.ca.us/citydepts/cd/apd/tod_whisman.htm, accessed February 20, 2005.

CHAPTER EIGHT

1. The marginal effect is

$$\sum_{i=1}^{n} \left(\partial y_i / \partial x_i \right) / n$$

where y = the probability of selection of a given neighborhood type; x = transportation and land-use preference score; n = number of observations in sample; and i = an index for an individual observation.

CHAPTER NINE

1. The urbanized area of Salonika has more than 60 people per acre. In 1997, comparable figures for U.S. metropolitan areas were Los Angeles, 8.31; New York, 7.99; San Francisco, 7.96; Chicago, 6.02; Washington, D.C., 5.88; and Boston, 5.65 (Fulton et al. 2001).

REFERENCES

Advisory Commission on Regulatory Barriers to Affordable Housing. 1991. *Not in My Back Yard: Removing Barriers to Affordable Housing.* Washington, DC: Department of Housing and Urban Development.

Aldenderfer, Mark S., and Roger K. Blashfield. 1984. *Cluster Analysis.* Beverly Hills, CA: Sage.

Allen, John C. 1972. Comment: The Municipal Enforcement of Deed Restrictions: An Alternative to Zoning. *Houston Law Review* 9: 816–40.

Alonso, William. 1964. *Location and Land Use.* Cambridge, MA: Harvard University Press.

Altshuler, Alan, with James P. Womack and John R. Pucher. 1979. *The Urban Transportation System: Politics and Policy Innovation.* Cambridge, MA: MIT Press.

Aumente, Jerome. 1971. Domestic Land Reform. *City* 5: 56.

Bartlett, John. 2002. *Bartlett's Familiar Quotations: A Collection of Passages, Phrases, and Proverbs Traced to their Sources in Ancient and Modern Literature.* Boston: Little, Brown.

Bay Area Rapid Transit District. 1999. *Policy Framework for System Expansion.* Oakland, CA: BART Board.

Ben Akiva, Moshe, and Steven A. Lerman. 1985. *Discrete Choice Analysis: Theory and Application to Travel Demand.* Cambridge, MA: MIT Press.

Boarnet, Marlon, and Michael Greenwald. 2001. Land Use, Urban Design, and Non-Work Travel: Reproducing for Portland, Oregon, Empirical Tests from Other Urban Areas. *Transportation Research Record* 1722: 27–37.

Boarnet, Marlon, and Randall Crane. 1997. L.A. Story: A Reality Check for Transit-Based Housing. *Journal of the American Planning Association* 63(2): 189–204.

———. 2001. *Travel by Design: The Influence of Urban Form on Travel.* New York: Oxford University Press.

Boarnet, Marlon G., and Sharon Sarmiento. 1998. Can Land-Use Policy Really Affect Travel Behavior? A Study of the Link between Non-Work Travel and Land-Use Characteristics. *Urban Studies* 35(7): 1155–69.

Bogart, William T. 1993. "What Big Teeth You Have!": Identifying the Motivations for Exclusionary Zoning. *Urban Studies* 30(10): 1669–81.

———. 1998. *The Economics of Cities and Suburbs.* Upper Saddle River, NJ: Prentice-Hall.

Bollens, Scott. 1992. State Growth Management: Intergovernmental Frameworks and Policy Objectives. *Journal of the American Planning Association* 58(4): 454–66.

Brener, Katia. 1999. Note: Belle Terre and Single-Family Home Ordinances: Judicial Perceptions of Local Government and the Presumption of Validity. *New York University Law Review* 74: 447–84.

Briffault, Richard. 1990a. Our Localism: Part I—The Structure of Local Government Law. *Columbia Law Review* 90(1): 1–115.

———. 1990b. Our Localism: Part II—Localism and Legal Theory. *Columbia Law Review* 90(2): 346–454.

Brownstone, David, and Arthur DeVany. 1991. Zoning, Returns to Scale, and the Value of Undeveloped Land. *Review of Economics and Statistics* 73: 699–704.

Brueckner, Jan K. 2000. Urban Sprawl: Diagnosis and Remedies. *International Regional Science Review* 23(2): 160–71.

Calabrese, Stephen, Dennis Epple, and Richard Romano. 2004. "On the Political Economy of Zoning." Working Paper, Carnegie Mellon University. Available at http://faculty-admin.tepper.cmu.edu/upload/wpaper_43205798535840_On_The_Political_Economy_of_Zoning_Final.pdf. Accessed February 12, 2005.

Calavita, Nico, Kenneth Grimes, and Allan Mallach. 1997. Inclusionary Housing in California and New Jersey: A Comparative Analysis. *Housing Policy Debate* 8(1): 109–42.

California Journal. 1997. Here Comes the Neighborhood. May 1.

Cervero, Robert. 1989. Jobs-Housing Balancing and Regional Mobility. *Journal of the American Planning Association* 55(2): 136–50.

———. 1996. Jobs-Housing Balance Revisited: Trends and Impacts in the San Francisco Bay Area. *Journal of the American Planning Association* 62(4): 492–511.

———. 2002. Review of Travel by Design: The Influence of Urban Form on Travel. *Journal of the American Planning Association* 68(1): 106.

Chadwick, Edwin. 1842. Report on the Sanitary Condition of the Labouring Population of Gt. Britain. Edinburgh, UK: Edinburgh University Press. 1965 edition.

Chapman, Michael. 1998. European Spatial Planning and the Urban Environment. In *Environment, Planning and Land Use*, edited by Philip Kivell, Peter Roberts, and Gordon Walker. Aldershot, UK: Ashgate.

Choppin, Timothy J. 1994. Breaking the Exclusionary Land Use Regulation Barrier: Policies to Promote Affordable Housing in the Suburbs. *Georgetown Law Journal* 82: 2039–77.

Clapp, John M. 1981. The Impact of Inclusionary Zoning on the Location and Type of Construction Activity. *American Real Estate and Urban Economics Journal* 9: 436–56.

Coase, Ronald. 1960. The Problem of Social Cost. *Journal of Law and Economics* 3: 1–44.

Conservation Law Foundation. 2004. Amicus Curiae Brief of the Conservation Law Foundation, GrowSmart Maine and the Maine Real Estate & Development Association in Support of Plaintiffs' Motion for Partial Summary Judgment. ALC Development Corporation and Raynan Properties, LLC, and Ronald B. Campbell, Plaintiffs, v. The Town of Scarborough, Defendant. Portland, ME: Cumberland County Superior Court. Civil Action Docket No. CV-03-498. Available at http://www.clf.org/uploadedFiles/CLF/Programs/Smart_Growth/State_Policy_Reform/Scarborough/amicus_brief_dunstan_20040726.pdf. Accessed March 4, 2005.

Crane, Randall. 1996. On Form versus Function: Will the New Urbanism Reduce Traffic, or Increase It? *Journal of Planning Education and Research* 15: 117–26.

———. 1998. Travel by Design? *Access* 12: 2–7.

Crano, William D., and Marilyn B. Brewer. 1986. *Principles and Methods of Social Research.* Boston: Allyn and Bacon.

Crone, Theodore M. 1983. Elements of an Economic Justification for Municipal Zoning. *Journal of Urban Economics* 14: 168–83.

Cullingworth, J. Barry. 1993. *The Political Culture of Planning: American Land Use Planning in Comparative Perspective.* New York: Routledge.

Danielson, Karen A., Robert E. Lang, and William Fulton. 1999. Retracting Suburbia: Smart Growth and the Future of Housing. *Housing Policy Debate* 10(3): 513–40.

Dowding, Keith, Peter John, and Stephen Biggs. 1994. Tiebout: A Survey of the Empirical Literature. *Urban Studies* 31(4/5): 767–97.

Downs, Anthony. 1992. *Stuck in Traffic: Coping with Peak-Hour Traffic Congestion.* Washington, DC: Brookings Institution.

———. 1999. Some Realities about Sprawl and Urban Decline. *Housing Policy Debate* 10(4): 955–74.

———. 2004. *Still Stuck in Traffic: Coping with Peak-Hour Traffic Congestion.* Washington, DC: Brookings Institution.

Duany, Andres, and Emily Talen. 2002. Making the Good Easy: The Smart Code Alternative. *Fordham Urban Law Journal* 29: 1445–68.

Ellickson, Robert C. 1973. Alternatives to Zoning: Covenants, Nuisance Rules, and Fines as Land Use Controls. *The University of Chicago Law Review* 40(4): 681–781.

Eppli, Mark J., and Charles C. Tu. 1999. *Valuing the New Urbanism: The Impact of the New Urbanism on Prices of Single-Family Homes.* Washington, DC: Urban Land Institute.

Ewing, Reid. 1995. Beyond Density, Mode Choice and Single-Purpose Trips. *Transportation Quarterly* 49(4): 15–24.

Federal Trade Commission. 1984. *An Economic Analysis of Taxicab Regulation.* Washington, DC: Bureau of Economics Staff Report.

Field, Charles G. 1997. Building Consensus for Affordable Housing. *Housing Policy Debate* 8(4): 801–32.

Fischel, William A. 1985. *The Economics of Zoning Laws: A Property Rights Approach to American Land Use Controls.* Baltimore: Johns Hopkins University Press.

———. Exclusionary Zoning and Growth Controls: A Comment on the APA's Endorsement of the Mt. Laurel Doctrine. *Washington University Journal of Urban and Contemporary Law* 40: 65–74.

———. 1999a. "Does the American Way of Zoning Cause the Suburbs of U.S. Metropolitan Areas to Be Too Spread Out?" In *Governance and Opportunity in Metropolitan Areas,* edited by Alan Altsuler, William Morrill, Harold Wolman, and Faith Mitchell. Washington, DC: National Academy Press.

———. 1999b. Zoning and Land Use Regulation. In *Encyclopedia of Law and Economics,* edited by Boudewijn Bouckaert and Gerrit De Gees. Entry 2200. Available at http://allserv.rug.ac.be/~gdegeest/tablebib.htm.

———. 2001. *The Homevoter Hypothesis: How Home Values Influence Local Government Taxation, School Finance, and Land-Use Policies.* Cambridge, MA: Harvard University Press.

Frug, Gerald. 1999. *City Making: Building Communities without Building Walls.* Princeton, NJ: Princeton University Press.

———. 2001. *The Legal Technology of Exclusion.* Manuscript. Cambridge, MA: Harvard Law School.

Fulton, William, Rolf Pendall, May Nguen, and Alicia Harrison. 2001. Who Sprawls Most? How Growth Patterns Differ across the U.S. Washington, DC: Brookings Institution, Center on Urban & Metropolitan Policy. Available at www.brookings.edu/es/urban/publications/fulton.pdf.

Garbett, Bryson. 2005. Personal interview, May 25. Developer, Garbett Homes, Sandy, UT.

Garvin, Alexander. 1996. *The American City: What Works, What Doesn't.* New York: McGraw-Hill.

Gibson, K., and C. Abbott. 2002. City Profile: Portland, Oregon. *Cities* 19(6): 425–36.

Gilbert, Gorman, and Jarir S. Dajani. 1974. Energy, Urban Form and Transportation Policy. *Transportation Research* 8: 267–76.

Girsh Appeal. 1969. 437 Pa. 237, 263 A.2d 395.

Giuliano, Genevieve. 1989. Is Jobs-Housing Balance a Transportation Issue? *Transportation Research Record* 1305: 305–12.

Glaeser, Edward L., and Joseph Gyourko. 2002. *The Impact of Zoning on Housing Affordability.* Working paper 8835. Cambridge, MA: National Bureau of Economic Research. Available at http://www.nber.org/papers/w8835.

Gordon, Peter, and Harry W. Richardson. 1997. Are Compact Cities a Desirable Planning Goal? *Journal of the American Planning Association* 63(1): 93–104.

———. The Sprawl Debate: Let Markets Plan. *Publius: The Journal of Federalism* 31(3): 131–49.

Green, Richard K. 1999. Land Use Regulation and the Price of Housing in a Suburban Wisconsin County. *Journal of Housing Economics* 8: 144–59.

Gyourko, Joseph. 1991. Impact Fees, Exclusionary Zoning, and the Density of New Development. *Journal of Urban Economics* 30: 242–56.

Hamilton, Bruce W. 1975. Zoning and Property Taxation in a System of Local Governments. *Urban Studies* 12: 204–11.

———. 1976. Capitalization of Intrajurisdictional Differences in Local Tax Prices. *American Economic Review* 66: 743–53.

Hemmens, George C. 1967. Experiments in Urban Form and Structure. *Highway Research Record* 207: 32–41.

Hylton, Joseph Gordon. 2000. The Supreme Court: Prelude to Euclid: The United States Supreme Court and the Constitutionality of Land Use Regulation, 1900–1920. *Washington University Journal of Law and Policy* 3: 1–37.

Inam, Aseem, Jonathan Levine, and Richard Werbel. 2002. *Developer-Planner Interaction in Transportation and Land Use Sustainability.* San Jose, CA: Mineta Transportation Institute, College of Business, San Jose State University. MTI Report 01-21. Available at www.transweb.sjsu.edu/publications/01-21.pdf.

Kahneman, Daniel, Jack L. Knetch, and Richard H. Thaler. 1990. Experimental Tests of the Endowment Effect and the Coase Theorem. *Journal of Political Economy* 98(6):1325–48.

Kennedy, Duncan. 1978–1979. The Structure of Blackstone's Commentaries. *Buffalo Law Review* 28: 205–382.

Kim, Ann S. 2005. Scarborough Developers Win One; A Judge Finds Flaws with the Zoning that Would Prohibit the "Great American Neighborhood." *Portland Press Herald*, February 18, B2.

Kirp, David L., John P. Dwyer, and Larry A. Rosenthal. 1995. *Our Town: Race, Housing and the Soul of Suburbia*. New Brunswick, NJ: Rutgers University Press.

Kitamura, Ryuichi, Patricia Mokhtarian, and Laura Laidet. 1997. A Micro-Analysis of Land Use and Travel in Five Neighborhoods in the San Francisco Bay Area. *Transportation* 24: 125–58.

Krizek, Kevin J. 2003. Residential Relocation and Changes in Urban Travel: Does Neighborhood-Scale Urban Form Matter? *Journal of the American Planning Association* 69(3): 265–81.

Landis, John D. 1992. Do Growth Controls Work? A New Assessment. *Journal of the American Planning Association* 58: 489–508.

Lansing, John B., and Eva Muller with Nancy Barth. 1964. *Residential Location and Urban Mobility*. Ann Arbor, MI: Survey Research Center, Institute for Social Research. Prepared for the U.S. Department of Commerce, Bureau of Public Roads.

Lansing, John B., Robert W. Marans, and Robert B. Zehner. 1970. *Planned Residential Environments*. Ann Arbor MI: Survey Research Center, Institute for Social Research. Prepared for the U.S. Department of Transportation, Bureau of Public Roads.

Lehrer, Eli. 1998. Burbsprawl: Room to Be Free? *Insight on the News*, November 23.

Levine, Jonathan, and Aseem Inam. 2004. The Market for Transportation-Land Use Integration: Do Developers Want Smarter Growth Than Regulations Allow? *Transportation* 31(4): 409–27.

Levine, Jonathan, Aseem Inam, Richard Werbel, and Gwo-Wei Torng. 2002. *Transportation and Land Use Alternatives: Constraint or Expansion of Household Choice?* San Jose, CA: Mineta Transportation Institute, College of Business, San Jose State University. MTI Report 01-19. Available at http://transweb.sjsu.edu/publications/LandUse.pdf.

Levine, Jonathan, Aseem Inam, and Gwo-Wei Torng. 2005. A Choice-Based Rationale for Land-Use and Transportation Alternatives: Evidence from Boston and Atlanta. *Journal of Planning Education and Research* 24(3): 317–30.

Levinson, Arik. 1997. Why Oppose TDRs? Transferable Development Rights Can Increase Overall Development. *Regional Science and Urban Economics* 27(3): 283–96.

Levinson, David M., and Ajay Kumar. 1997. Density and the Journey to Work. *Growth and Change* 28: 147–72.

Levinson, Herbert S., and F. Houston Wynn. 1963. Effects of Density of Urban Transportation Requirements. *Highway Research Record* 2: 38–64.

Lewis, Paul G. 1996. *Shaping Suburbia: How Political Institutions Organize Urban Development*. Pittsburgh: University of Pittsburgh Press.

Lochner v. New York. 1905. 198 U.S. 45, 25 S. Ct. 539, 49 L. Ed. 937.

Lucas, David H., Petitioner v. South Carolina Coastal Council. 1992. 505 U.S. 1003, 112 S. Ct. 2886, 120 L. Ed. 2d 798.

Lund, Hollie M., Robert Cervero, and Richard W. Willson. 2004. *Travel Characteristics of Transit-Oriented Development in California*. Final Report. Funded by Caltrans Transportation Grant, "Statewide Planning Studies," FTA Section 5313(b).

Maiorana, J.J. 1994. *Corridor Preservation*. Washington, DC: Transportation Research Board, NCHRP Synthesis of Highway Practice.

Malizia, Emil E., and Susan Exline. 2000. Consumer Preferences for Residential Development Alternatives. Working Paper 2000-02. University of North Carolina at Chapel Hill, Center for Urban and Regional Studies.

Maser, S.M, W. Riker, and R.N. Rosett. 1977. Effects of Zoning and Externalities on the Price of Land: An Empirical Analysis on Monroe County, New York. *Journal of Law and Economics* 20(1): 111–32.

Massachusetts Executive Office of Environmental Affairs. 2002. Massachusetts Geographic Information System. Boston. Available at http://www.mass.gov/mgis/. Accessed March 4, 2005.

McMillen, Daniel P., and John F. McDonald. 1991. A Markov Chain Model of Zoning Change. *Journal of Urban Economics* 30: 257–70.

McNeil, Donald, Jr. 2004. Barred from Testing for Mad Cow, Niche Meatpacker Loses Clients. *New York Times*, April 18.

Meligrana, John. 2000. British Columbia's Growth Strategies Act: A Policy Critique. *Canadian Journal of Urban Research* 9(1): 94–107.

Metropolitan Transportation Commission. 2005. Smart Growth/Transportation for Livable Communities: Housing Incentive Program. Available at http://www.mtc.ca.gov/planning/smart_growth/hip.htm.

Miceli, Thomas J., and Alanson P. Minkler. 1995. Willingness-to-Accept versus Willingness-to-Pay Measures of Value: Implications for Rent Control, Eminent Domain, and Zoning. *Public Finance Quarterly* 23(2): 255–70.

Mitchell, James L. 2004. Will Empowering Developers to Challenge Exclusionary Zoning Increase Suburban Housing Choice? *Journal of Policy Analysis and Management* 23(1): 119–34.

Mitchell, Robert B., and Chester Rapkin. 1954. *Urban Traffic: A Function of Land Use*. Westport, CT: Greenwood Press.

Morag-Levine, Noga. 2003. *Chasing the Wind: Regulating Air Pollution in the Common Law State*. Princeton, NJ: Princeton University Press.

Moss, William G. 1977. Large Lot Zoning, Property Taxes, and Metropolitan Area. *Journal of Urban Economics* 4: 408–27.

Myers, Dowell, and Elizabeth Gearin. 2001. Current Preferences and Future Demand for Denser Residential Environments. *Housing Policy Debate* 12(4): 633–59.

Nelson, Arthur C. 1999. Comparing States with and without Growth Management: Analysis Based on Indicators with Policy Implications. *Land Use Policy* 16(2): 121–27.

———. 2000. New Kid in Town: The Georgia Regional Transportation Authority and Its Role in Managing Growth in Metropolitan Atlanta. *Wake Forest Law Review* 35(3): 625–44.

———. 2002. Comment on Anthony Downs's "Have Housing Prices Risen Faster in Portland than Elsewhere?" *Housing Policy Debate* 13(1): 33–42.

Nelson, Robert H. 1999. Privatizing the Neighborhood: A Proposal to Replace Zoning with Private Collective Property Rights to Existing Neighborhoods. *George Mason Law Review* 7: 827–80.

Newman, Peter W.G., and Jeffrey R. Kenworthy. 1992. Is There a Role for Physical Planners? *Journal of the American Planning Association* 58(3): 353–62.

O'Halloran, Suzanne. 2004. Personal interview, February 26. Realtor, Kohler Meyers O'Halloran Inc., Gresham OR.

O'Toole, Randal. 1999. Dense Thinkers. *Reason*. Available at http://reason.com/9901/fe.ro.densethinkers.shtml.

Oregon Administrative Rules: Division 12, Transportation Planning, Section 660-012-0045(5)(a)). Available at arcweb.sos.state.or.us/rules/OARS_600/OAR_660/660_012.html.

Oregon Transportation Planning Rule. Oregon Administrative Rules: Division 12, Transportation Planning, Section 660-012-000. Available at arcweb.sos.state.or.us/rules/OARS_600/OAR_660/660_012.html.

Orfield, Myron. 2002. *American Metropolitics: The New Suburban Reality*. Washington, DC: Brookings Institution Press.

Pasha, Hafiz A. 1996. Suburban Minimum Lot Zoning and Spatial Equilibrium. *Journal of Urban Economics* 40: 1–12.

Peeples-Salah, Dionne. 1996. Rezoning for Transit Traps Downtown Homeowners. *Portland Oregonian*, January 18, AJ4.

Peiser, Richard B. 1989. Density and Urban Sprawl. *Land Economics* 65(3): 194–204.

Pendall, Rolf. 1999. Do Land-Use Controls Cause Sprawl? *Environment and Planning B: Planning and Design* 26: 555–71.

———. 2000. Local Land Use Regulation and the Chain of Exclusion. *Journal of the American Planning Association* 66(2): 125–42.

Penn Central Transportation Company et al., Appellants, v. City of New York et al., Respondents. 1977. 42 N.Y.2d 324, 366 N.E.2d 1271, 397 N.Y.S.2d 914.

Peterson, Paul E. 1981. *City Limits*. Chicago: University of Chicago Press.

Podgodzinski, J.M., and Tim R. Sass. 1994. The Theory and Estimation of Endogenous Zoning. *Regional Science and Urban Economics* 24(5): 601–30.

Portland Press Herald. 2005. Scarborough Lets Downsized "Neighborhood" Move Ahead. June 2, B2.

Purvis, Chuck. 2003. *Commuting to Silicon Valley*. Oakland, CA: Metropolitan Transportation Commission. Available at http://www.mtc.ca.gov/datamart/census/county2county/Commute_SiliconValley.pdf.

Quigley, John M., and Larry A. Rosenthal. 2004. The Effects of Land-Use Regulation on the Price of Housing: What Do We Know? What Can We Learn? Working Paper W04-002. Berkeley, CA: Institute of Business and Economic Research, Fisher Center for Real Estate and Urban Economics. Available at http://urban-policy.berkeley.edu/pdf/QRHUD0404.pdf (accessed February 12, 2005).

Rao, Nirmala. 2002. London: Metropolis Redux. *GeoJournal* 58: 3–9.

Rein, Martin, and Christopher Winship. 1999. The Dangers of "Strong" Causal Reasoning in Social Policy. *Society* 36(5): 38–46.

Rothblatt, Donald N. 1994. North American Metropolitan Planning: Canadian and U.S. Perspectives. *Journal of the American Planning Association* 60(4): 501–20.

Rubin, Jeffrey I., Joseph J. Seneca, and Janet G. Stotsky. 1990. Affordable Housing and Municipal Choice. *Land Economics* 66(3): 325–40.

Santa Clara Valley Transportation Authority (VTA). 1998–1999. *Travel Patterns of Employees in Rail Transit Station Areas.* San Jose, CA.

———. 2002. *Travel Patterns of Residents in Rail Transit Station Areas.* San Jose, CA.

Schultze, Charles L. 1977. *The Public Use of Private Interest.* Washington, DC: Brookings Institution.

Shlay, Anne B., and Peter H. Rossi. 1981. Keeping Up the Neighborhood: Estimating Net Effects of Zoning. *American Sociological Review* 46(6): 703–19.

Siegan, Bernard H. 1997. *Property and Freedom: The Constitution, the Courts, and Land-Use Regulation.* New Brunswick, NJ: Transaction Publishers.

———. 2001. Smart Growth and Other Infirmities of Land Use Controls. *The San Diego Law Review* 38(3): 693–746.

Smart Growth Network. 2002. *Getting to Smart Growth: 100 Policies for Implementation.* Available at http://www.smartgrowth.org/pdf/gettosg.pdf.

———. 2003. *Getting to Smart Growth II: 100 More Policies for Implementation.* Available at http://www.smartgrowth.org/pdf/gettosg.pdf.

Song, Yan, and Gerrit Knaap. 2003. New Urbanism and Housing Values: A Disaggregate Assessment. *Journal of Urban Economics* 54(2): 218–38.

Sorensen, Andre. 2003. Building World City Tokyo: Globalization and Conflict over Urban Space. *The Annals of Regional Science* 37: 519–31.

Stevenson, Sarah J. 1998. Note: Banking on TDRs: The Government's Role as Banker of Transferable Development Rights. *New York University Law Review* 73: 1329–76.

Stilwell, Frank, and Patrick Troy. 2000. Multilevel Governance and Urban Development in Australia. *Urban Studies* 37(5/6): 909–30.

Sunstein, Cass. 1987. Lochner's Legacy. *Columbia Law Review* 87(5): 873–919.

———. 2002. *The Cost-Benefit State: The Future of Regulatory Protection.* Chicago: American Bar Association, Section of Administrative Law and Regulatory Practice.

Swainson, Gail. 2005. OMB Approves Oakville Condo. *Toronto Star*, January 22, B03.

Talen, Emily, and Gerrit Knaap. 2003. Legalizing Smart Growth: An Empirical Study of Land Use Regulation in Illinois. *Journal of Planning Education and Research* 22(3): 345–59.

Thessalonki Master-Plan Organization. 1999. 1999 Travel Survey.

Thorson, James A. 1994. Zoning Policy Changes and the Urban Fringe Land Market. *Journal of the American Real Estate and Urban Economics Association* 22: 527–38.

———. 1997. The Effect of Zoning on Housing Construction. *Journal of Housing Economics* 6: 81–91.

Tiebout, Charles M. 1956. A Pure Theory of Local Expenditures. *Journal of Political Economy* 64(5): 416–24.

Transportation Research Board. 2001. Making Transit Work: Insight from Western Europe, Canada, and the United States. Special Report 257. National Research Council Committee for an International Comparison of National Policies and Expectations Affecting Public Transit. Washington, DC: National Academy Press.

Tu, Charles C., and Mark J. Eppli. 2001. An Empirical Examination of Traditional Neighborhood Development. *Real Estate Economics* 29(3): 489–501.

Turnbull, Geoffrey K. 2004. Urban Growth Controls: Transitional Dynamics of Development Fees and Growth Boundaries. *Journal of Urban Economics* 55(2): 215–37.

Vanderkooy, Terry. 2004. Personal interview, February 19. Private Development Division Manager, City of Gresham, OR.

Van Doren, Peter. 2003. Letting Environmentalists' Preferences Count. *Regulation* 26(2) 32–35.

Village of Belle Terre et al. v. Boraas et al. 1974. 416 U.S. 1, 94 S. Ct. 1536, 39 L. Ed. 2d 797.

Village of Euclid et al. v. Ambler Realty Company. 1926. 272 U.S. 365, 47 S. Ct. 114, 71 L. Ed. 303.

Wallace, Nancy E. 1988. The Market Effects of Zoning Undeveloped Land: Does Zoning Follow the Market? *Journal of Urban Economics* 23: 307–26.

Walters, David, and Linda Luise Brown. 2004. *Design First: Design Based Planning for Communities.* Burlington, MA: Architectural Press, Elsevier.

Warth et al. v. Seldin et al. 1975. 422 U.S. 490, 95 S. Ct. 2197, 45 L. Ed. 2d 343.

Watt, Kenneth E.F., and Claudia Ayers. 1974. *Urban Land Use Patterns and Transportation Energy Cost.* Manuscript, University of California at Davis.

Webber, Melvin M. 1961. Transportation Planning Models. *Traffic Quarterly* 15(3): 373–90.

Webster, Chris, and Lawrence Wai-Chung Lai. 2003. *Property Rights, Planning and Markets: Managing Spontaneous Cities.* Cheltenham, UK: Edward Elgar.

Weitz, Jerry. 1999. From Quiet Revolution to Smart Growth: State Growth Management Programs, 1960 to 1999. *Journal of Planning Literature* 14: 267–338.

Wheaton, William C. 1993. Land Capitalization, Tiebout Mobility and the Role of Zoning Regulations. *Journal of Urban Economics* 34: 102–17.

White, James R. 1988. Large Lot Zoning and Subdivision Costs: A Test. *Journal of Urban Economics* 23: 370–84.

Yerolympos, Alexandra. 1995. *The Replanning of Thessaloniki after the Fire of 1917: A Turning Point in the History of the City and the Development of Greek City Planning.* Second edition. Thessaloniki, Greece: University Studio Press.

INDEX

Affordable housing, 81–85, 186
    See also Single-family homes; Apartment
        building exclusions
Alternative development
    financing of, 129
    immediate and future benefits of,
        200–202
    seen as intervention, 29
    See also Compact development; Smart-
        growth regulation
Ambler, Euclid v., 51, 89–95, 103–4
Amenities, public, 115
American dream, 15–16, 27, 150
Apartment building exclusion, 51, 89–95,
    103–4
Associations, homeowners' and condo-
    minium, 107
Atlanta-Boston study
    background, 149–51
    clustering methodology and results,
        152–54
    regions, 151–52
    survey methodology, 154, 160–62
Australia, 197
Auto-oriented development, as default, 28

Bargaining over rights, 55–59
Bay Area Rapid Transit (BART) District, 15,
    194
Belle Terre et al. v. Boraas et al., 96–97

Boraas et al., Village of Belle Terre et al. v.,
    96–97
Boston. *See* Atlanta-Boston study
Boulder (CO), 112–13
Briffault, Richard, 97–99
Builder's remedy, 133, 136–37
Buildout, 78–79
Burden of proof in land use issues, 2–11,
    46–49, 187–88

Canada, 198
Capital-to-land limits, 110
Chadwick, Edwin, 89
Classification system, Hamilton three-way,
    68–75
Clustering of neighborhoods, 152–54
Coase model of bargaining, 55–59, 64, 77,
    84
Codes, smart-growth, 111–13
Collective property rights, 22, 59–64, 80–81,
    99–102, 177–80
Community objections through regulations,
    11–14, 40, 128–29, 137–47
Compact development
    advocates of, 29
    defined, 126–27
    developers' interest in, 120–21, 125–32
    obstacles to, 11–14, 137–47, 205n
    in Pennsylvania-New Jersey study,
        132–37, 147

transit use and, 146
under UGB, 120
See also Smart-growth regulation
Compartmentalized thinking, 185–86
Condominium associations, 107
Congress for the New Urbanism, 191
Constitutionality of zoning, 51, 89–95,
  103–4
Cost-benefit analysis, 179
Costs of exclusion, 70–73
Court decisions
  Euclid v. Ambler, 51, 89–95, 103–4
  exceptional treatment of zoning, 97–100
  Girsh Appeal, 133
  history of, 90–95
  Lochner v. New York, 92–95
  Mount Laurel, 132–33
  Village of Belle Terre et al. v. Boraas et al.,
    96–97
  Warth v. Seldin, 71
Covenants, 105–7

Davidoff, Paul, 82
Dearborn (MI), 141–43, 147, 191
Deed-restriction regimes, 105–7
Default, neutral
  assumptions, 9–10, 21–23
  history, 92–93
  status quo as, 175
Demographic changes, 76–79
Dense development. *See* Compact develop-
  ment
Density bonuses, 115–16, 132, 192
Department of Housing and Urban Develop-
  ment (HUD), 81–84, 126–32
Developers. *See* Land developers; Market forces
Development impact fees, 192
Discrete choice modeling, 162–67

Economics-based views
  assumptions in household choices, 68–70
  bargaining processes, 57–58
  grounded in Tiebout research, 67–68
  on zoning, 53, 59–64, 64–65
Economy, changes in, 76–79, 124
Ellickson, Robert C., 102–7
Empirical findings, role of 65, 74
Endowment effect, 61–64, 65, 70
Environmental interests, 199
Euclid v. Ambler, 51, 89–95, 103–4
Evolution of metropolitan areas, 171–75
Exclusionary zoning

alternatives to, 74–75
as barrier to affordable housing, 81–82
costs of, 70–73
as foundation of inclusionary policies, 116
as insufficient to prevent "musical suburbs" game, 177
motives for, 39–41, 51–53, 67–70
See also Municipal regulations

Fairfax County (VA), 203n
Federal regulations, 42–43, 81
Fee designs for mandatory inclusionary zon-
  ing, 117–18
Financing for alternative development, 129
Fischel, William, 63–65, 76–80, 84, 99–100,
  177–78
Form-based coding, 192
Free market. *See* Market forces
Free-rider problem, 64, 75
Fruit Heights (UT), 12–14

Georgia Regional Transportation Authority,
  193
Girsh Appeal, 133
Gresham (OR), 113
Growth control, 104

Hamilton three-way classification system,
  68–75
Hard-look doctrine, 96
Historical status of municipalities, 87–89
Homeowners' associations, 107
House prices, 36, 188
Household preferences
  Hamilton's three-way classification system
    and, 68–75
  neighborhood choices and, 146–47, 148,
    160–68
Housing affordability, 81–85, 186
  See also Single-family homes; Apartment
    building exclusion
Housing and Urban Development, Depart-
  ment of (HUD), 81–84, 126–32
Housing Incentive Program of the Trans-
  portation for Livable Communities Ini-
  tiative, 194
Houston (TX), 105–6
Hunt Valley (MD), 45

Immutability of municipal regulations,
  41–43
Incentive zoning, 115

Incentives
    for developers, 112–13, 115–16, 132, 192
    for municipalities, 193–94
Inclusionary zoning, 116–18
Interventions into the market
    alternative paradigms, 2–7
    as a product of resident preferences, 22
    market forces and, 109–11
    master-planned versus less planned com-
        munities, 25–26
    outside United States, 197–99
    travel behavior research and, 181
    ubiquity of, 25, 175–76
    alternative designs as, 29
    zoning as exceptional form of, 89–93,
        97–100
    See also Municipal regulations; Smart-
        growth regulation
Investors, 110–13
    See also Land developers

Jobs-housing balance, 47

Kemp, Jack (Housing and Urban Develop-
        ment), 83–84

Laissez-faire regimes, 6-7, 103–5, 108
Land developers
    cities working actively with, 141–44
    impact of zoning on, 186–87
    incentives for, 112–13, 115–16, 132, 192
    partnering with environmental interests,
        199–200
    views on alternatives, 125–32, 205n
    See also Market forces
Land use
    affordable housing and, 83–84, 85, 186
    alternative paradigms in, 2–7
    industrial, 90–91
    normal vs. subnormal development status,
        76–80
    transportation planning and, 30–37,
        161–62
    See also Research, travel behavior; Travel
        behavior
Land-Use policies
    developers' responses to, 186–87
    exceptional treatment of zoning, 87,
        89–90, 97–100
    outside United States, 197–99
    suburban development and, 29
    See also Interventions; Municipal regula-

tions; Policy reforms
Land values, 52–53
Liebmann, New Skate Ice Company v., 93
Linear programming methods, 27
Lochner v. New York, 92–95

Mandatory inclusionary-zoning ordinances,
        116–18
Market forces
    collective property right and, 177–80
    developers' perceptions of, 127–28
    incentives as indicator of investor interest,
        115–16
    local zoning as, 38–41, 64–66, 176–81
    low-density development and, 2–7, 21–22
    municipal regulations and, 11–14, 17–20,
        22, 27–30, 44–45
    opposing views of, 8–10, 38–41, 107–8
Massachusetts development data, 78
Master-planned environments, 25
Mission Valley Planned District Ordinance,
        143–44
Mitchell, James L. 134–37
Monocentric cities, model of, 71–73
Mount Laurel decisions, 132–33
Mountain View (CA), 139–41, 147, 193
Multifamily housing, 51, 91–92, 204n
Multinomial logit models of choice, 162–67
Municipal regulations
    alternatives, 102–7
    community growth and, 54–55
    as community right, 22, 59–64, 80–81,
        98–102, 177–80
    constitutionality of, 50–51
    constraining choices, 6–7, 11–14, 52, 185,
        204n
    history of, 16, 89–97, 202
    immutability of, 41–43
    impact of, 2–7, 21–22, 130–32
    as market force, 38–41, 64–66, 176–81
    market forces and, 11–14, 17–20, 22,
        27–30, 44–45
    nature of zoning, 86–87
    as obstacles, 11–14, 40, 128–29, 137–47
    profit potentials and, 110–11
    regional/state involvement and, 44,
        194–200
    suburban, 76–80
    See also Policy reforms; Smart-growth reg-
        ulation
Municipalities
    Hamilton's three-way classification system

of, 68–75
history of, 87–89
importance of planning powers, 148
as state agencies, 97–100
taxes in, 75
as voluntary associations of members, 176
"Musical suburbs" game, 74–75, 177

Negotiation, Coase model of, 55–59
Neighborhoods
    perceived opposition as force in develop-
        ment, 22, 128–29
    self-selection in, 30–36
    survey measuring preferences for, 160–62
    variables used to characterize, 169–70
Neutral defaults. See Default, neutral
Neutrality, as constitutional requirement,
    92–93
New Deal, 96
New Jersey-Pennsylvania study, 132–37, 147,
    195
New Skate Ice Company v. Liebmann, 93
New Urbanism. See Smart-growth regulation
New York, Lochner v., 92–95
Normal development standards, 63–64,
    76–80
"Not in my backyard" label, 5
Nuisance-based rationales, 22, 91–92,
    103–5, 107

Obstacles to alternative development, 11–14,
    40, 128–29, 137–47, 205n
Ontario Municipal Board, 198
Oregon Transportation Planning Rule,
    43–44, 80

Paradigms of metropolitan development, 4-5
Pembrooke Park (MI), 137–39, 147
Pennsylvania-New Jersey study, 132–37, 147,
    195
Planning process
    curtailing compact development, 137–41
    encouraging compact development,
        141–45
    failures in, gauged by travel behavior,
        45–46
    market forces and, 201–2
    vs. "the market" dichotomy, 107–8, 180
Pleasanton (CA), 45
Policy reforms
    differing opinions of, 73–74
    encouraging land-use innovation, 112

external incentives, 193–94
by municipalities, 191–92
rationale for, 23, 47, 190–91
by shared authority, 194–200
subsidies, 205n
trading of zoning rights, 61
See also Research, travel behavior
Political power in land-use, 42, 70–71
Polycentric urban form, 72
Portland (OR), 119–20, 195
Preference-choice modeling, 167–68
Private entities, municipalities' acting as,
    87–89
Private property protection, 92
Profits, development. See Investors; Land
    developers
Progressive taxation, 75
Property values, protection of, 95
Property-rights view, 108
    in Girsh Appeal, 133
    limitations of, 75–81
    normal-behavior standards, 76–80, 84
Publicly provided goods, 54–55, 204n

Rail transit, 146
Receiving zones, 114–15
Regional incentives, 193–94
Regional regulations, 22–23, 43–45
Regulatory streamlining, 144
Rental housing, 82
Rent-seeking actions, 95
Research, travel behavior
    compartmentalized thinking and, 185–86
    complexity and importance of empirical
        findings, 65, 74
    dangers of strong causal reasoning,
        182–83
    dilemma of proving benefits, 2–11,
        46–49, 184–86, 187–88, 203n
    history and challenges of, 23–27, 123–24
    implications of, for additional research,
        188–90
    intervention justification in, 7, 175–76,
        181
    politics of, 7–11
    self-selection bias in, 30–36
Residential preferences, 22, 34, 150–51,
    160–68
Revealed-preference research, 150–51
Rights, collective property, 22, 59–64, 80–81,
    99–102, 177–80
Rio Vista West project (CA), 143–44, 147

Salonika, Greece, 171–73
San Diego (CA), 143–44, 147, 191
San Francisco Bay Region (CA), 45
Scarborough (ME), 199–200
Scientific default and low-density policies, 46–49
Scientific proof. *See* Research, travel behavior
Seattle (WA), 115
Seldin, Warth v., 71
Self-selection, 30–34, 33–34, 162, 183–84
Sending zones, 114–15
Silicon Valley development (CA), 77, 173–74
Single-family homes
   American dream and, 15–16, 27, 150
   as nonconforming use in Gresham (CO), 113
   zoning for, 76–79, 204n, 205n
Smart-growth regulation
   codes for, 111–13
   developers and, 186–87
   encouraging, 120–22
   incentive zoning, 115–16
   inclusionary zoning, 116–18
   for promoting compact development, 109–11
   transfer of development rights, 113–15
   urban growth boundaries, 119–20
Social benefits of development, 55–59
Socioeconomic factors and residential preferences, 34
South Street Seaport District (NY), 113
State growth-management programs, 44, 194–95
State regulations *vs.* collective property rights, 99–102
Stated-preference research, 150–51
Subnormal development, 76–80
Subsidies, 205n
Surveys, 125–32, 154, 160–62

Tax reform policies, 74–75
Theory *vs.* empirical evidence, 73–74
Three-way classification system, Hamilton, 68–75

Tiebout, Charles, 54–55, 64, 68–70, 84, 176–77, 204n
Trading of zoning rights, 60–64
Traffic analysis zone (TAZ), 151–52
Transfer of development rights (TDR), 113–15, 192
Transit-oriented development (TOD), 143–44, 145
   See also Smart-growth regulation
Travel behavior
   explained by attitudinal variables, 34–35
   free market and, 27–29
   long- and short-term changes in, 200–202
   neighborhood self-selection and, 30–36, 162, 183–84
   as test of policy reform, 45–46
   See also Land use; Research, travel behavior

Urban design factors, 35
Urban growth boundaries (UGB), 10, 119–20, 195–96
Urban planning profession, 191–92
Urban sprawl
   causes of, 2–7
   implications of, 1
   as market failure, 8
   as planning failure, 9
   as seen by compact development advocates, 29

Village of Belle Terre et al. v. Boraas et al., 96–97

Walkable neighborhoods, 32–36
Warth v. Seldin, 71
Washington, D.C., 115
Wealth effect, 62
West Bloomfield Township (MI), 137–39, 147
West Village (MI), 141–43, 147
Westminster, (CO), 14
Whisman Station (CA), 139–41, 147, 193
Will of the people, 42–43
Winfield (IL), 112

Zoning. *See* Municipal regulations

ABOUT THE AUTHOR

Jonathan Levine is Associate Professor and Chair of Urban and Regional Planning Program in the A. Alfred Taubman College of Architecture and Urban Planning at the University of Michigan.